The Complete Idiot's Reference Card

Five Things You Should Never Serve for Breakfast

1. **Leftovers.** They *will* notice that this morning's Southwestern Omelet Surprise looks eerily similar to yesterday's breakfast burrito!

2. **Exotica.** Although it's fine to get creative with breakfast, remember that you are trying to satisfy many different tastes with one meal. Different is good—unidentifiable isn't.

3. **Anything that isn't fresh.** *Never* try to pass off stale food. At best your guests will notice; at worst they'll end up in the hospital with food poisoning—and you'll end up in court!

4. **Food that's the wrong temperature.** You don't like hot OJ, warm fruit salad, tepid eggs, and cold coffee, do you? Neither will your guests!

5. **And the worst thing you could serve for breakfast?** A grumpy disposition, of course!

Five B&B Naming Tips

1. Check those guidebooks and make sure your name is not already used by dozens of inns around the United States!

2. Pick a name that you can also use as a domain name (not as easy as you think!).

3. Be sure to pick a short, memorable name that can easily be spelled and understood over the phone.

4. Consider choosing a name that starts with a number or with the letters "A," "B," or "C" if you are in an area with many inns. This will put you at the top of any alphabetical list!

5. Naming the inn after yourself is popular with some people, but consider the day when you want to sell. The new owners will want to change the name, and, as a result, the inn's value will lessen.

Our Top Web Site Picks for Inn-Keepers

➤ www.bedandbreakfast.com

➤ www.staples.com

➤ www.inndoors.com

➤ www.americanhotel.com

➤ Your own! (Check out Park's at www.benchmarkinn.com.)

alpha books

W9-CGR-602

The Top Ten Suggestions from Inn-Keepers Who Know

"Be patient, don't lose sight of your dream, and have a lot of money at the start!"

—Jay Lesiger, Chelsea Pines Inn, New York, New York

"The B&B business is often like marriage. That which attracts us to the other partner is the very thing that drives us a little crazy."

—Nancy Saxton and Jan Bartlett, Saltair Bed & Breakfast/Alpine Cottages, Salt Lake City, Utah

"It's important that you have an idea of how to draw customers, do budgets, and become profitable. This is a business, not something that most of us can afford to do for the fun of it!"

—Michael MacIntyre and Bob Anderson, The Brass Key, Provincetown, Massachusetts

"Be prepared to cook, clean, shop, greet guests, and be a concierge every day with a smile on your face. You might be tired, ill, or feeling blue, but your guests don't want to know that. For them you *will* smile and be cheerful."

—Rick and Ruth-Anne Broad, Anne's Oceanfront Hideaway B&B, Salt Spring Island, B.C., Canada

"We always say to our customers that if they stay here more than once, we'll know them by their first names; twice, and we'll know what they like to drink and have for dinner."

—Dennis Radtke, County Clare—an Irish Guesthouse and Pub, Milwaukee, Wisconsin

"To make guests happy without losing your sanity, don't promise anything you can't deliver in normal routines."

—Tom and Janice Fairbanks, The Old Wailuku Inn at Ulupono, Wailuku, Hawaii

"Do Fast. Be Fast. Go Fast."

—Dr. Daniel and Evelyn Shirbroun, Joshua Tree Inn, Joshua Tree, California

"Remember that no matter how busy you are, you have only one chance to make a first impression—whether that impression is on the phone, through e-mail, or in person."

—Sabrina Riddle and Lynette Molnar, The Fairbanks Inn, Provincetown, Massachusetts

"No matter how long you're in this business, how much you've learned, and how well you've anticipated every problem, some new one will come along."

—Nancy-Linn Nellis, 1794 Watchtide by the Sea, Searsport, Maine

"It is so important to do your very best with everything. *You* are your best advertisement!"

—Ken and Karen Sharp, The Barn of Rockford Bed & Breakfast, Rockford, Illinois

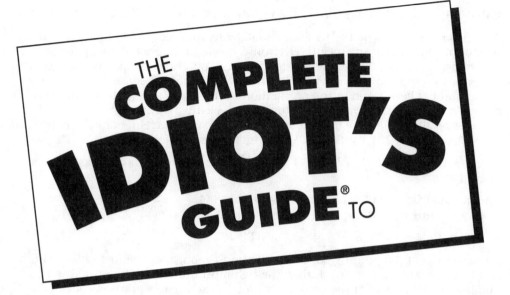

THE

COMPLETE IDIOT'S GUIDE® TO

Running a Bed and Breakfast

by Park Davis and Susannah Craig

alpha books

201 West 103rd Street
Indianapolis, IN 46290

A Pearson Education Company

International Standard Book Number: 0-02-864000-4
Library of Congress Catalog Card Number: available upon request.

03   02   01   8   7   6   5   4   3   2   1

Interpretation of the printing code: The rightmost number of the first series of numbers is the year of the book's printing; the rightmost number of the second series of numbers is the number of the book's printing. For example, a printing code of 01-1 shows that the first printing occurred in 2001.

Printed in the United States of America

Publisher
Marie Butler-Knight

Product Manager
Phil Kitchel

Managing Editor
Jennifer Chisholm

Acquisitions Editor
Amy Zavatto

Development Editor
Doris Cross

Senior Production Editor
Christy Wagner

Copy Editor
Rachel Lopez

Illustrator
Jody Schaeffer

Cover Designers
Mike Freeland
Kevin Spear

Book Designers
Scott Cook and Amy Adams of DesignLab

Indexer
Amy Lawrence

Layout/Proofreading
Svetlana Dominguez
Daryl Kessler
Lizbeth Patterson

Contents at a Glance

Contents

Foreword

➤ You love to entertain. Arranging flowers, setting a lovely table, preparing mouth-watering meals are among your favorite activities. Being an inn-keeper would be the perfect way to make the most of these talents, right?

➤ You've taken an early retirement package from a Big Corporation and are ready to sell your house in the suburbs. Opening a bed and breakfast in the mountains would make the ideal change of pace, no?

➤ You're known as Mr. or Ms. Fixit. From leaky faucets to weird wiring, you can always get the job done. Stripping wallpaper and paint is a piece of cake. Who better than you to restore that ramshackle Queen Anne Victorian as an inn?

If you could answer yes to any of these or similar questions, and you've long dreamed of being a bed and breakfast inn-keeper, then this book is for you. Not only is it easy and fun to read, but it's an excellent investment. If you decide to follow your dream, you'll find its invaluable advice a great help. If you flunk the inn-keeper wannabe test in Chapter 1, you'll be thankful that you purchased the book that saved your fantasy dream from becoming a reality nightmare.

Over the past 15 years, we've seen the bed and breakfast industry evolve from modest homestays where shared baths were the norm to today's sophisticated operations, where in-room whirlpool tubs, fireplaces, media centers, and telephone and Internet access are commonplace. Not long ago, not many Americans even knew what a B&B was, much less stayed in one. Today bed and breakfast inns are an accepted sector of the lodging industry, and are mentioned often—and not just in ads—in magazines, on radio and television, and in movies.

The widespread use of computers and the Internet has sparked the biggest change of all. Combining the high-touch world of innkeeping with the high-tech world of Web sites, online bookings, e-mail newsletters, and computerized property management software, is both a challenge and a tremendous opportunity; authors Park Davis and Susannah Craig do a great job of leading you through the maze of software and online options you now have open to you.

It used to take years to get listed in the best guidebooks; now it takes a month or two to be included in the top online directories. Inn-keepers who used to agonize endlessly about the expense of creating a lavish color brochure now can create an extensive Web site at a fraction of the cost, yet have thousands of additional readers. Print newsletters, which cost a small fortune to mail, can now be sent free via e-mail. All this information—*and much more*—is outlined by Park and Susannah, liberally salted with comments from experienced inn-keepers around the country, plus lots of helpful tips and thoughtful suggestions.

In addition to giving you all the technical savvy, hands-on practicalities and strategic planning advice, the authors never lose sight of the key quality that sets ordinary inns apart from the extraordinary ones—*the inn-keepers themselves*. These amazing folks can sense which guests need a little extra time and advice and which ones want only privacy. These inn-keepers have learned to create a gracious atmosphere where guests can be pampered, and they also know how and when to recharge their own batteries. They're able to keep their inn running smoothly, yet avoid having a long list of rules that would be more appropriate for a youth hostel than for a B&B. After you read this book, you'll either be on your way to becoming just such an inn-keeper, or, if you decide not to quit your day job, we're sure you'll have a new appreciation for the challenging job of running a B&B.

Eric Goldreyer and Sandra W. Soule

Eric Goldreyer is the president of BedandBreakfast.com, which he founded in 1994. In a few short years Goldreyer has made BedandBreakfast.com the leading online publisher in the B&B industry, with information on more than 23,000 bed and breakfasts and inns throughout the United States and internationally. In 1999, Goldreyer formed a partnership with WorldRes, Inc., the leading online hotel distribution network connecting hotels to leisure travelers.

Sandy Soule published America's first B&B guidebook in 1982. She's gone on to write her own guidebook series, inaugurate the Internet's first inn directory, establish her own Web site, and tour hundreds of B&Bs. At BedandBreakfast.com, Sandy writes the *BedandBreakfast.com Report* for consumers, the *Innkeeper News* for inn-keepers, and has led workshops at dozens of inn-keeping conferences.

Introduction

It's 8:45 A.M. Saturday morning. You slowly wake up to the sound of bluebirds and the warmth of summer sun. A few yawns, a good stretch, and that's all you need to start your Saturday, your day off. No work, no plans, a day all to your ... wait a minute, it's 8:45 A.M.! You have guests waiting downstairs for an 8:30 A.M. breakfast. You have three rooms to get ready before 1:00 P.M., and seven loads of laundry to finish. Your housekeeper is still out sick. The phone rings. It's your great Aunt Thelma calling to say that she and Uncle Henry will stop by today, say around 1:00 P.M., dear?

Okay, you get the idea. Running a bed and breakfast is not all hearts and flowers. Our preceding scenario certainly is not meant to discourage you; instead, think of it as your B&B wake-up call. If you've stayed at a few B&Bs and have met owners who seemed calm and pleasant, you might have thought, "Wow! What a dream job. I can do that!" You're right—with a lot of hard work, some cash flow, and an endless pantry of perseverance, you *can* do this. Just remember, there's a lot more to this business than serving coffee, cake, and tea. The pleasant B&B owners you've met don't have it easy; they're just doing their jobs right by keeping any behind-the-scenes mishaps from being visible to their guests.

Our goal in writing this book was to give you the real scoop on the small-time accommodation business. Opening a B&B is fast becoming the dream of many couples, retirees, small families, and singles. Whatever category you do or do not fit into, we wrote this book to help you fulfill that dream—and alert you to some of the possible nightmares you could have along the way. We've tried our best to pack it with information that you can't get anywhere else. We petitioned dozens of real live B&B, inn, and guest house owners for their best advice and anecdotes so you could get a taste of the real thing.

It's important that you find out as much as you can about the B&B lifestyle before you take the plunge. If you haven't stayed in many B&Bs, you have some homework ahead of you. Find a few spare weekends, some spare spending cash, and some B&Bs in areas you've never stayed in before (see a list of contributing B&B owners later in the Introduction and some Web sites that list B&Bs in Appendixes B and C). If you already know what type of B&B you're interested in opening (historical, ranch, seaside) try to stay at similar establishments. Take this book with you, along with your best observation skills. Make notes about everything you like and don't like. Ask the owner if he or she has some spare time to talk with you and share some experiences. If you have a not-so-great time, don't give up; try staying at another B&B.

What's not to love about a job that lets you work at home, get a tax break, and meet interesting people all day long? You're absolutely right. These—and more—are all known perks in this business. You may not be able to sleep in on weekends anymore but you will discover that owning your own B&B is the best decision you ever made.

How to Use This Book

We've divided this book into six parts. With each part you'll step further into the complex business of running a B&B. We take you from your very first thought of starting a business to branching out and expanding your success.

Part 1, "Home Sweet Home," tells you what this industry is all about, what it takes to run a B&B, and what kind of B&B you might like to run.

Part 2, "Taking the Plunge," plunges right into startup basics. Learn how to get your house and finances in order.

Part 3, "Getting the Word Out," gives you the lowdown on marketing, advertising, word of mouth, and more.

Part 4, "Making It Your Own," tells you how to make your B&B stand out from others, and how to get supplies and set house rules.

Part 5, "Getting Down to Business," details everything you need to know about daily operations, from breakfast to bedtime.

Part 6, "The Next Level," helps you review your progress, make plans to expand, and stay in business!

A Little Something Extra

Look in Appendixes B and C for lists of B&B organizations and handy resources of all kinds. For important points and extra information, check out the following boxes throughout the book:

Inn the Know

In these boxes you'll find tips and inside information that will give you an advantage.

B&B-eware!

Look for these red flags to warn you of problems so you can avoid them.

Coffee Talk

Get advice and tips from experienced and successful B&B owners and professionals.

Shoestring Solution

Great ideas on how to accomplish a lot with a little.

Acknowledgments

Here's our chance to thank the many people who've given us their support and guidance during the months of writing and researching this book. Here goes: Amy Zavatto for being both sin sister and editor extraordinaire, Meredith Blakely for her colorful guidance, Ruthanne Corazzini for her patient counsel, Doris Cross for her never-ending perseverance, Nana Phinney for pizza rolls and the traveler's perspective, and Bonnie and Ken Craig for letting Susannah pick their brains on small business quirks. Park honors his lovable Mom and loves the relatives who honored him with an inheritance. Susannah would like to thank Casey Edwards for his stealth-like support and Cosmo for not eating the manuscript. We would also like to thank Christy Wagner and all those behind-the-sceners at Alpha Books who have really made this book possible.

Special Thanks to the Technical Reviewers

The Complete Idiot's Guide to Running a Bed and Breakfast was reviewed by experts who double-checked the accuracy of what you'll learn here to ensure that this book gives you everything you need to know about owning and managing a bed and breakfast. Special thanks are extended by Park to Michael MacIntyre and Bob Anderson of The Brass Key Guesthouse in Provincetown, Massachusetts, for their inspiration and friendship and by Susannah for their keen eye and ultra-expert advice. Their expertise and invaluable contributions helped give this book a brass polish!

Special Thanks to the Contributors

We also would like to send a special warm-fuzzy thanks to our contributing innkeepers and professionals who helped make this book wonderfully down to earth, incredibly insightful, and funny, too:

Kerry Adams
Fireside Insurance Company
10 Shank Painter Common
Provincetown, MA 02657
Phone: 1-800-286-9045

Jane Bertorelli, Co-Owner/Inn-Keeper
The Union Street Inn
2229 Union Street
San Francisco, CA 94123
Phone: 415-346-0424
Fax: 415-922-8046
Web site: www.unionstreetinn.com
E-mail: innkeeper@unionstreetinn.com

Meredith Blakeley
Cape Cod Interiors, Inc.
78 Route 6A
Orleans, MA 02653
Phone: 508-240-0880
E-mail: ccdesign@mediaone.net

Rick and Ruth-Anne Broad, Owners/
Inn-Keepers
Anne's Oceanfront Hideaway B&B
168 Simson Road
Salt Spring Island, B.C. V8K 1E2
Canada
Phone: 250-537-0851
Reservations: 1-888-474-2663
Web site: www.annesoceanfront.com
E-mail: annes@saltspring.com

Ken Burnet and Greg Nemrow
(Owners), Sue Burnet (Inn-Keeper)
Gaige House Inn
13540 Arnold Drive
Glen Ellen, CA 95442
Phone: 707-935-0237
Reservations: 1-800-935-0237
Fax: 707-935-6411
Web site: www.gaige.com
E-mail: gaige@sprynet.com

Richard and Sam Corcoran
Hell's Blazes
PO Box 635
Old Mystic, CT 06372
Phone: 860-535-2335 or 1-888-MY-
DEVIL (1-888-693-3845)
Fax: 860-535-2628
Web site: www.visitmystic.com/
hellsblazes

Jerry and Sara Cross
Victoria Crossing
922 Beaumont Highway
Lebanon, CT 06249
Phone: 860-642-6998
Web site:www.ctquietcorner.org

Tom and Janice Fairbanks,
Owners/Inn-Keepers
The Old Wailuku Inn at Ulupono
2199 Kahookele Street
Wailuku, HI 96793
Phone: 808-244-5897 or
1-800-305-4899
Fax: 808-242-9600
Web site: www.mauiinn.com
E-mail: host@mauiinn.com

Claude and Mariette Gagne, Publishers
*The B&B and Country Inn Marketplace
Resource Guide*
926 Lenoir Rhyne Boulevard SE
Hickory, NC 28602
Phone: 828-324-7291 or
1-800-871-8977
Web site: www.innmarketing.com
E-mail: innsales@charter.net

Peter Garza and Christopher Covelli,
Former Owners/Inn-Keepers
Christopher's by the Bay
8 Johnson Street
Provincetown, MA 02657
Phone/fax: 508-487-9263
Reservations: 877-487-9263
Web site: www.capecod.net/
christophers
E-mail: christophers@capecod.net

Tari Hampe
Tari's, a Premiere Café and Inn
123 North Washington Street
Berkeley Springs, WV 25411
Phone: 304-258-1196
E-mail: thampe@intrepid.net

Mark Hancock, former owner
(New Owner: Crystal Castellanos)
Miss Molly's Hotel Bed & Breakfast
4550 Waycrest Drive
Fort Worth, TX 76180
Phone: 817-919-7188
Web site: www.missmollys.com
E-mail: missmollys@travelbase.com

Rainer Horn and Jürgen Herzog,
Owners/Inn-Keepers
Carpe Diem Guesthouse
12 Johnson Street
Provincetown, MA 02657
Phone/fax: 508-487-4242
Reservations: 1-800-487-0132
Web site:
www.carpediemguesthouse.com
E-mail: carpediem@capecod.net

Jeffrey Houston
Advanced Payroll, Inc.
PO Box 521
Provincetown, MA 02657-0521
Local: 508-487-2320
In-state toll-free: 1-877-487-2320
E-mail: advpayrollinc@aol.com

Michelle and Allen Kruger, Owners
Arbor House Bed & Breakfast at
Kruger's Farm Winery
75 Chester Maine Road
North Stonington, CT 06359
Phone: 860-535-4221
Web site:
www.visionthing.com/ArborHouse
E-mail: arborhouse@visionthing.com

Warren Lefkowich, Owner
West End Inn
44 Commercial Street
Provincetown, MA 02657
Phone: 508-487-9555 or
1-800-559-1220
Web site: www.westendinn.com

Jay Lesiger, Owner
Chelsea Pines Inn
317 West 14th Street
New York, NY 10014
Phone: 212-929-1023

Michael MacIntyre and Bob Anderson,
Owners/Inn-Keepers
The Brass Key Guesthouse
67 Bradford Street
Provincetown, MA 02657
Phone: 508-487-9005
Reservations: 1-800-842-9858
Fax: 508-487-9020
Web site: www.brasskey.com
E-mail: ptown@brasskey.com

Stephen Mascilo and Trevor Pinker,
Owners/Inn-Keepers
Beaconlight Guesthouse,
12 Winthrop Street
The Oxford, 8 Cottage Street
Provincetown, MA 02657
Beaconlight:
Phone/fax: 508-487-9603 or
1-800-696-9603
Web site: www.capecod.net/
beaconlight
E-mail: beaconlite@capecod.net
The Oxford:
Phone/fax: 508-487-9103 or
1-888-456-9103
Web site: www.capecod.net/oxford
E-mail: oxford@capecod.net

Martha McGinn and Simone Evans,
Owners/Inn-Keepers
Lizzie Borden Bed, Breakfast and
Museum
92 Second Street
Fall River, MA 02721
Phone: 508-675-7333
Web site: www.lizzie-borden.com
E-mail: lizziebnb@earthlink.net

John and Suzanne Munn
Vista Verde Ranch
PO Box 465
Steamboat Springs, CO 80477
Phone: 970-879-3858 or
1-800-526-7433
Fax: 970-879-1413
Web site: www.vistaverde.com
E-mail: vistaverde@compuserve.com

Nancy-Linn Nellis, Inn-Keeper
Watchtide by the Sea
190 West Main Street
Searsport, ME 04974
Phone: 207-548-6575 or
1-800-698-6575
Fax: 207-548-0938
Web site: www.watchtide.com
E-mail: stay@watchtide.com

Reonn Rabon, Inn-Keeper/Partner
Green Gables Guest House
1503 Second Avenue West
Seattle, WA 98119
Phone: 206-282-6863 or
1-800-400-1503
Web site: www.greengablesseattle.com
E-mail: info@greengablesseattle.com

Dennis Radtke, Manager
County Clare—an Irish Guesthouse
and Pub
124 North Astor Street
Milwaukee, WI 53202
Phone: 414-272-5273 or 1-888-
94-CLARE (1-888-942-5273)

Fax: 414-290-6300
Web site: www.countyclare-inn.com
E-mail: ctyclare@execpc.com

Sabrina Riddle and Lynette Molnar,
Owners/Inn-Keepers
The Fairbanks Inn
90 Bradford Street
Provincetown, MA 02657
Phone: 508-487-0386
Reservations: 1-800-324-7265
Web site: www.fairbanksinn.com
E-mail: info@fairbanksinn.com

Col. (ret.) John and Julie Rolsen,
Owners/Inn-Keepers
Garth Woodside Mansion Bed and
Breakfast
11069 New London Road
Hannibal, MO 63401
Phone: 573-221-2789 or
1-888-427-8409
Web site: www.garthmansion.com
E-mail: garth@nemonet.com

Nancy Saxton and Jan Bartlett
Saltair Bed & Breakfast/Alpine Cottages
164 South 900 East
Salt Lake City, UT 84102
Phone: 801-533-8184
Reservations: 1-800-733-8184
Fax: 801-595-0332
Web site: www.saltlakebandb.com
E-mail: saltair@saltlakebandb.com

Ken and Karen Sharp, Owners/
Inn-Keepers
The Barn of Rockford Bed & Breakfast
6786 Guilford Road
Rockford, IL 61107
Phone: 815-395-8535 or
1-888-378-1729
E-mail: BarnRkfd@Juno.com

Dr. Daniel and Evelyn Shirbroun,
Owners/Inn-Keepers
Joshua Tree Inn
61259 29 Palms Highway
PO Box 340
Joshua Tree, CA 92252
Phone: 760-366-1188 or 1-800-366-1444
E-mail: joshuatreeinn@thegrid.net

Robyn and Wolfgang Wendt,
Owners/Inn-Keepers
Rhythm of the Sea
1123 Beach Drive
Cape May, NJ 08204
Phone: 609-884-7788 or
1-800-498-6888
Web site: www.rhythmofthesea.com
E-mail: rhythm@algorithms.com

Trademarks

All terms mentioned in this book that are known to be or are suspected of being trademarks or service marks have been appropriately capitalized. Alpha Books and Pearson Education cannot attest to the accuracy of this information. Use of a term in this book should not be regarded as affecting the validity of any trademark or service mark.

Part 1

Home Sweet Home

The best way to prepare for entering this business is to start with yourself. You'll need to do some heavy analyzing of your current lifestyle, whether you (and the family) can handle running a bed and breakfast, and if you can hack it as a host. When you get up from the therapist's couch, learn about growth in the B&B industry and where current trends are heading. Discover the many options you have to make your B&B uniquely yours!

Open, Sez Me!

This is it. The dream of opening up your own bed and breakfast could come true very soon. Running a bed and breakfast may be the best adventure of your life, and, as in any new adventure, you'll encounter pitfalls, triumphs, and a lot of "in betweeners."

Before you dive into this book and the B&B way of life, you need to be armed with the best advice first. Our advice is this: Hear everyone and listen to no one. Don't get us wrong, we wouldn't have written this book if we believed you should head into this business willy-nilly, without doing some research. We've done our best to bring you solid and useful information that will give you real insight into what this business is all about.

The lifestyle is rewarding, demanding, and a great way to earn extra income. Keep in mind, though, that it also is completely different from anything you've ever experienced. First, take the test: Find out if your personality and abilities will give you a good shot at running a successful B&B—and enjoying it. If you decide to plunge in, this book will prepare you for the many challenges you'll encounter in planning, setting up, and running your very own bed and breakfast.

The Tradition of Welcoming Strangers

In the United States, the B&B business is relatively new. In other parts of the world, particularly Europe, the industry is centuries old. As you might have guessed, the business of charging strangers to sleep in your house has been a way to make a few extra nickels, francs, or marks for a long time. Pre–twenty-first-century travelers didn't have Best Westerns to check in to, so they had to rely on strangers to give them a bed for the night and to send them off with a hot meal in the morning.

It wasn't long before the casual services homeowners offered to travelers grew into a business, and throughout North America the bed and breakfast became an alternative to the commercial hotel.

Inn the Know

Guests would pay cash or trade something for their night's lodging and breakfast, sometimes choosing stops because they were known for their excellent rolls or comfortable beds.

Do You Have What It Takes?

As a host, you'll need to have the right balance of charm, generosity, humor, and professionalism. As an employer, you'll be striving for a positive working environment for your staff and efficiency without micromanagement. As an owner, you'll need to anticipate and plan for every aspect of the business, from marketing to taxes.

B&B-eware!

Knowing your own strengths and not-such-strengths before you open a B&B can save you a lot of grief. Taking our test is a good start.

Your skills as a host, employer, and owner are not all it takes to make it as a B&B owner; you need emotional and mental strength, too. If you have a short fuse or you lack the natural tendency to look after the needs of others, it might not be the right business for you, or you might need to do some work in these areas.

You, or you and your partner if there are two of you in the enterprise, need to know how to instantly put your guests at ease. A good B&B host radiates an easygoing nature and genuine charm. We're not talking an Eddie Haskel, "Boy, ma'am, you sure do look lovely today" kind of charm. You need to truly like—and be interested in—people. If you're not fond of dealing with strangers, your guests will pick up on it right away; the worst thing you can do is to make them feel like intruders! But don't despair: It is possible to bump up your charm quotient. (See "Hosting 101: Improve Your Score," later in this chapter.)

Before you start picking out carpet and hanging numbers on guest rooms, find some time to analyze yourself in every way. In addition to being personable and confident, a good host is efficient, accommodating, energetic, humble, observant, humorous, and able to troubleshoot with the best of them.

Just think, owning a B&B means that you'll run a business out of your home. No more boss, no more lousy commute, no more 9 to 5! That's all true. You'll be your own boss, which can be great—and also a great responsibility. The commute certainly is a short one if your B&B is the home you live in. And, if you think you won't be working 9 A.M. to 5 P.M. anymore you're right—prepare for a 9 A.M. to 9 A.M. workload (translation: 24 hours a day)!

Now is the time—before you knock down walls and buy pillows—to decide if this business is for you. Running a B&B is not a job; it's a lifestyle. You'll start going to the grocery store at 2:00 P.M. on Tuesdays because it's the best time to miss the crowds. Your Sunday morning routine of reading the paper and taking the dog for a walk now will move to Monday evening, during your manager's shift. You'll learn to buy your favorite GAP jeans online instead of wasting time at the mall. These might seem like small adjustments now but they'll become big sacrifices if you're not fond of changing routines.

When imagining what your life will be like as the inn-keeper, do yourself a favor and consider how every part of your life will be affected. Take into account your daily routine, your evenings, your family's routine, your vacations, and your weekends. Make sure your trade-offs will not undermine your happiness. If you're determined to make this lifestyle change you will find ways to compensate for whatever you have to give up. For more on determining whether this lifestyle is for you, check out Chapter 3, "What It's Really Like."

This Is a Test; This Is Only a Test

Cheat on this test and you'll be cheating on—that's right—yourself. If you plan to co-own your B&B, have your partner take this test, too, and then match up the scores. You might discover (or confirm) that one person will make a better host whereas the other has better organizational skills. Be honest in your answers and then keep reading to find out how to improve your score.

1. **Social misfit?** Your partner drags you kicking and screaming to a boring but swanky corporate party. During the evening, your partner gets into an involved conversation with the company's head cheese. You …

    a. Sit in the corner and sulk.

    b. Talk to the office clown.

    c. Walk over to the bar and get plastered.

    d. Find an outsider like yourself to talk with.

    How you did: You probably didn't pick **a** or **c** because you knew those were the "wrong" answers (although some of us have, at one time or another, sulked in a corner or drunk our sorrows away). If you picked "talk to the office clown," it shows that you're social, but you won't go out of your way to make conversation. Talking with an outsider shows that you have no problems conversing with a total stranger. When your guests first stay with you they will be, after all, just strangers.

2. **Persistence potential.** Your B&B has been up and running for two months now. All that time you've been trying, unsuccessfully, to get a particular travel writer to swing your way. You …

    a. Give it a rest and maybe try again next month.

    b. Call your mom.

    c. Keep calling the writer, even if you get voice mail every time.

    d. Send a clever package; maybe a picture of a toothbrush with the words, "Now that you've packed, we'll take care of the rest" on your business card, tucked inside a brochure.

How you did: You might have chosen **c**, but if someone won't talk to you or get back to you, take the hint. Don't take it personally, but do stop calling. If you chose **a**, you're closer than you think to giving up altogether. Choosing **b** definitely is a sign of giving up. Probably **d** was an obvious answer, but stop and think about why this option can work so well. You haven't spent tons of money, you're not being a pest, and you've made yourself and the business stand out in an unusual way. Not getting what you want can be frustrating, especially when it comes to the success of your business. Persistence will always pay off, especially if your tactics are understated but you still get your point across. Being persistent doesn't mean you need to be pesky. If one game plan doesn't work, figure out why and switch to something else.

3. **Time management technique.** Your last set of guests just checked in for the day. You have a spare hour so you decide to …

    a. Organize your messy kitchen, starting with the cereal.

    b. Call your mom.

    c. Write out the breakfast menu for the coming week and make a shopping list.

    d. Go out food shopping.

How you did: Guests just checked in, so **d** is not a good choice; **c** is okay, but it won't take the full hour; and **a** is ambitious, but the kitchen's condition might be making you crazy and slowing you down as well. If you think you can plan the menu, write the list, and give ma a ring, good for you. If you can organize the kitchen and call mommy, you'll be destined for B&B greatness. (Remember to tell her about your clever idea of sending a package to the travel writer. She'll be so proud!)

4. **Crisis control.** On a particularly crazy day, a staff member shows up an hour late, just when guests are eating a sit-down meal. At the same time, a guest calls

to say there's no soap in the bathroom. While you're on the phone, you notice that your tardy employee is gabbing with another staffer who is trying to get things done. You ...

   a. Quickly apologize to the guest about the soap and offer to send someone up right away. When you get off the phone, you speak to the tardy employee in private.

   b. Take care of the tardy employee right away because the guests who are eating breakfast need tending to while you're on the phone.

   c. Take orange marmalade and scrawl the words "get back to work" on the kitchen counter.

   d. Ignore your employees, finish your phone conversation, and then tend to the dining area yourself.

How you did: Although **c** will get the job done, your employees will receive it as a very hostile act; choosing **d** means you need to work on confrontation; if you chose **b**, you will have insulted the guest on the phone and been seen as unprofessional. Taking each situation as it's presented to you usually works best. Choosing **a** means being gracious and responsive to the angered guest on the phone and handling your tardy employee in private. This is not just a test of how well you handle your employees or your guests. Handling everyday situations quickly and correctly will make your B&B run smoothly. Think of yourself as the wizard behind the curtain (or in the kitchen). All your guests are Dorothys who can never know your behind-the-scenes secrets. To accomplish this, you need to make fast decisions that keep the show rolling.

5. **Confrontation cool.** At check-out guests inform you that they had not received towel service that day nor did they sleep very well either night because of noise from a nearby room. They demand a full refund. You ...

   a. Give them sincere apologies. You then gently point out that, if you'd been informed of the problems the day before, you could have done such and such about them. You offer them a discount, but not a full refund.

   b. Buckle, and give them a full refund. After all, you need returning guests.

   c. Show them the door. Who needs guests like that?!

   d. Apologize over and over and over again. Tell them you'll do anything to satisfy them except give them any type of refund on the bill.

How you did: Choosing **c** feels bad all around; you feel as if you've failed somehow (even if you haven't). The **b** choice feels all wrong. You want guests to return, but do you want *these* guests to return? Choosing **d** is a wishy-washy way to handle this situation. Trying to get the guests to leave without making any amends at all could develop into a riotous situation. The **a** choice lets your guests know that you would have taken care of the problem. Offering a compromise enables you to stand your ground while letting them feel as if they've won. Situations such as this are tricky. You want your guests to be happy but you can't give in to every request, either. You won't have (if all goes well) every guest asking for a full refund, but it will happen.

6. **Team spirit.** A staff member is out sick and your other employee is struggling to ready four guest rooms in two hours, before all guests check in. You're busy paying bills and answering the phone, which has been ringing off the hook. You ...

    a. Keep doing what you're doing.

    b. Put the bills down, let the machine get the phone, and help your staff.

    c. Put the bills down, take the phone with you, and help your staff.

    d. Decide to go to the store to get away from the madness.

How you did: If you chose **a** or **d**, those rooms will not be ready when guests arrive. The choice between **b** and **c** is tricky; it's up to you and how you like to operate. If you don't want to miss any calls or have to return any, take the phone with you. If you know that answering the phone will distract you too much from the work at hand, let the machine take care of it. If you have staff helping you out, remember that they are helping you out. Having hands-on, go-getting blood in your veins is the only way to run a B&B. You or your partner as well as your manager will need to approach the daily work this way so that nothing suffers.

7. **Flexibility fitness.** Potential guests who've visited your Web site call for a one-night, mid-week stay during a normally slow period. They inquire about a corporate rate. You ...

    a. Tell them you're closed mid-week, thinking you don't want to be bothered for one night at a lower rate.

    b. Tell them you can't speak English.

    c. Tell them you're not equipped to handle business travelers and mention that there's a Ramada Inn nearby.

    d. Ask them how much they're looking to spend and what services, if any, they need.

How you did: There are two tricks to this question. First, how flexible are you willing to be to get a room filled? The second, more understated, consideration is, are you asking the right questions? Maybe the potential guests actually are three travelers looking for three rooms. If you chose **d**, be sure to mention a range of rates to get a better sense of what the guests need. Also find out exactly what they need in business services. If these guests request the use of a fax machine and you don't have one, **c** is a good choice, and also can be the best one if you really don't want to be bothered for one night during the week. You'll just resent their being there, especially if it's not worth it financially. The important thing is to be flexible when you get the call, find out what the situation is, and then choose how you'll handle the caller.

8. **Funny bone factor.** A guest calls down from the room to say there's an emergency. You rush up to find the guest grasping onto the cord of an air conditioner that's dangling from the window—above your car! You and the guest try to get the AC up but, when it looks ready to give way, you get the idea of moving your car. You run down, start the car, and get it out of the way—just as the AC comes crashing down. Not a scratch on the car, just the busted air conditioner. You …

   a. Charge the guest for the replacement value of the AC and for opening the window in the first place.

   b. Joke with the guest that there are easier ways to get cool, such as turning on the AC instead of taking it out of the window. Then, strike a deal.

   c. Give the guest a piece of your mind.

   d. Clean up the mess, move your car, and then give the guest the silent treatment until he or she leaves.

How you did: If you can't laugh at some situations, you'll be a very rigid and stressed-out host. We chose the "dangling air conditioner" scenario because, believe it or not, we've heard this story from several inn-keepers! Most guests will feel very silly in a situation like this and will, let's hope, offer to pay for the AC. If they don't, we'd be inclined to choose **b**—make a joke of it and strike a deal with the embarrassed guest. If the guest is arrogant, shoot for most or all of the replacement value. Worse things than this can happen, and you, too, will have an air conditioner story to tell.

Hosting 101: Improve Your Score

Assessing what you're good at—and not so good at—is tough. A lot of the questions we asked made you react to situations based on your personality. There isn't, and shouldn't be, a set of rules that each host must follow. Everyone is different (a very good thing), and each B&B will provide a different atmosphere based on, well, you.

Do you find it easy to talk to anyone or only to people in similar situations, or people of your age or race? Are you nervous or self-conscious, and is that obvious to other people? Do they just smile and move quietly away, or are they engaged and put at ease by you? These are all things that can be improved upon.

Start by making conversation with total strangers and pay attention to how they react to you. The more people you talk to, the easier this will get. If you're lacking in the confidence category, this is something that needs to change right away. Don't be intimidated by a person's blank stare or sharp comment. If you have the confidence to break the ice with people, they'll respond in a positive way. If they don't, laugh it off and move on. The important thing is that you make the effort, and by doing that, you're well on your way to becoming a charming and genuine host.

Coffee Talk

Managing your day is not always easy, especially when unexpected situations pop up. If you have a good handle on how long projects actually take and when you can get them done, each day will become smoother than the one before.

If you need to manage your time better, put yourself to the test. Work a typical day and keep a time log of what you did. When you look at it at the end of the day you'll find holes or places where you could have been doing something more productive. The following day, schedule in projects that you know can be completed in the time you allow. Have several projects waiting in the wings in case you need to switch to something that can be completed in a shorter time period.

There are certain skills, such as being flexible, managing your time, and dealing well with conflict, that are must-have skills. If you've discovered through our test that you need work in some of these areas, do the work. Put yourself in situations that require those skills. If you're low on people skills, start talking to strangers. If you give up on things, take on a project that you know will require persistence to complete. If you're used to being in a management position, volunteer for a hands-on community project to get a feel for being part of a team.

Inn the Know

If we had the space, we could ask you a gazillion more questions that would help you assess your capabilities. With a friend or your partner, try thinking up situations on your own to test your responses. Some suggested areas are your enjoyment of providing services to others, acceptance of all types of people, handling of finances, everyday stamina, how well you take care of yourself, and how honest you are with yourself when things aren't going right.

Any steps you take to improve on your skills will be of help. Just having an awareness of your inn-keeping capabilities is enough to put you ahead.

Common Misconceptions

If you're like most people who have come to this life decision, some good experiences at B&Bs have sparked a dreamy notion of B&B ownership. The key here is that you had those good times as a B&B guest. If running a B&B were like staying at a B&B, everyone would be doing it! There are a lot of misconceptions about being a B&B owner, such as …

➤ **Working at home is bliss.** Working at home definitely can be great. Advantages such as a short commute and no required dress code have more and more people looking for ways to work from home. If these are your main reasons for owning a B&B, however, think twice before making the decision. "I work at home" would be the last way a B&B owner would describe how he or she makes a living. It would be more like "I own my own bed and breakfast." Owning your own B&B is a profession, not a part-time job. Even if you plan to run a very small operation, make sure you head into this new career with a professional head on your shoulders.

➤ **I'll own a B&B when I retire.** To retire means to "withdraw," "retreat," or "go away from." In other words, to stop working! If you've worked hard at your current job for 40 years and then decided to "relax" by owning a B&B, you're in for a rough ride. A lot of people assume that cleaning, cooking, and "mingling" with guests are light duty. After all, you do it for your family or yourself, why not do it for a few extra people who will pay you? Again, keep in mind that this is a business, not a cocktail party (although opening up a B&B is a great reason to have one!).

➤ **People will be lined up outside my door.** Well, maybe if you bought an existing operation that kept excellent books, or found *the* spectacular location that was crying out for lodgers. Otherwise, nearly all new B&Bs can expect a slow start, mostly because no one will know you exist for a while. Although you'll be itching for income, growing gradually and working out the day-to-day kinks will give you a good foundation for the future.

➤ **This friend of my uncle's cousin's sister opened up a B&B six months ago and already makes a ton of dough.** It is possible to make good money in this business; but be prepared to not see a major profit in the first year or even few years. Let's hope you get lucky and have 100 percent occupancy in your first year—but that's rare. Your best advertisement is word of mouth and because your first few months will see a limited amount of guests, the word can be spread only so far. Plus, you'll dish out a fair amount of clams for start-up expenses, which will eat into your profit for the first year and beyond.

➤ **After the house is renovated and decorated, my job will be done.** Having your property ready for business will be one of your most gratifying accomplishments, primarily because you'll feel a sense of completion. As you joyfully suck

11

down eggnog at your open house, though, don't allow yourself to think that your work is done. Your newly renovated house is the start of your newly renovated life. The preparation is over, now on to the adventure!

➤ **The neighbors will love having a B&B next door!** Don't count your chickens (unless you're on a farm, silly). Neighbors might not welcome 5, 10, or 20 cars coming and going at all hours. They might have had a quiet existence until you showed up, and they'd probably like to keep it that way. Talk to your neighbors before you move ahead with the business. Tell them about your plans for construction (if any) and for keeping them happy (building a fence or creating a different parking area). Try to involve them in the process and listen to their suggestions. However, be careful to not let them push you around. Property lines get fuzzy when someone decides to make improvements.

More Than Making Beds and Breakfast

Starting up a B&B is exciting and anxiety inducing at the same time. Before you have heartburn trouble or sweaty palms, do all you can to prepare yourself mentally and physically for the experience.

Running a B&B is more than just making beds and serving breakfast, because it requires you to be much more than housecleaner and chef. The roles you take on and the challenges you must meet will stretch from one end of your patience to the other. The only way to prepare for this undertaking is to do your homework. Find out about this business from those who've been there. Get to know the process of start-up, and watch out for the challenges to come.

Finding Out the Real Deal Firsthand

It's one thing to imagine grandma's apple pie and quite another to have a slice. Take time out to learn about the B&B business firsthand from owners and managers. It's the only way to get a real taste for the everyday life of an inn-keeper!

➤ **Level One: Start by sleeping around.** Try to visit a few B&Bs of different sizes. If you can, stay in at least one that's in a completely different part of the country. By staying at a few B&Bs you'll get a different perspective from each experience and a better sense of what makes you comfortable in a B&B.

➤ **Level Two: Go back to school.** There are many conferences, seminars, and courses that you can take related to this business. If you plan to operate a 23-room inn and restaurant, consider taking some heavy courses in hotel management, accounting, and food preparation. Even if your B&B is smaller, it certainly won't hurt to sign up for a few weekend seminars. You may find that the interaction between people who are going through start-up and those who've been in the business for years is worth the experience. See Appendix C, "More Re-sources," for some organizations and inn-keepers that give seminars in different areas of the country.

Inn the Know

When you call to make reservations, it's not a good idea to let the inn-keepers know why you're planning a visit. When you visit, if hosts seem receptive, broach this in the middle or near the end of your stay. Observe closely, but be unobtrusive. When you're there, talk casually with the owners about how they got into the business, tricks they've learned, and odd guests they've had. Take notes about what you like and don't like about the rooms, the policies, breakfast, and how the inn-keepers interact with other guests.

➤ **Level Three: Get out there.** Getting some experience will really put you ahead in your own business. Even if you can find only part-time work at a hotel, it will help. If you already have management experience look for work as an inn-sitter. Some B&B owners want to take a vacation or even take a few afternoons a week off. By doing some inn-sitting you can gain priceless familiarity with the day-to-day life of owning a B&B. For more on acting as an inn-sitter, see Chapter 20, "Help Wanted."

As an inn-keeper, the best investment you can make is in yourself. Do all you can to fill your noggin with as much information and work experience as possible and you'll soon be on your way to success and peace of mind.

The Best Decision You Ever Make

We hope you come to feel that opening up your home to paying strangers is well worth the time and trouble. Running a B&B can be a great experience. If you enjoy hosting and entertaining in your home, that's a good start. If you're willing to take the baggage that comes with hosting every day, such as endless cleaning and cooking, that's even better.

Although you won't know until you're in the business if this is the life for you, you can start preparing now for the adjustments. Get ready to find strength and persever-ance that you didn't know was in you! Your world will now revolve around your B&B

business. If you run that business with professionalism, smarts, and a lot of laughs, you'll learn to love the way of life that goes with it. Only then will you decide that this was the best decision you ever made.

The Least You Need to Know

➤ Before you plunge ahead and open a bed and breakfast, find out if you have the personal characteristics and abilities you need to be successful at it.

➤ Owning a B&B is not only a career change; it's a lifestyle change. Explore the effects that changing your way of life will have on you and yours.

➤ There are many common misconceptions about owning a B&B. Do your homework before you make your decision.

➤ The best way to prepare for life as an inn-keeper is to visit B&Bs, take courses, go to seminars, and gain work experience.

Big Things in Small(er) Packages

The trend toward B&Bs began about 15 to 20 years ago. You might even remember the first time you said, "What's a B-n-B?" Now most everyone knows what B&B means (and that it's not "Bed & Brothel"), or at least they think they know. The classic definition of a cute old couple in a cute old farmhouse with cute lace curtains, home-baked biscuits, and decorative ducks definitely has changed. There are still very nice country-style B&Bs out there but they are no longer the only option. What started as a trend has turned into a steadily growing industry. And all in about a decade!

B&B vs. Inn: What's in a Name?

What's the difference between a B&B and an inn? Good question. Here's another good one: Does it matter which term you use? Not really. Although there are some basic guidelines for the distinctions between B&B, inn, B&B inn, guesthouse, homestay, manor, house, mansion, lodge, and plantation, the terms differ in meaning from place to place anyway.

The most important part of your business's name will be what you add to "Inn," "B&B," "Lodge," or the like. Spend some time on this and come up with something that represents you as the owner, the area you're located in, or the house itself. Pick something catchy, historical, or quaint. If the house was built before 1900, find something from the past to use in the name. A lot of houses built in the eighteenth century use the year of construction in their names, such as "The 1776 Hale House."

Inn the Know

Some owners wisely describe the type of B&B they have in its name by adding, for example, "Farm," "Tavern," "Beach House," "Chateau," or even "Maison" if the house has a French theme. Some houses that are linked to a second business reflect it in names such as "Inn and Golf Course" or "B&B and Antiques."

Here are some of the common distinctions among types of B&Bs and their counterparts:

➤ **Bed and breakfast.** Because of its designation, this type of establishment must provide some kind of meal in the morning. Typically, a true B&B will serve a full breakfast or something close to one. B&Bs that do not serve hot breakfasts usually will have buffet-style fare with a wide range of muffins, bagels, breads, cereal, toasting waffles, and fruit. The majority of them have an area set off for breakfast. Some B&Bs have a dining area with an outdoor patio, but all have some kind of area conducive to sitting down for a spell to enjoy morning coffee. B&Bs usually are smaller than inns, and average about three to six rooms, although some have as many as 15 rooms or even more. The owners of B&Bs typically live on the premises, which is not always the case with other types of houses.

Amenities in B&Bs have been minimal in the past but that is changing as more of them are adding such extras as whirlpool tubs and other special facilities to their rooms. (See "All the Rage," later in this chapter.)

➤ **Inn.** Like B&Bs, a lot of inns offer a full breakfast. The major distinction of most inns—and this is the classic definition—is that they usually operate as a full-service restaurant for guests and nonguests. Inns also tend to be larger than B&Bs, with six or more guest rooms. There are, however, many smaller inns that do not have restaurants but use the term "inn" because they don't offer a full breakfast (or any breakfast) and don't want to give guests the false hope of full morning fare. As you can see, anything goes in the name game!

➤ **B&B inn (or inn B&B).** Some use both "B&B" and "Inn" in their names. What for? Hard to tell. Some want to be known as an inn and also want to make it clear that breakfast is included in the room rate. Maybe others just couldn't choose between the two terms!

➤ **Guesthouse.** B&B and guesthouse are almost interchangeable except that breakfast is not expected in a guesthouse. It sometimes is served but it is rarely a full breakfast. Guesthouse is more commonly used in some parts of the country, such as in the South, whereas in New England, for example, owners are more inclined toward B&B or Inn.

Coffee Talk

Sam and Richard Corcoran of Old Mystic, Connecticut, have the hottest spot in town. When they started up their B&B four years ago they wanted a name that would "eliminate people looking for Aunt Tilly's Tea Room and would ensure that our guests have a sense of humor." Richard was a heating engineer for 30 years; the B&B is painted flaming red, and has five fireplaces and gargoyles as the main décor. All of these factors led to naming the B&B "Hell's Blazes." Sam and Richard say the name alone attracts business. "If you don't have an interesting name, you won't stick out. You have to have a gimmick to give you an edge."

➤ **Homestay.** A homestay typically is the most casual of all types of establishments. Usually three rooms are the most you'll find in a homestay. They rarely have private baths for any of the rooms but breakfast usually is included in the rate. Homestay owners usually live on the property, renting rooms within the family quarters (hence the name) but reserving most of the space for the family. Because homestays are born of a need for extra cash, few have state licenses or signs out front. Breakfast is not necessarily served and most guests are passersby who need a place to crash for the night and find the homestay by asking around.

Inn the Know

Old Bates-type motels (remember *Psycho?*), built from the 1950s through the 1970s, have become another recent trend among fixer-uppers. Some restore the rooms with kitschy décor from the period.

➤ **Manor, house, mansion, lodge, homestead, ranch, or plantation.** These are some of the more typical designations used for special types of houses or houses set in special locations. Manor and mansion can be interchangeable, but sometimes "manor" is used for a house that is not quite big enough to be considered a mansion. When "house" or "homestead" is used, it usually refers to a historic period or past owner; the "Captain Morgan House," for example. Lodges typically are set in the mountains and have a distinctly woodsy décor. Plantation

B&Bs usually are found in the South, and owners have restored or kept up their original charm. Some ranch B&Bs are extensions of operating ranches, created for supplemental income.

Insights into a Booming Industry

People from all walks of life—from cell phone salespeople to kindergarten teachers, and computer geeks to travel agents—are leaving their commuting jobs and starting up B&Bs. Those with experience in the service and hotel industry are learning from the bigwigs and then applying their knowledge to their own business. It's a smart way to go, especially as the outside world and B&B owners start to take the profession more seriously. Guests now are expecting more service at B&Bs, or at least more hotel-like amenities, such as TV/VCRs with remotes and small bottles of high-quality shampoo, and they're getting it, particularly in touristy and bustling areas where there's more competition among B&Bs for guests who increasingly pass up hotels for cozier lodgings at the "little guy."

Boutique guesthouses are fast becoming a popular trend among investors. These properties have a distinct character based on what they were originally; a property could have been something as unique as a prison, as common as a bank, or have simply been a hotel that went on to operate as a rooming house in the late 1800s or early 1900s. Owners have restored the original structures but updated the amenities, and they typically offer pampering guest service.

Utilizing all manner of unlikely buildings, *boutique hotels* tend to have 50 or more rooms and are filling a gap in the expanding hotel market here and abroad. These often quirky, sometimes trend-setting properties are springing up all over the place, even in big cities where there simply is not enough space to build conventional hotels.

B&B Owners: A Growing Breed

More and more potential B&B owners are considering this lifestyle change for two main reasons. First, the industry has grown because of exposure through the Internet and because people are traveling more than ever. As B&B owners look to sell, they've been able to use the Internet as a marketing tool to reach investors they might not have found otherwise. In addition, the increasing number of travelers who stay in B&Bs gain insight into B&B life or, at least, what they imagine B&B life is like, and are drawn to it.

Second, more people who are making money in other fields are looking for either a lifestyle change or an investment property to use as a tax shelter. This growing breed of B&B owners looking for a piece of the B&B lifestyle has created a lot of turnover in the business. Some find out that they bit off more in workload than they could chew, and others fix up and sell B&Bs to make a profit.

Coffee Talk

Claude and Mariette Gagne, publishers of *The B&B and Country Inn Marketplace Resource Guide,* have seen a wave of new and unprepared buyers enter the marketplace. "Because of the Internet, B&B for sale properties are easier to find. Many folks are lured into this laid-back lifestyle before doing much research or taking an inn-keeper's seminar. As far as owning a B&B, it's a lot easier getting into one than getting out. Consequently, buyers go into this new venture ill prepared. Many are professionals with sizable cash reserves, and are used to making quick decisions. On the other hand, we also work with buyers who really go overboard in getting prepared. In the long run these folks will make a success of their inns."

According to the Professional Association of Inn-keepers International (PAII) in the 1998 B&B/Country Inn Industry Study, "An overwhelming majority of inn-keepers are part of a couple, although for many only one part of the couple is fulltime at the inn." Also according to PAII, the average age range for inn-keepers is "30 to 65+ years old with a heavy cluster in the 40 to 55 range." So you're not retired—you're not even part of a couple—can you own a B&B? Of course! Although it's true that couples own a good portion of B&Bs, singles are starting to get into the mix, too. As the industry has grown from a Mom-n-Pop operation, more and more singles are moving from their respective fields into the B&B business.

Coffee Talk

Sara Cross, co-owner (with husband Jerry) of Victoria Crossing in Lebanon, Connecticut, suggests getting any kind of work experience at a B&B before opening up your own. "Because I worked at a B&B there were no surprises. Go and do the work. See if you enjoy it before you pour heart and soul into something you may not like at all!"

Michael MacIntyre, co-owner and inn-keeper of The Brass Key in Provincetown, Massachusetts, has some insights into why older rather than younger inn-keepers are more typical. "I see the average B&B owner as being between 40 and 65 years old. I think it's due to the fact that this population has already gone through the first phase of the typical work environment. They no longer want to work for others. They also have more money put away to invest in a B&B. Young people don't normally have the resources and life experiences that the older age bracket has."

The biggest attraction for a lot of future B&B owners is the ability to work at home. Most haven't done enough research, and don't realize just how much work they'll be doing at home when they run a B&B. Buying this book is a good start, and so is attending seminars and classes, and talking to other B&B owners.

Best Areas to Raise the Roof

Location, location, location. Learning a few things from your brothers and sisters in the real estate business will serve you well. If you live in Boonietown, USA, where very few people pass by in any season or for any reason, you might want to reconsider your location. If, however, you live in Boonietown but there's a reason for people to come your way, such as great hiking, you might have a reason to be in the business there.

Most B&Bs are found in coastal areas, in the mountains, near lakes, by rivers, and in other vacation areas. One of the biggest trends in location, however, is big cities. A lot of B&Bs are cropping up in New York City, Boston, Seattle, San Francisco, and other urban locations. Wherever you decide to locate your B&B, first find out how other businesses are doing. Get to know the area by talking with owners of lodging houses, restaurants, gift shops, and bookstores, and anyone else who can give you insight into the economy and your business prospects.

> **Inn the Know**
>
> The Chamber of Commerce can give you the scoop on the scope of tourist business in the area you're looking at. If it's near urban life, find out what city B&Bs and boutique hotels are offering and create an alternative!

> **Coffee Talk**
>
> "Always remember location, location, location, but don't forget supply and demand," advise Robyn and Wolfgang Wendt, owners of Rhythm of the Sea in Cape May, New Jersey. "When we first came to Cape May to look at the house we called into a café where we knew the proprietors through a mutual friend. When we mentioned that we were looking at an inn to purchase but were sworn to secrecy as it was a private sale, they said, 'No matter which one it is, you must check out Rhythm of the Sea, as we've heard it might be on the market. Even if it's double the price of the other inns in town, their location will make it work for you.' No exaggeration!"

Growing Pains

We've all had growing pains; so do growing industries. Many newer B&Bs and inns and other types of small lodging have become just a little bit sleeker, leaving older ones to fall by the wayside. Some new B&Bs fail, too, when owners eager to jump into a growing industry take a big leap before looking both ways. It's a good idea to talk to people who've given up a B&B, if they'll talk to you. Why not learn from their mistakes? Listen closely to their advice, but don't let it dishearten you. Just because they couldn't make it work doesn't mean you can't!

The B&B Appeal

A couple of decades ago, those travelers who frequented B&Bs were mostly looking for a quaint getaway. They knew what to expect: minimal amenities, a quiet house, a shared bath, and morning chatter with the host over home-baked biscuits and tea. These guests expected to travel a bit out of their way but would do so for lower room rates or relaxed ambiance.

Times do change mighty fast and, although some of these experiences still exist, the industry is growing up. As it grows, B&Bs become more sophisticated. Gone from most of them are lace doilies under candy dishes and pictures of grandma's kids in the hallways. Gone are the days of hosts eating breakfast with guests and telling stories of the "Guest of Christmas Past." The biggest trend among new ownerships is a movement into more hotel-like guest services. Guests might opt for your B&B over a Holiday Inn, but they'll still look for those little bottles of shampoo and big white towels.

We're not saying that the charm and quaint appeal of B&Bs has been tossed aside. Absolutely not! It's okay to be nostalgic; those were good times. Some of those good times still exist, especially in B&Bs run by the same owner for many years. Your guests will stay with you in hopes of having a more personal experience. They're looking to you and your B&B for the comfortable and relaxed atmosphere that they know hotels can't offer. It's the combination of these two worlds—a charming atmosphere with more amenities and services—that has broadened the B&B's appeal and brought the industry into a new era.

You've Got ... Personality

Guests will choose your place over the Holiday Inn because they want a different experience. Do you know what a major part of that experience is? You!

You are an extension of your business and your business is an extension of you. In larger inns (25 rooms or more) guests don't anticipate having much—if any—contact with the owners, although they still expect employees to be more charming and personable than hotel staff. The smaller the establishment, the more the guests look forward to making a personal connection with you and your troupe. This doesn't mean that guests expect, or even want, a host who follows them around or spends the evening with them, but before guests walk through your door, they'll assume that you have an easygoing, charming nature and that you'll want to make their stay memorable. That is exactly what they should find! As the lodging industry grows and changes, the factor that continues to distinguish the B&B from the more commercial establishment is—again—you. If hosting is not your cup of tea (or your partner's), you have some work ahead of you. Take the hosting skills test and learn how to improve your score in Chapter 1, "Open, Sez Me!"

All the Rage

Some trends such as platform shoes and the Smiley Face tend to float in and out like, well, platform shoes and Smiley Faces. The B&B and country-style inn, however, is a trend that began about 15 years ago and is now a booming industry. The current industry-wide emphasis on guest services seems to be less of a trend and more of a response to a general change in the lifestyle of B&B clientele.

Although the contemporary B&B retains much of its traditional warmth and charm (due in great part to the host), guests expect more in the way of room amenities. Some of the "extras" that guests are looking for are a phone with voicemail; TV/VCR; minifridge with freezer for ice; iron/ironing board; alarm clock/CD player; hair dryer, bathrobes, shampoo, soap, and lotion; and control of heat and air conditioning. Most guests don't expect bigger attractions such as a whirlpool tub, small kitchen, fireplace, or deck or patio access, but those perks do appeal to those who are willing to pay more.

B&B-eware!

Watch out for white lie fever! You sometimes might feel the urge to "enhance" your description of a room or of your B&B with a little more, shall we say, glitter? Don't do it! If the "poolside room" turns out to be a third-floor room above a small, barely visible pool, you just lost a returning guest. Don't coat your descriptions in spice unless you have the rack to back it up with.

It's important when taking a reservation to tell guests as much as possible about the amenities in each room. Put your best feature forward once you get a sense of what your future guest is looking for in a room (see Chapter 17, "One Day at a Time," for more on taking reservations).

Other expectations guests might have are services such as a fax machine and phone lines with data ports, popular in B&Bs that service a lot of business travelers. For vacationers, it's becoming more common to provide concierge-type services such as making reservations for meals and tours. B&Bs looking to pamper their guests will offer bath salts for their whirlpool tubs, and full turn-down service.

In whatever direction you decide to take your B&B, remember that you are not limited in your choices. Guests will be pleasantly surprised by even the smallest touches that reflect you and the personality of your house. For more on guest services see Chapter 18, "Guest Services with a Smile."

The B&B Guest

There are some classic traits of the typical B&B guest. Does this mean that all your guests will either be fun-loving honeymooners or sweet old couples? Not by a long shot. You'll encounter a wide range of interesting and not-so-interesting folk from around the world. Major segments of the B&B guest market, however, do fall into categories. Here are some of them from a 1998 study created by YBR Marketing and the Professional Association of Innkeepers International:

➤ 77 percent of guests are middle-aged (age 25 to 54).

➤ 92.8 percent attended college and/or graduate school.

➤ 47.9 percent will pay you from their household income of $75,000 or more.

➤ $88.96 is the average amount that guests spend for a night's lodging.

Your typical guest will vary according to your type of operation and location. If you're near a college town expect a lot of middle-aged parents and traveling speakers. A B&B in a touristy town, particularly by the ocean, will see all types. Historical areas typically draw older folk or historians. Convention center areas fill up fast, so if you're near one expect to see a lot of suits at your breakfast table.

Inn the Know

According to YBR Marketing and the Professional Association of Innkeepers International, "Inn guests travel primarily as couples, sometimes with children or another couple. Inn guests' primary activities are dining out, sightseeing, shopping, and relaxing."

The Least You Need to Know

➤ The delineation between a B&B, an inn, and other similar terms has blurred. Choosing a name for your B&B is important, but don't get too hung up on labels.

➤ A decade ago the B&B was a trend. Now it's a booming industry with changes in ownership, style, and guest services.

➤ Location is important to your success. If your house exists in a remote area, be sure to offer something that guests can't get in busier towns.

➤ The B&B tradition of a welcoming and affable host is what continues to lure travelers to B&Bs.

What It's Really Like

Think about the office worker bee, the standard nine-to-fiver. Maybe you are one: You go to work, do your thing, pack up, and go home. The day is done until it starts up again tomorrow. Even if you really like your job, we're sure you'll agree that there's a lot of satisfaction in leaving it at day's end.

You've no doubt considered that operating a B&B will be different. One minute you'll be taking a reservation over the phone, the next minute you're solving a plumbing problem. Just when you start cleaning up after a guest who checked out late, in walks an arriving guest who is two hours early. Sit down and eat that sandwich? Not a chance.

We don't want to scare you off from owning a bed and breakfast. What we are suggesting is that you follow your own path. Some people have an image of what a B&B should look like and how it should operate but, in reality, no two B&Bs are the same. Heed the advice and suggestions of other owners (we've gathered quite a wide spectrum in this book alone) and draw on what you've learned from them when you have choices to make and problems to solve. The best thing you can do for yourself and for a successful B&B is to learn as much as you can about the business and then apply it to your own situation. Whatever happens with your new business will be your own unique experience—as it should be!

Staying Positive at the Get-Go

No matter what you're told about something you have yet to experience, it will always be different from what you imagine. Sometimes knowing this can provide peace, but keeping your spirits up during a transition to an unknown world can be difficult. Not impossible, but difficult.

Staying positive is easy when you're looking for a B&B property or going over plans to renovate your house with the architect. Picking out colors for your rooms and buying linens also are cheerful tasks. But when you become doubtful of your abilities as a host or you stress over making the mortgage payments you might start to lose your Pollyanna attitude. The best way to stay positive during the lengthy and challenging process of starting a B&B is to keep your feelings in check. Your first day, your first week, maybe even your first month might really, really stink. It's possible, and it happens. Just remember that you're new to this business. You won't get everything right the first time even though you will place those demands on yourself. If you keep plugging away and attacking each day with humility and a fierce, Rocky-style attitude, you'll make it.

Dealing with the Work-at-Home Way

Making the adjustment to working at home might appear easy; it's the reason a lot of people go into the B&B business. Working out of your home, however, can be a huge adjustment. Your contact with the outside world ceases, and people tend to think that because you don't go out to work you're not working. Your best friend calls to see if you can tape *Oprah* while she's "at work." Your partner, who works outside the home, asks you to run errands because he or she thinks you don't have much to do. On checking out, a guest asks, "So, is this *all* you do?" It's difficult to get others to understand that what you're doing at home is working.

It's easy to become frustrated when people don't understand what it takes to run your business. Don't give in to anger: Firmly and with good humor, bring them into the program. If you take your profession seriously everyone else will, too. Tell your best friend that you wish you had time to watch television, never mind figure out the VCR. Tell your partner that you can do one errand while you're out shopping for the B&B, and that any more than that will interfere with your business—*your source of income*. And last but not least, say this to the know-it-all guest: "No, I have other jobs too. I'm also a cook, housecleaner, plumber, decorator,

Inn the Know

Since the Industrial Revolution, we've been programmed to think that professional careers exist only outside the home. How many of you have had a parent say when you were a teenager, "Go out and get a job"? "Staying in" to generate income is just not seen as hard work. Ironically, running a B&B in your home is some of the hardest work around.

manager, receptionist, and host. I just don't leave my home to do those jobs." And don't forget to smile and crack a joke. After all, taking *any* job too seriously wouldn't be much fun!

Say Good-Bye to Saturday Night

If you've said to yourself, "Oh, I barely do anything on Saturday nights anyway. How bad can it be?" you're about to find out. The only way you won't mind giving up your Saturday nights is if you understand the real trade-off. You're not making an even swap from "nothing to do" to "something to do." You'll be staying home on Saturday nights because you have to. A house full of guests, especially if they stay in on a rainy night, means work for you.

If you like dining out, catching a movie, or cutting a rug or two at your favorite club, imagine what it will be like without these escapes. You might not have to completely erase these pleasures from your life, but they might be limited. You'll need to find ways to compensate for them or, during slow times, go out during the week. Even if you can afford to hire a manager to take your place when you're out, it will be a long while before you feel comfortable leaving the house in someone else's hands.

Owning a B&B can be a real catch-22. As owner, you run the business, but most of the time it ends up running you! There are ways to keep your sanity, and pencil in some private time. Just make sure that you can live without your Saturday nights.

Considering Family Members

As the owner of a B&B, having the support of your family is not only nice, it's necessary. If you have a wife, husband, or partner, whether or not he or she pitches in, you'll need this person's full support. If you have school-age kids, let them know what will change around the house and how they'll need to lend a hand.

Involve everyone in the process. Sit down with household family members and discuss all possible changes such as routines, meals, and even simple chores. For instance, running the washing machine at midnight won't be an option anymore if the laundry room is right below a guest room.

Make sure you listen to their concerns after the business gets underway, too. No one will know exactly how things will change until it actually happens. As long as you talk about the adjustments and smooth out the kinks that come along with new territory, you'll be able to get through it.

Inn the Know

If you already give your kids allowances or incentives for doing chores around the house, consider bumping up their duties in exchange for better perks. Try not to Cinderella them; just see if they can pitch in enough, for example, to let your house-cleaner leave two hours early on Tuesdays and Thursdays.

What You'll Gain Besides Income

Aside from shooting for a profit (keep your fingers crossed), there are other great advantages to owning a B&B:

➤ **Become the host with the most.** Hosting can be very satisfying, especially if your guests think that you're doing it right! If you have a lot of fun entertaining in your home and would enjoy doing it a lot—a whole heck of a lot—you will gain a lot of pride in your new career. If you haven't had a lot of experience hosting in your own home, what's stopping you? Have a couple of dinner parties for family and friends. It will give you a taste of both sides of hosting: the feel-good side of preparing a meal for other people and the unglamorous side of behind-the-scenes preparation and clean-up.

➤ **Top executive status.** Owning your own business can be very rewarding. If you've ever worked for someone else, you'll particularly love being your own boss! If you also enjoy the challenges and responsibility of being head cheese, this business is for you.

➤ **You can work in your slippers.** Well, not in front of the guests, but working at home can be a comfortable way to spend your day. Although every perk has its downside, this one is especially two-sided. When you work at home there's nowhere else to go at the end of your day! Keeping comfortable private quarters will help you to enjoy working at home because it will provide an escape from the business itself.

B&B-eware!

Watch out for the urge to turn rooms in your private quarters into guest rooms in hope of earning more income. Determine if the extra money is really worth it; don't sacrifice the sanity of private relaxation for a few extra bucks a week. You might end up missing your privacy so much that you bag the business altogether.

➤ **Live in your dream house.** Many innkeepers would not be able to afford their homes if they didn't rent out rooms for the extra income. You might not become wealthy in this business but having a B&B can afford you a better lifestyle.

➤ **Shortest commute in town.** For those who live at their B&Bs, being able to avoid traffic and long drive times is a real plus. If you plan to own a B&B that is farther than 10 to 15 minutes away from your home, consider it carefully. Some hindrances are that you'll need to hire someone to be at the property 24 hours a day, and you'll spend most of your days and nights at the B&B anyway! (See Chapter 4, "The B&B of Your Dreams," for more on the absentee B&B owner.)

> ➤ **Gimme a break, Uncle Sam!** If your B&B is run out of your home, you can get tax breaks on the house, food, and supplies (see Chapter 9, "Setting Up Your Business and Financial Structure").

You probably have even more personal reasons for choosing the B&B way of life. Before you dive in, be sure to take time out to make a list of all the conceivable advantages and disadvantages of it. If your cons outweigh your pros and you still decide to move forward, at least you know what you're diving into.

A Day in the Life

The following example is not typical of every B&B but it's a close shot at what a day in the life of an owner can be like. This scenario is based on one person running a six-room B&B, without staff or much help from a partner, who works outside the home.

6:00 A.M.: Alarm sounds, hit snooze bar and mentally prepare for the morning.

6:10 A.M.: Get up, take three-minute shower (full house of early risers). Wake up partner (two-minute shower allowed); get dressed.

6:30 A.M.: Start preparing breakfast items for cooking or baking; double-check eating areas to make sure all is in place from setup the night before; have juice and cereal.

7:00 A.M.: Prepare coffee and hot water for tea for early risers; continue working on breakfast.

7:23 A.M.: Pack up, as pre-arranged, muffins, fruit, and coffee for business travelers in suites 5 and 6 who are checking out at 7:30.

7:50 A.M.: Check out business travelers who are running late, and give them the best, quickest directions to their next destination.

8:00 A.M.: Guests start filing down for full breakfast (served buffet style).

8:15 A.M.: Serve breakfast and apologize for the wait (due to late check-out of business travelers).

8:27 A.M.: Phone rings, couple needs room for the weekend. Ask if you can arrange to call in 10 minutes.

8:31 A.M.: Return to dining area to check on guests and refill coffee.

8:40 A.M.: Return call and complete sale.

8:56 A.M.: When last guest files out, clean up eating area and kitchen; load dishwasher but don't run it (in case of any late showers).

9:15 A.M.: Clean suites 5 and 6.

Coffee Talk

"To make guests happy without losing your sanity, don't promise anything you can't deliver in normal routines," suggest Tom and Janice Fairbanks, owners of The Old Wailuku Inn at Ulupono in Wailuku, Hawaii. "Be sure that in your service plan you anticipate, meet, and exceed the normal guests' needs, so they won't be calling you after hours. Have high quality tea, hot water, soft drinks, fruits, cheeses and snacks available for them to help themselves. Provide dining information and offer to take care of their dining needs in the morning so it's all done for them by evening."

10:30 A.M.: Take a phone reservation; send out reservation confirmation; organize office; hang around desk for 11:00 A.M. check-outs for rooms 2 and 4; and check e-mail.

11:30 A.M.: Make dinner reservations as requested by guests in rooms 1 and 3 during breakfast; leave messages on guests' voicemails confirming reservations were made; run the dishwasher.

11:50 A.M.: Drink a protein shake and glance at the newspaper.

12:00 P.M.: Start cleaning rooms 2 and 4.

1:30 P.M.: Start a load of laundry.

1:40 P.M.: Change towels and tidy up rooms 1 and 3.

2:17 P.M.: Greet arriving guests, get remaining balance of payment, give tour of house, answer questions, and show them to room 4.

2:50 P.M.: Put first load of laundry into dryer and start a second.

3:00 P.M.: Eat a late lunch of ...

3:05 P.M.: Answer more questions from newly arrived guests.

3:15 P.M.: ... tuna salad; unload dishwasher.

3:30 P.M.: Clean common sitting areas and bathroom; start on third load of laundry; fold first set; call cable company.

4:30 P.M.: More laundry; run to store for a few breakfast items.

4:55 P.M.: Greet guests returning from their day out on the town; give them directions to restaurants; chill wine in your fridge for room 1 to drink later that evening.

5:20 P.M.: Sweep front steps; tidy outside common areas (this includes stomping down unearthed lawn created by pesky mole family).

6:00 P.M.: Finish laundry; stock linen closets.

6:20 P.M.: Set up common areas for evening time: low lights, candles, fireplace, classical music.

6:30 P.M.: Greet guests checking in very late for room 2.

7:00 P.M.: Greet partner who came home an hour ago.

7:05 P.M.: Make late dinner reservations for room 2; call room 2 to confirm reservation was made.

7:10 P.M.: Deliver fax that arrived for room 3.

7:15 P.M.: Meet room 2 guests in the hallway (they've decided to order in instead).

7:20 P.M.: Cancel dinner reservation and bring take-out menus up to room 2.

7:30 P.M.: Prepare tray with plates, napkins, silverware, glasses, and chocolates for room 2.

7:40 P.M.: Sit down to eat lovely dinner prepared by partner (wishful thinking?).

7:50 P.M.: Answer door, take tray and delivery person to room 2 and then show delivery person out.

8:00 P.M.: Finish dinner; do dishes.

8:20 P.M.: Put feet up and have a cup of tea.

8:40 P.M.: Write out some bills; check e-mail.

9:27 P.M.: Check breakfast areas for next morning meal: refill condiments; set up buffet table with plates and silverware ready to go; make muffin mix for next day and put in fridge.

10:11 P.M.: Write out notes for next day's schedule.

10:30 P.M.: Watch evening news.

11:00 P.M.: Close down common room.

11:20 P.M.: Hit the sack.

Phew! And that's a slow day!

Inn the Know

You've probably noticed in our "day in the life" example that running a B&B is a combination of repetitive action (things such as laundry are endless) and surprises (guests changing their minds). A lot of days, running a B&B is just full of repetitiveness.

Totally Devoted to You

It's 10:30 P.M. You finally have some spare time to yourself. Do you write out bills, check your e-mail, file paperwork, or call it a day? Demanding as this business is, you'll learn that setting aside time for yourself can be just as demanding.

Inn the Know

Taking time out to relax is not only good for your psyche, it's good for business. The best host is calm, well-rested, and happy. If you can't take a vacation, section off bits of time every day just for yourself. Part of the charm of your B&B is you. If you're cranky to your guests, it won't matter how charming your décor looks.

Inn the Know

If you give guests access to the kitchen, make sure that your own quarters are closed off from this area. Guests won't know where they're going and could wander into your private rooms. This also will cut down on late-night noise creeping into your quarters (usually guests in search of ice).

Finding Time and How Much You'll Need

Finding time for yourself sounds very passive, as if time is just hanging out there in space waiting to be caught. You'll need to make that time for yourself and your family. If you wait to stumble into some empty time you'll be waiting an eternity.

Determining how much time you'll need to make for yourself is a bit tricky. When you first start out you can expect to be consumed by the work. In part, this is a really good thing. Squeeze as much work out of yourself as you can while your enthusiasm is off the charts.

Be careful, though, to not go overboard. Burning out in the first few months is common. As you'll need that explosive enthusiasm to last you for more than the first few months, try not to trade in all your free time to work on the business. Stay alert to how this extra work affects you mentally and physically. Do you have to have someone drag you out of bed in the morning? Are you snapping at your 12-year-old? Do you find yourself fading in and out of concentration?

Everyone needs different amounts of personal time to keep them going. You might discover that running a B&B affords you more time than you thought. On the other hand, if you find that personal time is slipping away from you, take steps to get it back. Hire staff, if you can afford it, or shut down the business for two days during your off season. You might lose some income initially, but you'll be better prepared to stay in business for the long haul.

Balancing Your Life

Now that your work and home are in one place, you'll need to make some mental and physical adjustments. Melding work into your home life requires a great deal of organization. It also forces you to think and live differently from when you worked outside the home.

Physically, you need to arrange business and personal affairs as separate entities. Paperwork should be kept in different files, family food is separate from your guests', and your living quarters in the house are kept private for you and your family.

Mentally separating your business from your personal life is a bigger challenge. Turning the day off at night is difficult because if you live on the premises, you don't get to actually leave your place of work. Removing yourself from the house is a good way to mentally shift gears. When you do have some time to yourself, go to the gym or have lunch with friends. If you can't get out of the house, do your best to leave business out of your private quarters. Set a cut-off time in the evenings after which you and your partner do not discuss the business. Everyone needs down time. Whether you physically or mentally get away from work, either tactic will help you stay sharp during your workday.

Coffee Talk

From Ken Burnet, co-owner of the Gaige House Inn in Glen Ellen, California: "Do not assume you will be happy doing everything yourself for very long. *You will burn out.* Develop and implement a concept that sets you up as a business, one that you will continue to grow as the years go on. This means staffing, computer systems, renovation and marketing growth."

The Least You Need to Know

➤ Running a B&B requires that you alter your thinking (and that of others) about working inside the home.

➤ It's essential that you prepare yourself and your live-in family members for a change in lifestyle.

➤ A day in the life of a B&B owner is made up of repetitiveness sprinkled with surprises.

➤ When you live and work at home, making separate time for yourself and your family will keep you balanced and refreshed.

Chapter 4

The B&B of Your Dreams

In This Chapter

➤ Determining the type of B&B you want

➤ Choosing the services you'll offer

➤ Living away from the B&B property

➤ Discovering the many ways that your location affects your business

---

Everyone has his or her own idea of the perfect B&B—that's what makes this business so unique. Each B&B has its own flair, born out of the owner's style and handiwork. You can be sure that guests will look for your personal touch when staying at your B&B. They want to see the results of your dream! When you plan for your own dream B&B to come true, make sure that vision is attainable. What good is a dream if you can't make it come true?

The B&B of your dreams could be the B&B of someone else's nightmare. Hoping to own a 30-room mansion? Looking for a B&B lodge near a ski resort? These types of B&Bs will sound fascinating and achievable to some and downright frightening to others. Before you sign over your trust fund as a down payment, consider the type of B&B you'd like to run and how much work you can realistically handle. Figure out your perfect-fit B&B before you invest and you'll be able to turn that dream into a reality.

Working Up to Perfect

Brenda Fictional dreams of owning a B&B in Seal Beach, California, one with ocean views and "The Inn at Seal Beach" painted on a life preserver. If she could convince her Iowa family to go coastal, that dream could come true. When Brenda's grandmother offers to sell her her old, creaky, Victorian Iowa home at less than market value, Brenda says no. She thinks that it's too much house for her family, plus it needs a lot of work. Besides, she's still hanging on to a West Coast escape. Sigh. What to do? You can see where we're going with this little scenario. Brenda has a great opportunity to start a B&B in her hometown but she doesn't take it, even though the B&B of her dreams is not a possibility at this point in her life unless she wants to live apart from her family. Don't get us wrong; we're not suggesting that Brenda toss her ocean dreams in the dumpster. We are suggesting that Brenda (and you) keep your mind open to possibilities that don't exactly match your dream.

Don't get discouraged if the ideal property doesn't pop up right away. Fix up an old house in a contemporary style or buy a turnkey B&B and remodel it to your tastes. The best way to get ahead in this business is to work with the opportunities around you. Because it's not always possible to find your idea of utopia the first time, why not start with a less-than-perfect house, make it better, and then sell it for something else (known as a *flip*)? As great-grandma Ethel used to say, "When life hands you potatoes, make potato salad."

Shoestring Solution

A **flip** is a real estate term for fixer-upper properties bought with the intention of renovating and then selling them to make a profit. A flip is a good way to start out in the B&B business, especially if you haven't found your dream B&B yet, or your resources are limited.

Your B&B-to-Be

There are so many different types of B&Bs these days! If you haven't purchased a property yet, you probably have your ideal B&B in mind. Or, maybe you at least know how you'd like to run the business. Be realistic about your likes, dislikes, skills, and finances.

As you will learn in Chapter 8, "The Business Plan," when you're short on cash and experience, gradually increasing your level of service and guest capacity is the way to go. However you envision your B&B-to-be, make sure you choose to own one that you'll be able to handle financially. If you can't afford to hire staff right away for your new 15-room inn, fill up only five or six rooms at a time until you get some cash flowing. If you've never run a kitchen before, bring in someone who has! Staying in business is your main objective, so find a B&B that is suited to your tastes *and* your start-up ability.

A Sound Structure

Although newly constructed B&Bs are cropping up, restorations of old buildings are more typical. There's been a great movement in recent years to create B&Bs out of unusual dwellings such as lighthouses, old banks or post offices, adobes, motels, cluster cabins, barns, ranches, mills, old schoolhouses, boathouses, haunted houses, and even jailhouses! Having an unusual structure for a B&B, such as old train cars, is an easy way to lure clientele. More and more travelers seek out-of-the-ordinary accommodations, and the B&B business is responding.

The Lizzie Borden Bed, Breakfast and Museum in Fall River, Massachusetts, is an example. It's a cozy house, if you like axe murderers. Lizzie Borden was acquitted of murdering her father Andrew and her stepmother Abby in 1892, and the crime remains unsolved and the subject of many theories. So, what do you do with a house that has this kind of history? Turn it into a B&B! Owner Martha McGinn inherited the house from her grandparents and opened for business in 1996. "The main reason people stay with us is for the intrigue and mystery of whether or not Lizzie really committed the crime. Our referrals and repeat stays are because of our hospitality." Tours are given and those daring enough can stay in the room where Abby was murdered while she was making the bed. Guests are fed a breakfast similar to Abby and Andrew's last meal, and then treated to sugar cookies in the shape of an axe!

B&B-eware!

In a lot of small towns, B&Bs in existing commercial dwellings are an allowable grandfathered (also known as "pre-existing nonconforming") use of property in a residential district but they'll lose that allowance if the building is torn down. Before you move ahead to purchase property just for the land, make sure your proposal for a new B&B is possible (now and in the future) according to town zoning.

Your B&B probably couldn't top Martha McGinn's for bizarre appeal, and it might not even have an unusual structure; so if the outside isn't catchy, fill the inside with uncommon artifacts or create a theme. Have an affinity for Shakespeare? Name rooms after your favorite characters and soon you'll have guests calling for the "King Lear" suite. Go with your own interests and give your guests something to tell other potential guests about!

Coffee Talk

Joshua Tree Inn in Joshua Tree, California, was originally built as a motel. Say owners Dr. Daniel and Evelyn Shirbroun: "We think that most people that choose a place like ours tend to like something different. When we travel it seems everything is duplicated from place to place—the malls, the hotels—we always look for something different and unique to the area. Hard to find these days. Staying at an inn is a way to get a flavor of the neighborhood."

When owners are considering a name for their B&B, most of them typically choose something that reflects either a certain quality of the house ("Victorian" or "Gables," for example); a characteristic of the neighborhood or vicinity ("Mangrove B&B"); their nostalgia for a person or experience (such as using the last name of a grandparent); or their aspirations for the property (such as Four Diamonds Lodge or Benchmark Inn!). If you're going for a whimsical name or anything unique, find something that ties in directly to your B&B. Having a good story behind your name or having a name with an obvious connection to the property (such as the Four Coconuts Guesthouse because you have four coconut trees on the property) can have huge appeal. If you decided to name your special place Snowman's Rest because you're surrounded by water in a Louisiana bayou, then you have the option to draw on that theme throughout the house and in marketing tactics. Some guests will gravitate toward your B&B because of its unusual theme choice.

It's also important to think about what you *shouldn't* call your B&B. Best not to name your place the Doo Drop Inn if you're near a sewage treatment center, and watch out for licensing infringement: Naming your B&B the "Dollywood Inn" without permission could result in having your own D-cups sued right off!

What Services Will You Offer?

Guest services can range from having warm towels to a masseuse on premises. If you dream of offering every imaginable and possible kind of guest service on the day you open your doors, be prepared to put in impossibly long hours; or more realistically, consider starting with a few basic services. You can add things gradually, after you've worked out the kinks of getting the place up and running. If you try to do too much at once, staff or no staff, you might just find *yourself* needing a massage! The services you'll provide will depend on your type of clientele. If you mostly cater to retirees, a full business center might be a waste. If your spot becomes a popular honeymoon and anniversary destination, free sparkling wine for couples will be a huge attraction. If your clientele runs the gamut from singles to families, you'll need to have a little something for everyone. Try including the usual (such as daily towel service) along with a few extra special services (such as breakfast in bed).

In trying to provide a little something for everyone you might find that the quality of your service slips. Just as in life, there's danger in trying to be all things to all people! If you expect to (and hope to) have a really wide range of clientele, try out a few services to see what catches on the most. If you find that no one—singles to families—hangs around for afternoon tea, ditch it. Pay attention to what your guests really want. Weed out the less popular services and add new ones to see how they work. For more ideas on guest services to consider providing, see Chapter 18, "Guest Services with a Smile."

The Absentee B&B Owner

When you run a B&B that is not part of your home, there are a lot of factors to consider. First, it might not be that profitable for you if the B&B has fewer than six rooms and you have additional housing costs for yourself. If you run a B&B out of your home, you get tax benefits and offset costs. Second, you'll need a person on site at all times. That means you need to hire staff to either sleep there or work the night shift; that also will cut into your profit. Third, being absent means you have less control over how the property is run.

If you consider buying a B&B that you won't live in, weigh all the factors, including driving distance and time away from your own house. A big drawback to being an absentee owner will be the disappointment of your guests. A lot of them want to interact directly with the owner, who is a great part of the attraction of a B&B. People also look to the owner to give them the best service possible. You can counteract the problem, though, by hiring top-notch staff. Having at least one person who can fill your shoes when you're away from the house (whether you live there or not) is the only way to have happy guests!

Best Spots for B&Bs

If your B&B is near a college, vacation spot, cultural or historical area, convention center (or any place that attracts people!) you're already a step ahead. B&Bs that are a little farther out of reach can be a tougher sell.

Location also is one of the biggest determinants in how much you can charge (see Chapter 7, "All About Room Rates"). If you're in a remote location and not directly in the path of a "hot" destination it might be difficult to get as high a rate as B&Bs closer to the action. Adding amenities and services, though, will allow you to bump up your rates and be competitive with B&Bs in central locations.

When Traffic Is a Good Thing

There's no doubt that B&Bs on a main street have an advantage. Even if you're in a small town, you might not get a lot of drop-ins, but people will know you're there. Relatives and friends who visit your town for weddings and special events will more likely be referred to your B&B than to those at a distance. Even if someone doesn't know you or what your B&B is like, the fact that you're on a main drag makes you stick out ... "Hey, isn't there a B&B on Suchensuch Street? Let's drive by and get the name."

If you're close to a commercial district but off a direct route, find ways to reach business travelers such as offering a 10 percent discount to area businesses that book clients with you.

Inn the Know

Keep in mind that although guests will appreciate the convenience of reaching your house, once inside they won't want to be reminded of the traffic outside. Consider putting landscaping buffers in strategic places to minimize noise. Also talk with a knowledgeable heating engineer or handyman about adding extra insulation.

Trapping Tourists

To "visit" is a pretty light word for what most tourists do on vacation. Most out-of-towners like to immerse themselves in the areas they've chosen as getaways. In your brochure and when you talk with callers, use your area hot spots to advantage ("only a five-minute drive from the world's largest ball of wool" or "within walking distance of shops, restaurants, and museums").

If your B&B is near a touristy or vacation spot but not in the heart of it all, use both of those factors as sell points. "Close to downtown on a quiet, residential street" will sound like the best of both worlds to most tourists.

Off the Main Road

B&Bs located off the beaten-down path are starting to pop up all over the place. Have you ever been driving through a highly residential area, spotted a B&B, and thought, what is that doing out here? A big reason is that, when location isn't a strength, B&B owners are offering a lot more on the inside. Even though your neighborhood B&B might seem a little out of place at first, neighbors might come to be thankful for it after they've placed relatives in your comfortable home for the holidays instead of their overcrowded one.

B&B-eware!

Beware of the urge to exaggerate! When describing your location, it might be tempting to sweeten up the reality: Don't stretch truths. If your property is 30 driving minutes outside from a city, don't tout it as "close to downtown"!

If your B&B's address is Nowheresville, think about investing in big and small amenities that will keep guests going out of their way to get to you (see Chapter 13, "Getting the Most from Your B&B," for more on amenities).

When describing your B&B, highlight the attributes of its being in the boonies by using a phrase such as "getaway retreat" or "private and peaceful." If you're somewhat near an urban area, try to stay away from using language such as "far from the hustle and bustle." Most guests will want the option of going into town, so it's wise to play up everything that your location offers.

If you're really out there, you'll more than likely draw a different clientele by offering a lot of unusual amenities and services. Reserving hot air balloon rides or setting up day hikes will help your establishment become somewhat of a destination in itself.

Though some guests may be contented to hang around the house others will prefer to hover above it!

Your guests also would be looking for a home-cooked breakfast. If you serve only a continental breakfast and it's a haul to the nearest breakfast spot, your empty-stomached guests might be grumpy for the rest of the day. Having topnotch services and an outstanding breakfast will help keep them extra-happy and coming back for more getaways.

Coffee Talk

The Vista Verde Ranch in Steamboat Springs, Colorado, is a retreat and recreational haven with everything from cattle drives to its own nightly entertainment. Owners John and Suzanne Munn work hard to keep out the rest of the world so guests can completely relax. "We promote the fact that there are no phones in the room, the television is well hidden, and the newspaper is a day late. Once in a while we get a corporate tycoon who wants *The New York Times*—now. By the third day they forget about it."

Near an Event Center or College

Being close to the bustle of a college, boarding school, convention center, or anything that draws crowds is a great plus. Count on being booked for parents' weekends or the great annual Spoon Hangers Convention.

Keep on top of what events are happening when so you can get your highest rates during these times. Pay attention to how the incoming crowds will affect other businesses, too. If Stan's Bistro, the best restaurant in town, always books early, don't wait until 4:00 P.M. to make reservations for your guests. Develop a good relationship with the best restaurants in town and soon you might find that they're saving tables for you.

Shoestring Solution

Leave your business cards and brochures where people congregate such as on high-traffic college bulletin boards, brochure racks at convention centers, hospitals, nursing homes, food stores, and fitness centers. Make connections with people who can really spread the word for you. If the people aren't coming to you, go get them!

Startup Overview

Before you hang a sign on your door and wash your new white towels, you'll find yourself in the heart of a very involved process. The following is a short list of the major hurdles that all B&Bs must traverse before opening their doors. The chapters that cover them in detail are noted in parentheses.

➤ Creating a business and marketing plan (Chapter 8, "The Business Plan")

➤ Sorting out finances and gathering funds (Chapter 9, "Setting Up Your Business and Financial Structure")

➤ Planning construction or renovation of the house and property (Chapter 5, "Knocking Down Those Walls")

➤ Zoning and licensing approval from your town (Chapter 6, "Legalities and Liabilities")

➤ Purchasing of start-up supplies, big and small (Chapter 14, "Stocking Up on Supplies")

➤ Putting policies in place for guests and staff (Chapters 15, "Setting Guest Policies," and 20, "Help Wanted")

➤ Networking with area businesses and becoming familiar with what your area offers to travelers (Chapter 11, "Networking Works")

These obviously are just the very main parts of the processes involved with startup. Keep in mind that your road to starting up a B&B will not be a straight line. One thing you can count on is that all the aspects of startup will overlap, so prepare to adapt to changes. You'll find yourself buying those new white guest towels before your laundry room is even built!

Things might go as smooth as silk for you and your new business. If that happens, all the power to you. More likely than not, however, you'll fall into the 99 percent of B&B owners who've had a bumpy start.

Here's the thing: What's so bad about a few bumps? If running a B&B were easy to do everyone would be doing it. B&B owners are a tough breed, able to handle any type of situation and challenge. Some have had it a little easier than others but all have faced unexpected and unusual roadblocks on their way to a smooth operation.

Get used to the idea of hitting a few bumps so they won't hurt so bad. Of course you can never prepare yourself for the unexpected, but you can expect it. Know that meeting challenges will make you a stronger person and a smarter inn-keeper. After running a B&B, you'll be able to do anything!

The Least You Need to Know

➤ Buying less-than-desirable property, fixing it up, and selling it for profit is a good way to work up to financing and finding your dream B&B.

➤ Living off premises presents financial and other difficulties, but it can be done successfully.

➤ Out-of-the-ordinary B&Bs are a big draw for guests.

➤ A visible location gives B&Bs an advantage.

➤ B&Bs in Boonieville have to work a little harder to gain clientele but they can be attractive as getaway retreats.

➤ Startup is rarely without challenges, but overcoming them will make you a better inn-keeper.

Part 2
Taking the Plunge

Sit down in a comfy chair with a nice hot cup of your favorite something and no distractions. Then, plunge right into our crash course in the start-up basics of renovating a house, learning about your area's rules, determining what you'll charge for your rooms, and drawing up a business plan (accounting and taxes, too).

Starting the business will consume your life. There's a lot you need to know for the tasks at hand (such as putting up those walls) but there also are certain important steps to take at startup that will help your business succeed later on (such as determining your business structure). As we said, get comfy.

Knocking Down Those Walls

Now we're getting to the fun part. Well, the fun and kind of stressful part. Okay, the fun and anxiety-driven, migraine-inducing, face-squinching, head-shaking, shoulder-cringing part. So we exaggerate a bit, this much we admit, but chances are you'll find that waiting for your B&B to hurry up and get done already can be frustrating.

For most of you, major constructive surgery, or even minor renovations, will mean getting outside help. Having others work on your property will put things out of your control. Schedules fall behind; parts don't arrive; or a wall gets torn down and some major wood rot is discovered, delaying the project even more. The fun part of buying a turnkey property, converting your own home, or renovating your B&B is the transformation. Seeing your B&B vision become the real B&B will make any migraine evaporate.

Turning Your Home into a B&B

Maybe the kids finally moved out and you have extra space, or someone walked into your house and said, "Wow, this could make a great B&B!" Whatever your reason for turning your private residence into lodging, you'll need to do some serious research to make sure it's possible. It's not enough to know that guests will find the house

Inn the Know

For an excellent (and fun) orientation and guide to remodeling, check out *The Complete Idiot's Guide to Remodeling Your Home,* by Terry Meany. Considering renting out space to year-round tenants? Pick up *The Complete Idiot's Guide to Being a Smart Landlord.*

inviting or that the location is suitable, although these are major considerations. You need to be certain that you can get the legal green light, and that you'll be able to adjust to your new living space.

Potential Profit-Maker or Money Pit?

Maybe "money pit" is too strong, but you will need to determine whether your house will garner enough income to be worth it. All things are relative. If you have only two or three rooms and you plan for those rooms to generate partial income, it's probably worth it. If you count on what you make from those rooms as your sole income, you might have a struggle.

Time also is a factor in how much money you'll make. The more days that you can receive guests and the more rooms you have, the higher your income will be. Of course your workload also will increase.

Think creatively about how you can get your dream B&B to materialize. If you have a smaller house and wish to run a full-time B&B, can you add on or build some back cottages? Are there other ways to generate income such as displaying local artwork for a commission on sales? If you increase the number of rooms, can you handle the extra work, or will you spend your additional income on hired help?

B&B-eware!

When you're planning out your living quarters, keep in mind that you might be fine in a small space at first, but that it might wear thin over time. You could start resenting your guests for taking up space in your house— even though it was your idea!

There are many options and opportunities you can take advantage of to develop your B&B and plan for its future growth; your choices will depend on what you—and your house—can handle. Projecting your income is a basic part of the process, covered in detail in Chapter 9, "Setting Up Your Business and Financial Structure."

Don't Live in the Basement

If you're considering squeezing your private living space into one small area and converting the rest of your house into a B&B, think twice. What will you miss, and won't living in one small room get old, particularly if you don't have your own bathroom or private kitchen?

Maybe the structure of your house is such that sectioning off private living quarters would leave too little space for guests, or make the house less appealing in other ways. If this is the case, will you be able to add on for private quarters or more guest rooms? This option is costly (and might be tricky, depending on your town zoning laws) but it might be a good one if you're someone who needs a fair amount of space.

Some B&B owners build separate, private quarters on the property or convert an existing structure into living space. If you have kids and need a real "house" space to live in, that might be an option for you. If you consider moving out of the main house, make sure that the numbers add up. Don't lose sight of the reason why you decided to operate a B&B out of your home in the first place!

Checking in with Officials

Stop! Put down that prybar! If you're renovating your B&B, before you knock down any walls, check to make sure it's okay with the town officials. Even if your house is commercially zoned, you'll need to follow proper approval and licensing procedure (see Chapter 6, "Legalities and Liabilities").

Buying a House

There's a world of difference between buying a turnkey property and buying a house for conversion to a B&B. Apples and pineapples. Tomato and to-mah-to. Cats and ... well, you get the idea. A turnkey property, or one that is already operating as a B&B, will require a "dive in head first" approach, whereas buying a house that is not a B&B is a gutsy strategy that requires you to start from scratch. If you have little experience with renovating a building, or a lack of intestinal fortitude, you may opt to purchase an existing B&B.

Make Sure Your Turnkey Isn't a Turkey

You'll probably look at a few up-and-running B&Bs before you find the perfect fit. One house might have only shared baths and you're looking for rooms with all private baths. Another might have really small rooms with no room for improvement.

When you find a house that strikes your fancy, take some steps to make sure it's all that it appears to be. Get a hold of finance and tax records to ensure the business part of your investment is

B&B-eware!

If you're buying a property, find out what codes have changed in the town and what you have to do to bring it up to code. Get the advice of a good real estate agent or attorney about what the seller should do before handing it over to you. Your Chamber of Commerce can recommend someone who can get the job done.

sound. Before you sit down with the sellers to go over records (more on this in Chapter 9), thoroughly investigate the building and property. After you ask the owners why they're selling the B&B (they probably won't say "because it's falling apart" but you never know), ask yourself these questions:

➤ **What kind of major renovating will I need to do?** Check all things mechanical and physical to make sure the house is not rotting from the inside out or doesn't need new wiring. If there's a major problem, note it and use it during negotiations. Hire a professional inspector (see "Letting Professionals Take Over" later in this chapter) if you're unsure about what to look for. If you plan on financing, the bank will require an appraisal but probably will not require a home inspection. However, having a written report from an inspector might give you leverage before or during a closing.

➤ **Have the owners kept everything up to code?** Check into the property from behind the scenes and make sure that licenses and permits are current and that the building is up to code. Some towns allow business licenses to be transferred with ownership; others will require new owners to apply from scratch. Have your real estate agent or real estate attorney check into any changes in town regulations. When a business changes hands, the new owners will not be able get away with a property that is not up to code.

Coffee Talk

Jane Bertorelli, co-owner of the Union Street Inn in San Francisco, California, has some more questions you can ask yourself before buying an up-and-running B&B:

"Is the inn in a year-round market or is it seasonal? Could you operate without staff? Do you want to deal with employees? Is there a labor pool in the vicinity? What is the history of the inn? Has it had a succession of owners? The challenge of turning around a rundown inn is exciting but it takes time, energy, and additional investment! If you're paying top dollar for a property that is completely 'done' and has a high occupancy at maximum rates, you have limited options for increasing revenue, but life certainly might be easier!"

➤ **Is there room for improvement?** You'll be buying more than just a house; you'll be buying someone's reputation and clientele. Taking that business to the next level might be the only way to keep some returning guests who developed relationships with the previous owners. Structurally, can the house be added on? Your real estate agent or attorney can find out what can be done in your area.

➤ **What does everyone else think of the business?** If you buy into an operation with either a not-so-great reputation or no reputation at all, you'll have some extra marketing to do. If you buy a business with an excellent reputation, you'll have even more work to do to keep it up. If you buy a B&B that attracts clientele looking for a quaint, low-maintenance getaway, and you plan to implement full guest services to get a better rate, you'll have a ton of work to do!

➤ **Will I like where I'm living?** Check out the private quarters to make sure you can stand it. Look past the wallpaper and make sure the space has potential for comfort and coziness.

Shoestring Solution

As an item in your sales agreement, request a list of guest names and addresses to be included with the purchase of a turnkey operation. Though you can assume that some business will be lost (especially if you're replacing a well-liked inn-keeper), it might be minimized if you send out postcards to the more recent names on the list. Introduce yourself and announce any plans you have for upcoming renovations or promotions. Be cordial and brief, limiting the number of words to 75 or 100; about the same number as this paragraph!

Now you're ready to check out those records and find out if the house looks as good on paper as it does from the lawn!

Converting a House

If you're looking for a not-yet-existent-B&B house to purchase, you'll need to consider everything from scratch: location, potential for private quarters with a separate entrance, parking areas, and a definite "yes" from town officials to the question of whether you can make that house into a B&B.

You can't know everything it'll take to restore an old house or convert a modern one, but you should know what the major undertakings will be, such as a new septic system or a new roof. Some structures need to be completely gutted and have new walls, ceilings, and floors installed; others need a few areas fixed up or new plumbing installed. Whatever type of structure you decide to invest in, make sure you know exactly what you're getting into.

Even the seemingly smallest details can turn out to be a big deal. Why is there a musty smell when the house hasn't been empty? You like the style of the house but it doesn't match the style of your furniture. Can you make your stuff work or will you be picking out new duds? Things such as lead paint or asbestos are costly to remove. If the house seems like a great deal but has been on the market for two years, there's probably a reason.

Check out the condition of the house from every perspective:

➤ **Yours.** Inspect the physical and mechanical structures of the property before you make an offer. You won't know the real worth of the house until you do. Check the heating and electrical systems, foundation, paint, roof, pipes, water, and insulation. Find out if the house is connected to city sewers or has a septic tank. Make sure you know the ins and outs of the house or that you hire a professional who can tell you what they are.

Inn the Know

If you're "Inspector Clueless," hire a certified inspector, who will charge a flat fee (usually around $100 to $250) for the one- to two-hour inspection, and will provide you with a written report.

➤ **Someone who knows.** Make friends with either another B&B owner (stay out of your competitions' hair) or someone who really knows their stuff in construction. Take the person with you when you tour the house; you might learn that you can't knock down that wall because it turns out to be a load-bearing one. Not every house is right for a B&B, so make sure yours fits the bill.

➤ **The green light.** Once again, you'll need to check in with the powers that be, also known as your town, before you make any move. Investing in a big house with the hopes of turning it into a B&B and finding out later that it's not possible will make you regret your impulse. Are you zoned for residential, commercial, or mixed use? A good realtor will know this cold. You also can see the town assessor for the actual plans on how your area is zoned.

Fine-Tune Your Layout

After you've bought the house of your dreams, spend some time looking closely at the inside space. Imagine you're a guest looking at it for the first time. Where does your eye go first? What would make a room brighter? Does a small room have the potential for looking crowded with a queen-size bed? Some space considerations are …

➤ **More rooms vs. more room.** If you have the option of chopping up a space to make two rooms instead of one, is it worth it? Will one room be incredibly small with the other just a little better than small? Think about the comfort of your guests once they've entered the room and closed the door—remember they'll be calling those four walls home for a few days. If you're looking for the flexibility of adding a suite-like space to your room roster, investigate the possibility of a quality pull-out sofa or day bed instead. Privacy can be created with pull-back curtains or a folding, removable, and possibly decorative folding screen. If your property has appeal to business travelers, consider a user-friendly work space as an option.

➤ **Tips on creating common areas.** Guests might not spend tons of time in your common areas, especially if the rooms are small, but don't overlook these areas. Spend some extra time sitting down and looking at everything from their perspective. If the space seems small, think of other areas in the house that also could become common areas. Is there odd space near the top of the stairs where you could add a small sofa or table and chairs? Do you have a tough time renting out that really small room that could be turned into an upstairs sitting area? Look to the outside for areas, too. You might not be able to use a patio or garden area year-round but having this option in warmer weather will be a huge plus.

➤ **Making good use of space.** Whether the space is in your guest rooms, private quarters, kitchen, or storage area, there is space to be had. Buy furniture that can serve a double purpose, such as a cabinet with shelves or drawers that can hold a small television. Build shelves or small closet doors into an eave.

➤ **Building outside havens.** Don't have a lot of acreage? Perfect! Create a sitting garden, add a fishpond, build a patio or sunroom. Less grass to mow.

Getting to Work

Keeping up a house is a lot of work. Keeping up a house that has a lot of traffic from guests is nonstop work. Get ready to work on your house before, during, and after renovations. Just because renovations are "done" doesn't mean that you can take a load off. What will help in the future is buying products that last, learning some maintenance tricks for the things that always run amok, and hiring professionals for the big jobs.

Before you rip up even one floorboard, add up your numbers. Can you afford to do all the renovations at once? Will you attempt to do any of the work yourself? What will you live on, and where, while your house is a mess? For more on how to sustain an even blood sugar level without foraging in the woods for berries, see Chapter 8, "The Business Plan."

Inn the Know

Learn the basic inner workings of the toilets (blockage and flushing problems are more common than major repairs) and faucets (drips usually can be fixed by replacing a worn-out washer). Calling for outside help for small fixables is costly and will delay the work. You'll be amazed at how easy repair work can be if you know what you're doing.

Sturdy as She Goes

That carpet at Frank's Discount Carpet Warehouse is really cheap and there's a lot of it. There's enough to carpet all your guest rooms! Sure, this carpet might save you some bucks in the short run but how will it wear? Buying well-made furniture, carpets, paints, and appliances might lower your bank balance in the beginning, but it will save you headaches, and possibly cash, in the future.

Do-It-Yourself Renovations

You watch *This Old House,* you go to Home Depot or Lowe's every weekend, and you're confident that you can build that sun porch. There's nothing to it, really; some wood, some glass, a few nails; what's to know?

Coffee Talk

"To save money on renovations the only thing I could have done was to have been my own 'general contractor' but that's too long a story," recalls Mark Hancock, former owner of Miss Molly's in Fort Worth, Texas. "What we did was have the contractor sign a 'turnkey' contract with everything spelled out. I went so far as to write up all of the specifications of the job myself, not relying on the contractor. As it turned out, that probably saved me a lot of money, because the contractor operated on such a loose basis. We had several confrontations about 'changes' that weren't really changes at all when compared to the specifications that I had had the contractor sign."

Most of you will think the opposite—that it's easier to hire someone who actually does construction for a living. For the small percentage who will try to save some money and attempt a "DIY" (do-it-yourself) project, consider it only if you've had some building experience. How much money will you save if you have to hire a professional in the end anyway?

If you're really looking to save some money, pitch in on work that contractors are doing for you. If you can do the work (painting, for example), and do it at a pace that won't set back your own renovation schedule, your general contractor can hire one painter instead of two, and you can save some money.

Letting Professionals Take Over

Who are those professionals? If you're doing major reconstructive surgery, the major players will be the architect, general contractor, and interior designer. Crews that actually will do the nitty-gritty work include demolition, masons, framers, engineers (including septic engineer), septic installer, roofers, plumber, sprinkler installer, electrician, insulators, sheetrockers, plasterers, heating and cooling installers, landscapers, painters, and carpenters. Your general contractor most likely will have a crew that does demolition, framing, roofing, general carpentry, and finish work. Though the crew might include specialists in other areas, almost all general contractors will have a core crew of carpenters.

Before you run to an architect, interior designer, and general contractor, you first need to figure out what you want. Don't worry; even if you weren't an art major, you can still draw up sketches. Putting ideas down on paper will help you get to know your house intimately. You'll need to take measurements for each room and factor in where lighting and plumbing fixtures are (or will be) located. Your initial sketch also will be a good reference point when the work is in progress. An interior decorator might have some great ideas on room alterations but is that what you really want? A smart B&B owner will listen to an expert's advice but only take it if it's better than the owner's own original idea. To get your room designs down, head to an office supply store for some graph paper.

Treat each room as you would your children: You might enjoy being around one more than another, but you'd never tell them that. Spend some time in your least favorite rooms to figure out what could make them more appealing. For rooms with odd or limited space, use the walls, ceiling, and furniture to the room's best advantage. Put shelves in the walls or add drawers underneath the bed. Possibly brighten up a small, dark room with a skylight. Making a room more flattering will make you proud to call it one of your own.

Check out your contractors before hiring them. Ask to see examples of their finished products. Ask B&B owners whose houses you admire for referrals. Also, ask owners who have completed projects similar to yours about costs. Find out how happy they were, not only with the finished product, but with the contractors' willingness to listen to their ideas and make cost-efficient suggestions.

Decide on a delivery date that a construction company can really stick to. Having a performance contract with your general contractor is good insurance. Consider having a monetary penalty in place for late delivery of the finished product or overrun of costs. The penalty could be around $200 a day or whatever amount is agreed upon. Note that penalties may be hard to enforce. As a B&B owner you'll probably want to make some changes as the work progresses. How this might affect the delivery date is always a sticking point if the contractor is late in completing the project.

If you have a penalty, it's a good idea to have a bonus incentive too, if the workers finish early. Let the general contractor give you a final date, and then add 50 percent to that deadline. Add any less, and you'll just drive yourself and the construction workers crazy trying to meet the deadline.

Work closely with the general contractor at the outset and throughout the renovation process to be sure that the correct materials are ordered and that the schedule is going as planned.

Unless you're the general contractor, consider going away during some of the renovations. The best time to skip out is during demolition, the laying of a foundation, or the installation of something such as a septic system, all of which will shut the house down for a bit. If you're going to take any time away, the first third of the construction period probably is the best time to schedule some. Be sure to talk with your contractor before making any plans. You'll want to be there consistently for jobs such as framing, to make sure that those plans you and the general contractor put on paper translate to the walls.

Saving Your Sanity During Renovation

Your life won't stop completely while your house gets a makeover. The mortgage payments will still come, you'll have financial and marketing plans to work on, and maybe you'll need to start interviewing for staff. It's natural to think only of the construction while it's going on, but that could set you back in other ways.

Ease on into Business

Consider welcoming guests during some or all periods of the renovation if possible. Let's face it; you more than likely can use a little income, and guests' exposure to your work-in-progress can gain you some positive feedback. But make sure that your guests will be nearly as happy as they would be during nonhectic times and prepare to discount rates accordingly. Don't attempt to have guests if your water is shut off or there are dangerous work sites on the property. You

B&B-eware!

Keep your budget in mind during renovation. If construction work is part of a bank loan, you'll have to make the payments, so keeping some rooms rented might be a necessity!

want them to remember your blueberry pancakes, not coughing up dust or being unable to sleep late because of the cement mixer.

If you attempt to pre-open for business, offer your "trial run" guests extra-low rates. Make the situation clear before they show up so that there are no surprises. Involve guests in the process and take them on a tour of what "will be." This will help spread the word before you're up and running and might even garner some return guests who will want to see the finished product. You also will gain a little bit of income that you hadn't included in your budget.

Not That *Wall!*

Don't feel like a pest in your own home. If you see that something is a mistake, even after it's happened, get it corrected. The best way to keep contractors on the right track is to stay involved. Check in with them daily on the progress they're making. You don't need to be pushy to find out where things stand; you'll uncover and head off misunderstandings just by talking about the project at hand.

Using Your Time Wisely

Can't get away? Don't exactly know what to do with yourself while you wait for renovations to finish? Use this time to do some things that will save time later on.

Get to know your area from a tourist's point of view by visiting attractions, events, and restaurants. Fine-tune your marketing plan and work on ideas for a Web site (or get a Web designer on the job if you can spare the cash at this point). Attend an innkeeping seminar or take a cooking class. Think of things that really will benefit the business in the long run, whether it be in management or in better serving your guests.

Keeping the Neighbors Happy

You're excited about the coming overhaul to your property but not everyone will be. Noise, traffic, refuse, and the eyesore of demolition will keep neighbors on edge. The best way to ease their minds during these times is to let them in on the progress of the renovations. Keep in almost daily contact with them on a personal level, too. If you have an opening gala, invite them. If they can't make it, give them a tour when they do have time.

Unless you're dealing with a developed property, neighbors are almost always leery of change. Make sure they understand that this is a positive step. Your enthusiasm can be infectious, particularly if you can point out increased neighborhood property values or other benefits. If you get the sense that the neighbors won't be won over no matter what you do, try a more limited approach. Talk with them when you see them but don't go out of your way to do it. If people hold grudges that a few kind words won't dispel, don't expend your energy. You have better things to do.

Work on Your Hammer-and-Nail Skills

As you try to improve your hosting skills, consider working on your ability to keep the house up and running. If you have a small operation, you won't be able to afford a plumber or repair person every time something breaks. Even in bigger houses, it's good to know a few tricks of the trade.

If you are renovating the B&B, hang around the guys and gals working on the house. Get your hands dirty and work with them on laying down a floor or installing a boiler. These are heavy-duty jobs that you won't be able to do yourself but if you learn how things are installed, you'll have a better idea of what to do when they develop problems.

For basic repair, get to know the inner workings of these fine household items:

➤ **Ole John.** Plunging a toilet and knowing what to do when it doesn't flush are invaluable skills.

➤ **Faucets.** Leaky faucets are common, especially with strong water pressure. Usually you just need to replace a ring in the faucet head, which wears out quickly.

➤ **Hot water heater and boiler.** When these big boys go down, it's not always a major problem. Sometimes a switch gets tripped, causing the equipment to shut down completely. Talk to the installer about maintenance and about common problems and how to fix them.

➤ **Electrical stuff.** Most of this stuff you just shouldn't handle. Loose wires and such are dangerous and should be taken care of only by an electrician. What you can do is get to know your breaker box or, heaven forbid, fuse box. If the lights go out, don't panic. Flip the switches. If it happens a lot, you might need to have your wiring updated.

➤ **Mendable stuff.** Would you call a repairperson if one of your front steps were loose? If your tub needed caulking? If a door had a loose hinge? Really think about that repair before you call someone in. Fixing a hole in the wall is easily

Inn the Know

Don't get too ahead of yourself on bigger jobs; stay away from electrical and heating problems that should be handled by professionals. But for minor repairs, check out *The Complete Idiot's Guide to Trouble-Free Home Repair, Second Edition,* by David J. Tennenbaum. Time-Life also puts out a great series of how-to books, perfect for the novice.

Shoestring Solution

Want to cut down on excessive noise? Do it from the inside out. Hang large tapestries, quilts, or decorative rugs on the walls. Put area rugs on the floors. If you renovate, consider laying down cork underlay over subflooring. It's a great noise reducer.

done if you have the right tools and supplies. Sometimes a seemingly major headache can be easier to take care of than scheduling a contractor.

Most of you have had experience fixing small problems such as the preceding ones in your own house. If you've lived only in modern facilities and you just bought a post–World War II house, prepare to play catch-up, and remember that the more you do something, the better you'll get at it.

The Least You Need to Know

➤ If you're buying a house that needs work, it will save you money and headaches later on if you first determine whether it needs major repairs.

➤ Be sure your B&B property-to-be will comply with zoning regulations and is up to code.

➤ Stay involved in the more critical stages of the renovating process by discussing progress with the contractors on a regular basis.

➤ Making good use of the time you'll have during renovations (such as checking out tourist sites) will help your business when you get going.

➤ Head to the library or invest in a book or two on home repair. These how-to references can help you save time and money.

Chapter 6

Legalities and Liabilities

> ## In This Chapter
>
> ➤ Complying with the basic requirements of your state and local district
>
> ➤ Protecting yourself from property loss and becoming a good risk
>
> ➤ Finding the right insurance coverage

Every state, county, city, and town will differ when it comes to rules and regulations that govern such issues as zoning, licensing, and safety. If you happen to be the first B&B in your town, prepare to lay some heavy groundwork. There might not be many existing regulations for them, so town officials will watch you carefully and probably will use your business as a model for B&B regulations to come. If there are other B&Bs already operating in your area, you'll be expected to follow the rules and regulations that are in place.

The best way to head off surprises (what do you mean I can't build a back cottage?) is to do your homework. Find out about the zoning guidelines for the property, fire code and health regulations, and what licenses and permits you'll need. There also are state regulations to be fulfilled. The feds are primarily concerned with getting a chunk of your cash flow and making sure you file your taxes correctly (covered in Chapter 9, "Setting Up Your Business and Financial Structure").

Space does not allow us to provide more than a set of guidelines for dealing with typical rules and regulations, many of which might apply in your area. To get the scoop on regulations that will affect you, talk to your building department; ask your attorney, business manager (if you've hired one), or real estate agent (if the agent is wise in the ways of regulations); and talk with other local B&B owners.

Rules of the Locals

These days, town officials are less likely to be baffled by a proposal for a B&B than they used to be, thanks to a positive turn in the industry's growth. Even now, though, B&Bs remain something of an oddity; not a restaurant (in most cases), not a boarding house, and not a hotel. Your business will exist in a kind of regulation limbo at times. Official processes might take longer because officials might not know exactly how to classify your establishment. Consequently, they might impose very strict parameters to ensure that all bases are covered; or they could go in the opposite direction and your B&B's regulation could be looser than you expected.

Coffee Talk

Here are some tips about buying seaside property from owners/inn-keepers Rick and Ruth-Anne Broad of Anne's Oceanfront Hideaway B&B in Salt Spring Island, B.C., Canada. "Oceanfront is a very dear commodity in most areas of the west coast. Look into things like set backs and watershed areas before you buy, and decide if it fits both your budget and your plans. For example, you probably won't want a high bank, steep cliff waterfront if you're going to welcome children. If you're going to be wheelchair accessible you won't want steep access or a lot of stairs. We had a few minor difficulties getting our plans approved as this is a very conservation-minded area and they needed assurance we weren't building a 'mini hotel.'"

Naturally, you'll view your B&B as a positive addition to your local economy and your community, and some officials will agree with you. Others will need some convincing, and oddly enough, those who appear guarded at first sometimes can become your biggest supporters. They're the people who really want to do what's right for the town, and they'll pay attention to your proposal. So be prepared for the fact that your positive perspective on your B&B might not immediately be shared by everyone, and there probably will be a few who will never come around. Don't get discouraged; keep in mind that it's the job of the town officials to weed out the very bad ideas (Stan's Fire Breathing School for Kids) from the very good ones (your B&B).

There are a lot of politics involved in getting a business started. If you're new to the town, you'll have more ground to cover because you'll want to meet and talk to as many VIPs as possible. If you're a long-time resident, talk to town officials you know and find out which way the political wind is blowing. In either case, try to garner as much support as you can from those in decision-making positions. At the very least, make your presence known and get to know how things work in the town. Attend board meetings that might affect you or your property. Hire a respected architect and contractors, those with a proven track record with other local businesses. Establish yourself and gain the respect of the movers and shakers *before* you need their support.

Local Regulations

Most of your red tape will occur on the local level. Make sure you find out the protocol for procedures and the requirements in your municipality before you start the process of establishing your B&B.

Getting Legal

Depending on your town, you may or may not need to obtain every type of license and permit that exists for a small business. However, if having proper approval to conduct business will make your B&B stand out as a full-fledged and professional operation, it's worth the fees. Chances are you'll have to apply for one or more of the following types of local documentation to start up your business:

➤ **Business license.** Most towns require a license to conduct business. You can apply for one at the town hall (some areas have a department for licenses) and, once licensed, you will receive a certificate to frame on your wall. You also will be charged an annual fee for renewal of the license and your B&B will have to be inspected annually. This can include health inspections if you have a pool, hot tub, full-service kitchen, or bar. There also might be inspections by an electrical inspector from the fire department to test smoke alarms and make sure fire extinguishers are in place; and a building inspector who will ensure that exits aren't blocked and that your general maintenance and upkeep is acceptable (no broken boards, and so on). If the inspectors find anything amiss, most likely they will require you to fix the problem and be inspected again before they'll sign off on renewal.

➤ **Building permits.** If you're constructing a B&B from scratch, you plan on major additions, or even if you build a fence, you'll need to file for a building permit. Each permit involves a fee. Before you head down to the town hall, call to find out what documentation you'll need for a casual meeting

Inn the Know

If you plan to purchase a turnkey B&B, do some research on licenses and permits held by the current owners. As is the case for some liquor license rules, you might need to renew the license in your name or apply for a new one.

with the member or members of the building department. You'll likely need to leave copies of blueprints or plans with them for review. Your property might need to be inspected, and planning or zoning committees also might need to review your plans before a permit is issued. Issuing building permits enables towns to keep an eye on property improvements and to reassess them accordingly during tax time. Most areas don't require a permit for fixing an existing structure but it really depends on your level of reconstruction and the structure of the town's codes. If you buy from a respected real estate agent with commercial real estate knowledge, much of the licensing and registration legwork should have been done by your agent. If you don't buy through an agent—or even if you do—hire a real estate lawyer to follow through on the legalities.

➤ **Fictitious name.** Why, surely you can't mean that! Yes, we do, and don't call us Shirley. When you register your business name you file for a "fictitious name" statement with the county clerk. It doesn't mean that you register your business under a different name. Filing a fictitious name statement is for B&Bs that have a name separate from the owner's given name (such as Hideaway Cove Inn). If you do use your own name for the business ("Sue Ellen's B&B," for example), you're exempted from registering.

B&B-eware!

Don't try to get away with constructing something without a building permit. It might cause some serious complications when you try to sell the place down the road because you won't be allowed to get a certificate of occupancy, which you'll need to convey a deed at sale of the property.

Filing for the fictitious name most likely will require you to have a notice of your application published in the newspaper for a set amount of time. You'll be charged for filing the name and for the cost of publishing the notice. This procedure will alert the local world of its new prospect; you also might need it to open a business checking account, so be sure to save a clipping of the notice.

It's a good idea to register your B&B's name whether you're required to or not. When you file, the county double-checks your name against other registered B&Bs to prevent duplication. Registering will save you from being taken to court by another B&B of the same name that wants to stop you from using it.

Get in the Zone

Your town's appointed officials mapped out residential, commercial, and public areas because people don't want to live next to a fast-food joint and fast-food joints want to be near other businesses. For this reason, there are restrictions on where you can have a B&B (although this gets tricky because most of the time it's a business and a residence) and what it looks like from the street.

The town has the right to say no to you if the property resides in an area not zoned for B&B use. Getting approval from the zoning board means presenting your business plan, answering questions, and waiting for approval from the powers that be. It sounds simple but there can be even more steps added on, particularly if you need a building permit, which you can't get because the building department still needs to inspect your property, and so on.

B&B-eware!

Think you can miss that zoning meeting when approval for construction on your B&B is on the table? Think again. Although your local zoning commission can vote yea or nay on any project whether you're there or not, it only makes sense to show up. What if someone on the board has questions for you? What if half of the board wants to vote yea and the other nay; who will be there to persuade them? Don't be intimidated by these meetings. Go, armed with enthusiasm and answers for all conceivable questions. Pay attention to the board's concerns and dispel them with positive solutions.

In some towns, planning and zoning are combined into one commission; in others they're separate. The more committees that need to approve your plans, the more meetings you'll need to attend and the longer it will be before you can get your B&B started.

If an existing zoning bylaw is a stumbling block, it is possible to fight it (bylaws are covered later in the chapter). You can request a variance for your property or even the rezoning of an area. However, don't rely on this option and think, "Oh, I can get them to change their minds." It might not happen. Look at records of recent zoning board approvals and consider current town plans. You might have a solid case for your request if it conforms to plans for the future direction of the town or will break ground in an undeveloped area of the town plan. You could have town officials thinking that your proposal was their idea all along!

Some of the other procedures you might be required to go through involve …

➤ **Public works requirements.** The public works department is concerned with traffic and adequate access to buildings. Some public works departments are very strict about limiting the amount of off-street parking per guest room, the existence of a sidewalk, your curb cuts, and the width of your driveway. Check with public works before you buy a property that has no parking at all!

➤ **Historical society or review boards.** Some towns have boards that go beyond planning and zoning to manage changes in residential and commercial property. These boards will have guidelines on signage, fencing, house color, and consistency in architectural style. If your property is a historical landmark (or you think it should be considered one), it might need to be inspected and reviewed before it's officially recognized as such.

B&B-eware!

Stop! Before you build that front porch, check to make sure that no one will make you tear it down. In historical districts, local historical and preservation societies ensure that properties keep up their old world charm. Sometimes you can fight the nit-picky stuff, but adding a porch that will change the look of the house will be a tough battle. There is a saving grace: Most preservation boards care only about changes that can be seen from the road.

In-House Safety Check

In a business catering to overnight guests, health and safety should be taken seriously—and it will be by your local fire marshal and health department.

➤ **Fire codes.** Some of the requirements you might encounter in your area to bring your building up to code are hard-wired smoke detectors with battery back-up, exit signs (possibly lighted), fire extinguishers in strategic areas, sprinklers (mostly required only with new construction or major renovation), legal exits, and fire doors. Your fire marshal should supply you with fire safety brochures, a must-have for any business. A fire code violation can result in fines if you don't have it corrected, and could hold up your license renewal until the problem is fixed. Fire codes are becoming extremely stringent everywhere, especially with new construction and remodeling. Improvements to fire safety in an older building can be used as a bargaining point when you're seeking zoning approval or variances. In more densely populated areas, additional benefits include lowering the risk of burning down the neighborhood, insurance breaks, and better sleep for you.

➤ **Health department.** These people make sure that your staff and your operation (primarily food service) are fit enough to serve the general public. Inspection by the health department is extremely important. If you fail, you might be able to operate (with a probationary time period to get your act together); but do yourself a favor: Save your reputation and get it right the first time. Health departments typically will check your kitchen and bathrooms for cracks in the walls (which allow unwanted pesky critters in); proper ventilation; and washable floor, wall, and ceiling surfaces. If you offer a full breakfast you might be required to purchase a convection oven and commercial dishwasher. Depending on your operation, you might even need to get a food handlers permit. You'll also need to educate your staff on proper food handling and cleaning procedures. Check with your municipal or (if there isn't one) county health department for specifics on their guidelines so you'll be ready for an inspection. State health departments can be very rigid and have been known to make unexpected stops. Find out what your state and county guidelines are so you can be prepared.

Local Bylaws

Some communities will have detailed bylaws restricting what changes can and cannot be made to a B&B or to the property. Most of these regulations apply to small B&B and guesthouse operations existing in residential areas. Some municipalities have separate bylaws for inns and larger B&B businesses. Bylaws you might run into cover the following:

➤ **Seeing signs.** Restrictions on the size of signs and their height from the ground are common.

➤ **Regulations on food service.** Because most B&Bs are zoned in residential areas, you might not be allowed to serve any meals to nonguests, or might be restricted to serving only breakfast. The purpose of these restrictions is to prevent excessive noise and traffic in residential areas. Cooking facilities in guest rooms also might be prohibited.

➤ **Owner-occupied rules.** In some towns, to be classified as a B&B, you will need to live on the property. You might be able to circumvent this rule by hiring a live-in manager and notifying the town of his or her name.

➤ **Limits on guests and how long they stay.** The number of guest rooms might be limited, as well as how long guests can stay. These restrictions are put in place to distinguish B&Bs from boarding houses and other rental units.

Inn the Know

If you're entertaining the idea of using your B&B for parties or weddings in the future, check to make sure it's permitted. You might need to add extra parking or make other accommodations; things you'll want to know about before renovating.

➤ **Renovation considerations.** Some towns will not allow renovations that would rule out restoring a house to its original use as a single-family residence (usually determined by the number of kitchens in the building). Once again, local codes come into play that might affect your renovation and the future sale of your B&B.

Local Taxes

You will be required to pay local property tax based on your purchase price and the annually reassessed value thereafter. Your municipality or your state also might charge rooms tax. If you sell things such as gift items you'll need a separate permit for sales tax. For more on taxes and how to file, see Chapter 9.

Americans with Disabilities Act

If you operate a B&B with five guest rooms or fewer and live in the house, you are exempt from complying with the federal Americans with Disabilities Act (ADA). Old buildings are not exempt. If you buy a three-story inn, you will need to add an elevator (not required with one- or two-level buildings). ADA compliance may be required for making certain renovations (check out the ADA Web site for details).

Compliance with the ADA requires making provisions for those with physical disabilities, including the sight and hearing impaired.

Inn the Know

To find out more about what's required to comply with the ADA, contact them directly at Office of the Americans with Disabilities Act, Civil Rights Division/Department of Justice, PO Box 66118, Washington, DC 20035; 202-514-0301 or 202-514-0383 (TDD). The ADA home page at the U.S. Department of Justice is www.usdoj.gov/crt/ada/ adahom1.htm.

State Policies

Just as municipalities differ in their zoning, licensing, and regulatory requirements, so do the states. The following are some typical state requirements for B&Bs:

➤ **Room tax permit.** If you're "selling" the use of rooms in your house, in other words operating a B&B, your room charges will be taxed by the state. You'll need a room tax permit so that you can add this tax to your guest bills.

➤ **Sales tax permit.** If your state has sales tax and your property is zoned for selling products, most likely you'll need to obtain a permit to collect sales tax on anything other than rooms that you sell to your guests. Talk to your accountant about the best way to keep track of sales tax and when to pay it (monthly, quarterly, or yearly). The more tourism your town has, the quicker you'll be able to find out what's required (from another local B&B, for example).

➤ **State employer tax I.D. number.** If you have employees, states also collect taxes in the form of an "unemployment insurance tax." The state employment office will issue you an employer number automatically. You'll need this at tax time when you report payroll.

➤ **Worker's compensation.** This may be required, depending on state or local codes. See "Must-Have Coverage and Then Some," later in this chapter.

➤ **Liquor license.** States require one if you serve hard stuff and beer and wine (some states have a separate beer and wine license, which is easier to get because they assume you're serving food).

Getting Good Insurance

Having a solid homeowner policy is a start, but as you'll find out when you talk to your lawyer and insurance agent, it's not enough. Choosing insurance coverage carefully and wisely is your best protection. Find an agent that specializes in bed and breakfast coverage or is experienced in small businesses. There are a lot of good insurance packages for B&Bs now.

Becoming a Good Risk

Insurance companies want to have some insurance themselves. B&Bs that have good insurance policies (and with lower premiums) have taken steps to prevent liability. Here are some specific ways you can become a good risk:

➤ **Get inspected.** Even if they're not required, building, fire code, and health inspections will prove to the insurance company that you've taken steps to protect your business. Ask your agent what you can provide for the insurance company (inspection reports, for example) to get good coverage at a lower premium.

➤ **Prevent injuries.** Buy some carbon dioxide detectors, heat sensors, and smoke alarms for every room (these will be required anyway). Heat sensors and smoke alarms are typically required to be hard-wired by an electrician, particularly if you do a major renovation. Putting fire extinguishers in each room is an excellent idea, especially if you have an older house, and they're very affordable. Put handrails in bathtubs and showers, non-skid material under rugs, fix broken or loose steps, remove snow and use salt to melt ice on pathways, put baby gates at tops of stairs (if you accept young children), install emergency lights and motion lighting outside, and use double-bolt locks on all outside doors.

➤ **Prevent liability.** Before you offer services that can put guests in dangerous or precarious situations, such as offering use of your mopeds or picking up guests at the airport or train or bus station in your personal-use vehicle, talk to your agent to make sure you're covered for personal injuries to your guests. You probably won't be, and you'll need to buy extra coverage or a really good umbrella policy. Also have guests who use mopeds, for example, sign a disclaimer (ask your agent about the language to use). Don't feel bad about doing this—if they rented them somewhere else they'd have to sign a waiver anyway. But don't rely on insurance or a disclaimer as your only means of protection: Make sure those mopeds, horses, or snowmobiles are safe for use in the first place!

➤ **Train your staff.** Teach your staff the proper way to lift heavy objects (from the legs, from the legs!), and how to practice safety in the kitchen and when operating machinery. Don't expect them to be familiar with safety practices, even if they've worked at other B&Bs. If anything happens to an employee while on the job, Worker's Compensation will cover their expenses, but your insurance rates will rise as a result. Plus, what happens if an employee causes injury to a guest by failing to practice safety? Most likely you—not the employee—will be sued. Not familiar with work safety practices? Contact the U.S. Department of Labor's Occupational Safety and Health Administration at www.osha.gov for more information.

Protection from Loss

Your insurance company will require that you submit a list of all valuables and goods on the property. This list will help the company assess property value, and will be invaluable down the road if you need to make a claim of damage or theft. That way, if a guest burns down the entire floor, you'll know how much the furniture and other items in room 6 were worth. Be sure to list everything and its true value. If you're not sure what Grandma Betty's tea set is really worth, get it appraised. Underestimating the monetary value of your personal and business property can only hurt you later on.

Coffee Talk

Kerry Adams of Fireside Insurance Company in Provincetown, Massachusetts, suggests that you take pictures of rooms and of extremely valuable items. You might even get your agent to do it. Keep your list and the pictures in a safety deposit box at the bank and send copies to your insurance agent. Save copies of receipts for newly purchased items and don't forget to add the items to your list! If a fire wrecks the house, you might not remember everything that was lost. In a typical catch-22, insurance companies accept verification of loss only after a claim is made: Pictures can help establish that you had something, but you can prove that you had it only after it's gone!

Must-Have Coverage and Then Some

There's a lot of insurance coverage to be had in this business. The potential for something to go wrong is huge in any business and this especially holds true for B&Bs and their owners. The insurance game is all about getting the best deal for the most protection possible; but insurance coverage is something that you don't want to skimp on. If you don't pay for coverage now, you might pay a lot more in damages later on.

Coverage for the house and the business will split into two main parts: property and liability. Property insurance covers the house, everything in the house, and everything used to maintain it. Liability covers anything that could happen to someone while in your house or on your land. A package deal that includes property and liability insurance is your safety net.

B&B-eware!

Do not operate your B&B without having full insurance coverage! Getting standard coverage during renovation or construction is well worth the money, too. What happens if the kid next door falls into your newly dug hole for the swimming pool? It's a risk you can't afford to take.

Find a policy with broad coverage to protect against fire, theft, and weather damage. It's not easy to get full weather damage (it depends on where you live) but get as much coverage as you can. One hailstorm can break windows and damage siding for good.

Getting "business interruption" coverage might save you if something major, such as a flood, stalls your business from operating. How would you pay the mortgage and other bills that will still be coming in? If you can prove a steady history of your income in the months before the catastrophe, this coverage will kick in and cover your lost revenue in case of a disaster.

Worker's compensation coverage, even if it's not required in your state, is a must. If your chef cuts off his or her thumb while slicing apples on your cutting board, you won't have to pay the medical bills, physical therapy expenses, and lost wages. Worker's comp also can cover life insurance. Unless an employee can show that an owner's utter and extreme negligence caused an injury, you, the owner, will not be sued under this coverage. An owner might choose to be covered as an employee under worker's comp, but it will cost more.

Some other insurance that you should consider adding to the list includes ...

➤ **Food spoilage.** Especially if you are an inn or offer more than one meal, this is a good extra. During an extended power outage, you might lose a few hundred dollars in food, depending on what you have in your fridge and a separate freezer.

➤ **Products coverage.** If a guest gets food poisoning on your property and it is not your fault, but the fault of the producer of the tainted product, products coverage will protect you. This should be included in your basic coverage.

71

Inn the Know

Some basic policies will allow only 8 or 10 "perils." Typically, the basic eight perils are fire, lightning, windstorm, hail, aircraft, riot, vehicle explosion, and smoke. Broad-range policies will protect against every peril unless specifically excluded.

➤ **Personal liability.** Although the term implies physical damage to you, it actually refers to emotional injuries such as slander. Personal liability also protects you in case you stumble onto a naked guest, or overhear a private conversation (invasion of privacy), or a staff member walks into a room without knocking (unlawful entry). You'll most likely have a certain amount of coverage in your basic policy.

➤ **Protection from Mother Nature.** If you live by the coast, get flood insurance. If you live in California, get protection against earthquake damage. Mudslides have occurred in your area? Tornado country? You'll be thankful you're covered for these unforeseen happenings when the forces of nature release themselves on your property.

➤ **Ordinance or law replacement.** If you decide to rebuild after loss of property due to fire or "Act of God," you'll need to renovate in compliance with ordinances (once again). This extra coverage helps pay for work done to get your building up to code. Some towns might require you to update the building according to new fire and building codes that require adding such things as a sprinkler system or new plumbing. These costs might not fall under ordinance replacement coverage and will come out of your own pocket. This coverage is strongly recommended for older buildings that are not up to code: Things that you don't anticipate can cause you great expense.

➤ **Excess liability.** This is extra coverage put into use when your regular liability coverage runs out. Usually referred to as an "umbrella policy," this coverage kicks in when your regular coverage is maxed out.

A word to the wise: If you serve alcohol, whether you have a liquor license or not, you'll need some extra insurance. Usually called "liquor liability," it will protect you in court if any inebriated guest leaves your property and causes an accident. Be sure to get the correct type of liquor liability insurance. Inns that sell liquor in their restaurant need a different type of insurance from B&Bs that give it away. If you do give liquor away (to honeymooners or at an evening cocktail hour) it can be construed as part of the rate. Definitely add liquor liability if you do any heavy volume of liquor sales. If you're just giving it away, most likely coverage will be based on the minimum allowable amount.

When you're looking for protection for the business, don't forget about yourself! A lot of inn-keepers' partners keep their outside jobs for the medical and life insurance benefits. If you're not lucky enough to have this option, ask your local Chamber of Commerce and the national B&B associations (see Appendix B, "National and Local Associations") about their group coverage plans.

The Least You Need to Know

➤ Every state and municipality will have different regulations but most will require compliance with zoning, fire, and health departments.

➤ Local bylaws can dictate everything from the size of your sign to how many meals you can serve.

➤ Avoiding perilous situations and decreasing your liability exposure will get you better insurance coverage at a better price.

➤ B&Bs need more than basic homeowners insurance to cover the business and the property.

Chapter 7

Rooms ranging from 50¢ to 4 hundred jillion dollars

All About Room Rates

In This Chapter

➤ Weighing all the factors when calculating room rates

➤ Raising rates

➤ Being flexible about room rates

The hospitality industry "standard" for setting room rates can be complicated. Your highest rate might be $225 per night for your best room during July 4th weekend. Your lowest rate might be as little as $55 per night for your hardest-sell room during a weekday in February. The fluctuation is vast due to a lot of different factors but it mostly boils down to what you can get for the room.

A lot of inn-keepers just starting out can feel guilty or uncertain about placing a dollar figure on their rooms. That feeling will diminish over time, especially when you've been in business for a while and have a better grasp of the value of your property. Even if you can't afford to stay in one of your own rooms, there are guests who can!

Pricing Your Product

Overcome your uncertainty about what to charge by thinking of your rates as an economically calculated fee rather than a number pulled out of a hat. When a manufacturer of doorknobs prices out its stock, the management doesn't just pick a number that sounds good, willy-nilly. They factor in their costs, the prices that other manufacturers charge, and what people are willing to pay for their doorknobs.

Think of your rooms as products you are trying to sell and, as doorknob makers do, calculate the sell price of each room according to a set of factors. To help determine

your rates we've created a "class system" of sorts. Use the following as a loose guideline to develop and adjust your rates:

➤ Competition

➤ Location

➤ Amenities

➤ Service

➤ Season

Take a Clue from the Competition

The best way to find out about your competition is through Web sites, but there are still some B&Bs out there without them. Try to get hold of their brochures or try the Chamber of Commerce for information on them. Phoning B&Bs as if you were a potential guest used to be a good route, but these days you have to watch out for caller I.D.! Perhaps a friend or relative from another town can make the calls for you. Give the person a script that includes questions you want answered.

When you have your rate information, make a list of the B&Bs, what they charge for each season, and what they offer in amenities and services. Compare it with what your B&B has to offer.

Most tourists will try to save some money on room rates but B&B hoppers rarely will opt for the cheap motel over the beautiful house with breakfast included (unless they have a minivan full of kids). If you have a lot of amenities and a flair for hosting, don't be afraid to ask a little more. A whirlpool bath, a good night's rest, and home-made breakfast is worth a lot more clams anywhere. You might be surprised at how difficult it will be to get rid of your least expensive room. Most people think that the cheapest room has something wrong with it!

Location, Location, Location

What you can charge in your area will depend a lot on, well, your area. Factoring in location goes hand in hand with finding out what your competition charges. Their rates will give you a clue to what you can get in the general area, but the physical location of your house will be a variable.

Let's take the cases of Tom and Henrietta. Each owns a B&B in a seaside tourist town that bustles in the spring, summer, and early fall. Tom owns a five-room B&B that sits on a hill, has ocean views from three rooms, and is three minutes to the main drag. Henrietta owns a six-room inn at the bottom of the same hill, but has no ocean views, and is eight minutes (eight *up-hill* minutes) from the hustle and bustle. The two offer comparable amenities and service but Tom would be losing out if he didn't charge more for his ocean view rooms. Not to mention that the tax assessment on Tom's property will be higher for those ocean views. Charging more for ocean view rooms might be a necessity!

Just as airlines or large urban hotels are set up to make subtle rate changes based on traffic patterns, in time you'll be able to adjust your rates at will. Remember that rates reflect the equilibrium of supply and demand. Use a combination of information and intuition and you'll set the rates that will do the most for your business.

B&B-eware!

If you're conveniently located near a town center, city, college campus, boarding school, hospital or nursing care, event center, museum, sports arena, concert hall, or worm farm, don't hesitate to charge accordingly. If your area attracts a lot of traffic, your options for what you can charge guests instantly increase.

Rooms Have a Lot to Offer

The biggest amenity your room has to offer is a private bath. If you have rooms that share a bath, you'll have to take a hit on rates for those rooms. More often than not, people will pay the extra money to have bath facilities in their rooms. Because more and more B&Bs are opening up with only (or mostly) private baths, guests are starting to expect it.

When rating each room, consider starting with your smallest one (or the one with the fewest amenities) and working your way up. To make sure that you get the most out of each amenity you provide, you'll need to calculate its worth.

Inn the Know

Want to know the real appeal of your rooms? Become a guest in your own house. Sleeping overnight in a room is a good way to really know its value. Pay attention to everything in it: how it looks, sounds, and feels. How easy is it to maneuver around the bathroom? How loud are the sounds that float in and out during the wee hours? Is the bed too hard or soft? Is the room too cluttered? Too empty? How much would you pay to stay in that room?

If your B&B is comparable to another B&B in your area but you have a better location, you can charge more. If you live in a remote area where you're the only B&B, then whirlpool tubs won't be able to get you that much more.

To help establish the relative value of your rooms, take a close look at what your competition offers and prepare a list of amenities you hope to feature.

Amenities Checklist

Amenity	You Offer	Percentage of B&Bs That Offer This
Breakfast and Meals		
Full breakfast	No	61
Continental breakfast	Yes	84
Full breakfast only sometimes	Yes	67
Lunch (not included in room rate)	No	16
Dinner (not included in room rate)	No	23
Lunch and dinner (not included in room rate)	No	15
Business Services		
Voicemail or answering service in rooms	Yes	53
Fax accessibility	Yes	67
E-mail/Internet access in rooms	No	6
Mailing supplies	Yes	28
Stationery supplies (notepaper, pens, envelopes, etc.)	Yes	25
Conference or meeting room	Yes	9
Common Rooms		
TV w/VCR	Yes	96
DVD player	No	7
Stereo	Yes	98
Fireplace	Yes	69
Computer w/Internet access	Yes	12
Use of kitchen	No	17
Common baths	Yes	48
Icemaker	No	23
Common-Use Incidentals		
Video (and/or DVD) library	Yes	45
Book/reference library	Yes	58
Magazines and daily newspaper	Yes	90

Amenity	You Offer	Percentage of B&Bs That Offer This
Games	Yes	78
Umbrellas	Yes	75
Bicycles	Yes	24
Picnic baskets	Yes	47
Beach chairs/towels/accessories	Yes	38
Beach passes	No	35
Complimentaries		
Wine/sparkling juice in room (even just for special occasions)	Yes	38
Sherry	Yes	19
Snacks in room or common area	No	46
Wine and cheese hour	Yes	30
Afternoon tea	No	27
Grounds		
Swimming pool	No	12
Kiddie pool	No	7
Jacuzzi-type spa or hot tub	Yes	18
Sauna	Yes	8
Picnic/lounge area	Yes	72
Porch or patio	Yes	80
Playscape for kids	No	22
Rec equipment/outdoor games	Yes	32
Walking access to hiking trails	No	25
Walking access to beach or lake	No	15
Outdoor shower	No	6
Adequate parking	Yes	78
Guest Rooms: Big Stuff		
Queen- or king-size beds (the latter can be in some or all rooms)	Yes	95
Whirlpool tub	No	29
Fireplaces	No	38
Ceiling fans	Yes	60
TVs/VCRs	Yes	80
Eat-in kitchen in one or some rooms	No	44

continues

Amenities Checklist (continued)

Amenity	You Offer	Percentage of B&Bs That Offer This
Mini-fridge	Yes	78
Porches or decks	No	30
Dimmer lights	No	18
Heat/vent/light fixtures	No	11
Bathrobes	No	18
Extra blankets and pillows	Yes	89
Coffeemaker and supplies	Yes	65
Bucket w/ice and glasses	Yes	78
Iron/ironing board	Yes	70
Digital or mechanical safe	Yes	55
Extra-nice bedding (feather duvets, etc.)	Yes	67
Cots or roll-aways (and/or cribs) for extra guests	No	28
One or some rooms with sitting areas	Yes	82
Guest Rooms: Incidentals		
Phone in every room	Yes	45
Clock radio	Yes	92
Night lights	Yes	76
Bedside reading lamps	No	72
Videos/magazines/books	No	54
Bible or feel-good book	Yes	78
Mini-sewing kit	No	27
Aromatherapy scents (not candles!)	Yes	58
Guest Rooms: Baths		
Mini-shampoo/conditioner/lotion	Yes	87
Soap w/B&B name or shower gel	Yes	67
Bath salts (for tubs)	Yes	58
Hair dryer	Yes	78
Towel warmer	No	12
Makeup or shaving mirror	No	25
Hotel-Like Services		
24-hour manager	Yes	84
Airport/bus/train pick-up	Yes	32
Breakfast in bed (served or self-serve)	Yes	60
Dinner/show/other reservations	Yes	89

Amenity	You Offer	Percentage of B&Bs That Offer This
Turndown service	Yes	26
Discounts booklets for tourist attractions, car rentals, etc.	Yes	68
Masseuse	No	2
Shoe shine	No	5
Exercise equipment	No	16
In-house laundry service	No	32
Hold service for luggage	Yes	85

Your amenities list can differ from this one. Try not to be intimidated by what your competition offers. Focus on qualities that are important to you and take into consideration your property's limitations.

Breakfast is an amenity that carries some weight when determining rates. It's included in the rate, but *what's* included? Full breakfast B&Bs can charge a little more, and those that serve only a continental style breakfast should concentrate on guest services and amenities to compensate.

If you're near motels, use competitive rates, and highlight the fact that breakfast is included to pull people your way. Call the motels to find out their basic rates and use them as a gauge.

One Lump or Two?

Should you set rates as "per person" or "per room"? If you go with the per person rate, make sure you're explicit and clear when describing rates. Most establishments, including hotels, use a per-room rate, and that's what people expect. Sometimes the per-person rate is used in all-inclusive resorts that offer amenities such as golf, swimming, massages, health club facilities, and all meals as part of the package deal.

It's also legitimate for a B&B to charge extra if guests add a third or fourth person to their room; charging an extra fee of $15 to $75 (based on the quality of your property) is completely acceptable. Even though that extra person is not taking up another room, he or she is taking up space and eating your breakfast.

Also, don't allow too many extra folks in one room! It can compromise the quality of your establishment and we strongly advise against it. Blame it on a fire code violation. This works well because most people obey rules set by authorities without question. Have an "extra person" policy and rate in place before you need to use it.

Service Please

If you plan on going the extra mile with guest services, such as turndown service or airport pick-up, set your rates accordingly. Even if guests don't use some of your services, if they know what you provide, they'll be willing to pay for it.

Coffee Talk

Dennis Radtke, General Manager of County Clare—an Irish Guesthouse and Pub in Milwaukee, Wisconsin, says: "Guests are looking for personal attention and charm. Due to the volume of guests, it's very difficult for a large hotel to be charming. There are just too many guests. Our inn has thirty rooms, and we always say to our customers that if they stay here more than once, we'll know them by their first names; twice, and we'll know what they like to drink and have for dinner."

Knowing how much extra to charge for services can be tricky. A service is something you provide for someone else; so how do you measure it in dollars?

Determine just how far you'd be willing to go for a guest—every guest—who walks through your door. Some services will please some people and go unused by others. Services that are truly appreciated can't just be at your whim; you should offer services that guests will use. This could include carrying luggage, wake-up calls, making dinner or show reservations, and turndown service. Figure out what kinds of services are going to be of value to your guests to establish what you'll provide and how much they might raise those rates.

'Tis the Season

Most areas have a high, mid, and low season. Sometimes, B&Bs use "peak" and "off" to describe their busiest and least active times. This three-tier system, especially in tourist areas, is a good gauge to use for two reasons. First, you can track traffic to determine which days to charge your highest rates, and when you'll need to be flexible. Second, it's a good structure for determining how high and how low you're able to go. Discounting a room rate at the last minute to get a guest in is fine, but you risk losing that room to a guest who might have been willing to pay the going rate. Having room rate parameters will help you stay within the boundaries of potential profit.

Within the main seasons, it's wise to have weekend and weekday rates, especially for the shoulder season (mid or low). Using a lower weekday rate during slow times is a good draw. During peak season, when you can get higher rates, a lower weekday rate is not necessary. Again, the goal is to charge what you can get for the room without undercutting profit.

Inn the Know

If you're near an event center where concerts, conventions, and the like happen sporadically throughout the year, consider listing your rates for rooms as ranging from, say, $85 to $275 instead of specifying seasonal and weekend/weekday rates. You still need the foundation of a three-tiered rate system, but this will allow you some flexibility during busy times. If you have the chance to sell a room during typically slower times, use your mid-season rate to get the higher price tag.

City B&Bs or inns might not see the seasonal fluctuations that a primarily leisure-oriented destination might, because the mix of guests can include business travelers. If your location is in the heart of a city, base your rates on services, location, and competition. Knowing what your city competition charges is crucial. People expect to spend bucks in the city and they tend to do some extra shopping around to save on accommodations.

Coffee Talk

"Find ways to maximize your off season," suggest Sabrina Riddle and Lynette Molnar, owners of The Fairbanks Inn in Provincetown, Massachusetts. "While much of the focus is often on filling the inn during the high season, the potential for expanding profits lies in filling rooms during slow times. Encourage off-season stays beyond just the weekend through promotions like 'stay seven nights and pay for only five.' Or create special events at the inn so guests have a reason to come and enjoy the more relaxed off-season."

Inn the Know

Guests should not be charged to borrow anything from the house. We have yet to come across a small operation that charges for little extras. You wouldn't, however, want to offer the use of bikes free of charge if there's a bike rental place three blocks away. If you do let guests use your things, make sure you have the appropriate liability coverage (see Chapter 6, "Legalities and Liabilities").

Sometimes determining what to charge can be a tough call during busy times as well as during the low season. In setting rates, try to get the most out of the traffic that shuffles through your town. Charging more in the high season is a simple case of supply and demand. The "demand" from tourists for a roof over their heads is high during busy times and your "supply" of rooms is a valuable commodity; so of course you can charge more.

Charging for Extras

Making guests pay for extra offerings at your B&B usually is considered to be in bad taste. We're not talking about items you sell such as drinks (if you have an inn with a liquor license) or items purchased through a separate business connected with the B&B. We mean extras such as letting guests use bikes, fishing equipment, picnic baskets, or binoculars; or providing fare for a wine and cheese hour. Exceptions might include wash and fold service and babysitting services if you're able to or want to provide them.

If you're worried about lending out your property for fear of theft or damage, don't do it. Save your own sanity and offer services in other ways, such as arranging hikes or sitters for the kids.

Other Income

When you're calculating what to charge for non–room-rental sources of income—selling antiques, renting out space for weddings and small events, catering—find out what everyone else is doing. Your competition is the best indicator of how things sell.

Bill Notreal owns a small B&B but decided to start a catering business for evening functions. He undercut his rates based on one caterer he knew whose prices were somewhat high. After getting little business but rave reviews for his food, he decided to check out more of his competition and he discovered that they charged even less than he was charging for comparable fare. Now he was getting a reputation for good food but high prices. Although that's better than being known for bad food and high prices, some of Bill's potential customers will shop elsewhere. Offering something at a higher price will get you knocked out of the ring if someone else is able to undercut you.

As in charging for anything that you sell, factoring in costs and what you want for a profit is not enough. Make sure that you can get that price before you put your product out there. Realize that there is a minimum profit that you need to make to remain viable, and undercutting competitors is just not worth the effort, or the risk to your sanity.

Raising Prices

B&B owners have different formulas for increasing their rates every year. Some have no formula at all. Raising prices in small annual percentages, usually 5 to 8 percent, is one of the most popular methods. Others raise rates in dollar figures.

If you experience an 80 percent or higher occupancy during your high season, your property is on an upswing, and comments are favorable, it's time to raise your rates by 5 to 8 percent. If occupancy reaches 90 percent or more, your place probably is great and your rates might be too low. Try a 10 percent (or more) hike in rates. Conversely, if you feel that you're not doing enough business in shoulder or low season, your rates need to be trimmed a bit. Don't be too hasty in dropping your rate from $75 to $50. It might attract a few more guests but you'll need to sell 50 percent more rooms to achieve the same gross, and you'll have greater expenses for food, fuel, water, and other bills. Strategizing your rates so that you can get the maximum amount is known as "managing inventory." For more on this, see Chapter 23, "Stay in Business!"

When you're thinking about changing your rates, do some of the same kind of research you did when you first set them. Check out your competition. Reexamine each season and even each week and weekend of the preceding year and determine whether tourists would pay more during your busiest season. Take a good look around your property and the rooms. Have you added more amenities such as a coffee maker in every room? Do you provide more guest services now? Most additions to a business are minor and are done gradually, but when you add them together they can make your rooms worth a lot more. If you've renovated or added more amenities, always raise rates. After all, that's why you upgraded!

Some B&B owners won't raise prices unless they're living on tuna noodle casserole for fear of low occupancy rates. If you raise room rates and lose only a few customers, your income will level out, but it won't drop. Keeping rates super-crazy-bargain-low will make guests think twice about staying with you. They'll wonder, "Why is that

Shoestring Solution

When printing your first brochure, fight the urge to list your room rates. Instead, print separate sheets on a computer to slide into your brochure. The following year when you have more spending cash, have your rate sheet done by a printer. If you have a Web site, changing your rates is as easy as turning a doorknob, and doesn't cost a thing.

Inn the Know

If you've recently renovated your interior, added an outdoor patio, or are including a fancier breakfast, here's your opportunity to make back what you put into your business—or at least try to! Raise those rates more than your usual increment to match your improvements.

place so cheap?" and then they'll go somewhere else because they don't want to find out. Conversely, if your rates are low, you might get volumes of guests. Don't forget that this high traffic takes a toll on your inn. You'll make as much money as if your rates were higher but your expenses will be higher, too, because of occupancy wear and tear.

Most inn-keepers implement their new rates during slower periods when they've had time to reflect on the preceding seasons. Count your loot, if any, and then prepare to adjust your Web site and rate card.

However you decide to handle your rates, always make sure that they match what you have to offer. Raising rates too little will cut into future profit. If you implement too high a yearly increase, you might deter previous guests from revisiting; or if they do return, they might expect much more. Once you're established, you may not need to worry about losing some customers if you increase rates, as long as you have others who'll be happy to replace them.

Changing Your Mind

You'll probably alter your rates soon after you first set them and maybe even a few times after that. Don't fret about it too much. As long as you're not undercutting your room's worth or charging rates that are higher than your clientele will pay, eventually you'll find the perfect rates for each room and season.

Setting your rates doesn't mean you need to set them in stone. Flexibility is key in how you apply them. If you experience a slow time during your mid-season calendar, drop to your low rate. Determine in advance what your fallback position will be. When you have those rates in place you'll be able to say to a potential guest, "These rates won't be in place for another two to three weeks but I'd like you to stay with us so let me offer them to you now."

Use your upgrades to their fullest potential. If the nightly rate for room 1 is $95 but room 6 is available and has the same amenities but also an ocean view at $115, sell room 6 for $95. Upgrading within categories won't cost you anything. They're still paying for the same things but you're getting more because you've filled the room. But use this strategy only during low times. When there's a high demand you'll be losing out on that more valuable ocean view room. For more on strategies and controlling your inventory, see Chapter 23.

Having flexibility in your rates can only help you sell rooms. As long as your rates are at a high enough level

Shoestring Solution

If you have a minimum stay policy and your rooms are not filling up fast, book your lower-priced rooms for fewer nights. You can always drop the minimum stay of your most sought-after rooms later on.

to discount at times, you won't lose out. Don't feel as if you're being wishy-washy. After all you're the boss—you answer only to yourself when you change your mind!

Inn the Know

Don't be afraid to charge special rates for special people. If you have clientele coming back more than a couple of times, give them a break in your rate. Better still, use your upgrades. In high season, it's the same thing as giving a discount; in the low season, you're garnering more money. Try offering a good old "pay two, stay three" deal. If guests want to book for only two nights, offer an additional night free (during low season). They might not take you up on it if their plans are set but they'll know that you're going out of your way for them; making a unique offer to a returning guest will not only please them in the pocket, they'll feel special. You like them, you *really, really* like them!

At the beginning of your second year in business, look back at the first year before you recalculate rates. Check the previous year's calendar for a record of special events and weather conditions that may have affected occupancy. If there were two months out of the year when you were filled for only seven room nights, consider closing down for those months especially if you're paying staff to sit around. Before you do, though, talk to other local inn-keepers and make sure that they had the same low turnout. If they didn't, it might just be that you're doing something wrong! Make sure your rates are comparable and your house is up to snuff. If it's a case of "hidden-inn syndrome," kick that marketing plan up a notch.

Implementing the example of the C.L.A.S.S. system of competition, location, amenities, service, and season can serve as a handy reference in your freshman year. After you've been in the business for years, you'll likely have a well-established clientele and excellent word of mouth to use as a guideline for setting rates. Always remember that certain intangibles such as the charm of your house and your winning way should never be underestimated!

The Least You Need to Know

➤ When pricing out your room rates, consider the factors of included breakfast, your competition, location, season, amenities, and services.

➤ Charging for extras such as bike use or serving tea is a big "no" at B&Bs.

➤ Raising rates can be done annually or whenever improvements have been made to the house or rooms.

➤ By being flexible when quoting rates you'll be able to fill more rooms.

The Business Plan

If you were taking a road trip through Tanzania for the first time, what's the first thing you would do (after you were immunized for every killer-mosquito virus)? You'd get a map. Starting your business is like going to Tanzania (well, a little). You have an idea of what it's like but you don't really know because you haven't been there. Having a roadmap—your business plan—will get you going in the right direction and guide you through this new and unfamiliar territory: owning a bed and breakfast.

Yes, You Really Need One!

You might have notes in your head about finances or marketing strategies. You probably even know just how much you'll need to spend for startup and renovations. Putting these thoughts and figures on paper will help you see them as attainable goals.

If you're new to the B&B business (or relatively new), having a business plan is particularly important. It might be difficult to determine where your money needs to be spent or just how viable a B&B really is in your location. The business plan is a tool to use at startup and also a working document that you'll refer to as the business grows. As you proceed through your first year, you'll find it valuable to revisit the estimates and timelines in your initial plan. You won't find that they were all dead-on accurate, but they'll be the best guidelines you have to make projections for future growth.

B&B-eware!

Keep track of who sees your business plan. It will contain personal records and information that's not for all eyes to see. Make a list on your original draft of people who will receive copies.

Who Sees Your Business Plan?

Your business plan will serve as your roadmap, but that's not all it can do for you. Banks or other financial lenders will require some kind of written plan before they write you a check. They want to know that your dream will generate enough dough to pay them back. You'll want to show the plan to your attorney and your accountant to make sure everything in it is kosher, and maybe get your accountant's help in working up the numbers. You could show the plan to your insurance agent as well, to prove that the business has been thoroughly researched and is a good risk.

Buying an Established Business

When you buy a business that's already up and running it's still a good idea to have a business plan. The focus here will be on showing that the business is successful and that it will continue to grow under your management. Make sure you get hold of financial records from the previous owner: tax statements for every year in business (or at least the last three); room rental records, including any changes in rates; and occupancy figures—and make sure all the numbers make sense.

Coffee Talk

Claude and Mariette Gagne, publishers of *The B&B and Country Inn Marketplace Resource Guide*, make these suggestions: "When purchasing an inn, be sure to obtain all client records and the computer programs used for these records. Obtain ownership of telephone numbers, artwork, brochures, on- and off-property signage, the transfer of all transferable permits, agreement to not compete (against you) within 100 miles, copies and reimbursements of all gift certificates, and advance deposits. Also secure an agreement that the inn will continue accepting reservations until the date of the property transfer."

When you develop your financial and marketing plans, base them on the past accomplishments of the previous owners and how you'll generate even more growth. You'll also need to prove that tourism in the area is still strong and that the B&B is a staple in the local tourism business (or could be). Be sure to obtain a record of where your establishment is listed in print and on the Web, and get a copy of a guest mailing list if one exists.

Basic Components

Every book you read on starting your own B&B will suggest a different setup for the business plan. Yes, we're encouraging you to read other books (well, read ours first and then move on to those other books). Your business plan will differ completely from the B&Bs down the street and one in Tanzania. Review a bunch of different types of plans and then tailor the ideas to fit your situation. Our example includes basic business plan elements that you can adapt to fit your needs.

Opening Lines

For any proposal, you'll need a cover page with the business name, your name, and the date. Include a table of contents for the sections, along with page numbers.

Main Objective

After the cover page, the content of this next section is up to you. You need some kind of introduction to prepare the reader for what's to come. It typically takes the form of a summary, but we suggest that you use this space to state your goals and reasons for starting a B&B. Summaries work fine, too, but why not go for the gusto? Make a personal connection with people right up front by telling them how you arrived at this point in your life and why starting a B&B is the greatest idea you ever had. Okay, that's a little over the top, but you get the idea.

Inn the Know

Don't get fancy in a business plan. Use white paper, black type, and a readable font. If you're not computer literate, here's your chance. You won't really want someone else to write this up for you (unless it's a partner or other trusted individual); plus you'll need to learn how to work that computer for the business anyway.

Consider writing this portion last. After you've detailed all the facets of the business, writing out your goals and objectives will be easier. Keep the objectives short—less than a page—or people will just skim it.

Detailed Description

Here's your chance to get to know every little aspect of your business. Writing out a detailed description of your B&B (keep it to one page) is a good mind exercise. You'll have to repeat your spiel vocally as you build a support system and look for assistance; detailing your business on paper is good preparation.

When you describe the business, list everything. Include location; house specifics (number of rooms, style, age, renovations made and to be made); type of B&B (just breakfast provided, other meals); structure of business (sole proprietorship, partnership, corporation); and amenities and services provided.

Business Management

Who will run the place? Take one to two pages to write out specifics on what you'll do at the B&B, what your partner will do (if there is one), or if you'll hire an innkeeper. Be sure to give your rationale for the division of labor; for example, if you have an accounting background, it makes sense for you to do the office work. Attach your resumé and those of others who will be involved in managing the B&B (if they list relevant experience). Also mention plans to take inn-keeping seminars or classes, giving specifics on which ones and when.

On a separate page, list the names and credentials of those who will be your support team: attorney, architect, general contractor, interior decorator, consultant, and insurance agent. Include any affiliations you have with B&B organizations, reservation services, and of course, the Chamber of Commerce.

Market Research

Compile all of your efforts to research the market you're trying to reach and present them here; page length is up to you. You'll need to include specifics on clientele, attractions in town that will pull people your way, what guests will look for in accommodations (include your charming personality), and the particulars on your competition. See Chapter 10, "Marketing 101," for more on gathering market research.

Integrate basic statistics on the B&B industry with your own research. Get any local tourism records (call your local Chamber of Commerce) and any national statistics that demonstrate growth in the industry. If you join the Professional Association of International Innkeepers (PAII), you'll have access to their extensive research. Also check out your state associations.

Marketing Plan

Marketing plans will grow as your business grows, and vice versa. Listing strategies in calendar form will motivate you from month to month. Write down your ideas as they come to you—from gala opening to designing the Web site—and then slot each project into the month you'll begin to work on it. Marketing projects rarely end; they're usually built on previous ones. If a project doesn't yield very good results, replace it with something that will.

Having a detailed plan for marketing and promotion of roughly three to four pages (no more) will show you and those whose help you need that you're serious and dedicated to growing the business and you know how to get it done. See Chapter 10, which covers marketing plans in detail.

Financial Projections

Most people will turn to this section first. The rest of your proposal is important and will be perused by lenders but your financial plan is key. There are four basic components to the financial section: how much start-up cash you need, where you'll get start-up cash, how you plan to generate revenue, and what your estimated operating expenses will be. That's right, it's chart time.

Business Timeline

Here's your chance to prove that you've thought through your plan. In the timeline, cover how long it will take the B&B to get off the ground, at what rate the business will progress, and where you see yourself in two years. (If your answer to that is "on a beach in Maui drinking out of a coconut," don't put that in.) Do put in how you plan to expand the business such as by adding more amenities or more guest rooms or renting out space for events.

Make sure that you have real growth expectations. Shooting for a 90 percent occupancy rate in the first year will be unrealistic (unless you're buying a turnkey operation, and even then it's better to shoot low).

Inn the Know

A lot of investors are buying properties, renovating them, and turning them around for a big profit. They then take that profit and buy the B&B of their dreams, or they do another "flip." Don't tell a bank that you're going to flip a property unless you have an established track record as a proprietor.

Financial Projections: Uncut

To illustrate what goes into the financial section of the business plan, we've created a test case. His name is Dominick Invented. Dominick is buying a five-room B&B, an 1875 Federal-style home, from a couple who are retiring from the business. The house has three standard but very nice rooms and two suites that have private baths. The couple never developed the house to its greatest potential, so Dominick plans on doing most of his renovations to the rooms, where he'll add two private baths, join a common-use bath to one room, and update bathroom fixtures in the two suites.

Coffee Talk

"When purchasing our B&B we were determined to not put all of our money into the closing and down payment," recalls Ken Burnet, co-owner of the Gaige House Inn in Glen Ellen, California. "We did not want to own the inn unless we could add more rooms and redo it. It is very important to keep money away from the down payment for two reasons: You will want to renovate and you will need resources to carry the inn until it reaches the revenue to carry itself. Don't give in to the bankers! You will never have as much leverage to arrange the necessary financing as you will at purchase time."

Dominick's financial situation is a typical one. He needs to determine what kind of mortgage he can cover based on estimated expenses and income and his initial start-up costs. For the rest of this section, you'll step inside Dominick's world to see how he forecasted his financial future. Examples are always a good way to see how things are done. Just be sure to tailor these strategies to fit your particular needs.

Before you can determine how much money you need for startup or a mortgage, take personal inventory. Sit down and write out all of your assets and every source of financial capital you have access to. You can have your accountant work the initial numbers for you but we don't suggest it. If you don't do it yourself, you won't know the numbers cold; you want to be able to spout them when necessary. If you discover that your financial circumstance is less than attractive (like having all your money in one place), try to move funds around, or stabilize your finances as much as possible in other ways before you apply for a loan. Check with a financial advisor to know how your situation will appear to banks.

Determining Start-Up Costs

Not sure how much money you'll need for new construction and all those mattresses and bathroom fixtures? We've put Dominick's estimated costs in the following list, but be sure to use this only as a guide for expenses you might have. Call your interior designer and supply companies (if doing this on your own) to research your real costs. If you're like Dominick, you'll mix furniture you have with new pieces. If you're starting from scratch with furniture, the costs will be much higher than Dominick's. And don't forget to add a little more to the estimates from your architect and contractor. Be realistic about what things cost. Don't think you can live on ramen noodles to save a couple of hundred dollars.

To determine his start-up costs Dominick gets estimates on renovations from his general contractor, calculates costs for new furnishings, and estimates the expenses he'll need to cover during renovations.

Estimated Start-Up Costs

Major Renovation Costs

General contractor	$110,000*
Plumbing and heating	$9,000
Electrical work	$8,000
Architect	$8,000
Landscaping	$5,000
Interior design consultant	$2,500
Bribe to town official. (We kid! Just a little B&B humor.)	

Furnishings

Three rooms at $5,000 each	$15,000**
Two suites at $7,000 each	$14,000**
Kitchen	$11,000
Breakfast nook	$5,500
Hallways/other common areas	$6,000
Private living quarters	$4,000***
Common living room	$3,500
Outdoor furniture	$2,000

Office Materials

Computer	$3,000
Reservation software	$1,000
Business letterhead, envelopes, and cards	$1,500
Printer paper, files, booking calendar, etc.	$500

Marketing Startup

Web site	$4,000
Opening gala	$2,500
Brochures	$2,500

continues

continued

Estimated Start-Up Costs	
Other Start-Up Costs	
Working capital	$50,000****
Moving costs	$1,000
Licenses and permits	$500
Utility deposits	$400
Total $281,400	

*This cost includes demolition, building materials, labor, and any subcontractors, but Dominick plans on doing some of this work himself. A general contractor's fees include profit and overhead.

**All rooms will have private baths installed or renovated.

***To keep costs down, Dominick will do minimal renovations and redecorating to his private quarters but some things will need to be done by contractors to section them off from guests and make his living space more like home.

****This includes dough to cover living expenses, consulting or professional fees, and backup cash in case revenues don't kick in as hoped when renovations are finished.

The Income Operating Statement

Before Dominick heads to the bank to ask for a mortgage, he determines exactly what kind of mortgage he needs based on his estimated income and expenses. Detailing his income operating statement (also called a "Proforma" by some) will help give him an overall picture of his incoming and outgoing cash flow and how much he can spend on a mortgage payment every month.

In his income operating statement, Dominick estimated his potential earnings for each room and during each season (more later in the chapter on how to determine these calculations). He then listed his expenses for the year: everything from the "small stuff" such as office supplies, to the bigger ticket items such as staff paychecks. Notice that start-up expenses are not included here. This form determines what your cash flow will be like throughout the year so that you can estimate how much of a mortgage payment you can cover.

Income Operating Statement	
Location: 312 Village Hill	**Zoning:** Mixed-Use
Type of property: 5-room B&B	**Age of property:** 1875
Price: $285,000.00	**Construction:** Wood frame

Income Operating Statement

Lot size: 37,500 sq. ft.
Sq. ft. of building: 5,500

No. of guest rooms: 5
No. of common areas: 3

Value Per Room and Season

Room 1: $75, $105, $140
Room 2: $75, $105, $140
Room 3: $75, $105, $140

Suite 4: $115, $145, $185
Suite 5: $115, $145, $185

Estimated Income Per Season

(Formula: Available Room Nights × Potential Room Rents × Estimated Occupancy = Estimated Income for That Season)

High season: 100 nights × $790 × 75% = $59,250
Mid season: 84 nights × $605 × 50% = $25,410
Low season: 181 nights × $455 × 20% = $16,471
Total estimated gross income: $101,131

Estimated Annual Expenses	Comments
Food (cont. breakfast): $3,120	
Nonfood: $1,300	
Towels/linens/bedding: $3,000	
Property taxes: $3,500	
Liability insurance: $3,200	
Worker's comp: $1,800	
Auto insurance: $1,500	
Electric: $4,000	
Water: $500	
Oil (heat): $2,500	
Propane (stove/fp/water): $1,400	
Cable: $1,000	
Phone: $2,500	
Half-time assistant: $15,000	
Seasonal employee: $6,000	
Legal: $1,000	
Accounting: $600	
Seminars and assoc. exp.: $1,300	
Marketing/adv. costs: $3,500	

continues

continued

Estimated Annual Expenses	Comments
Adult ed. classes: $900	
Travel to seminars: $1,200	
Office supplies: $500	
Business meals: $750	
Landscaping: $1,400	
House maintenance/repair: $5,000	
Auto maintenance/repair: $1,000	
Gas for car: $500	
Payroll company: $780	
Trash pick-up: $1,000	
Snow removal: $500	
Chimney sweep: $150	
Misc.: $1,200	
Total gross expenses: <u>$71,600</u>	

Determining Feasible Mortgage (Per Month)

(Gross Income – Gross Expenses = Yearly Net Revenue)

$101,131 – $71,600 = **$29,531 (Yearly Net Revenue)**

(Highest Possible Monthly Mortgage Payment = Net Revenue ÷ 12)

$29,531 ÷ 12 = **$2,460.92 (Highest Possible Monthly Mortgage Payment)**

Proposed Financing

Mortgage required: $285,000	**Down payment:** $15,000
Mortgage: $270,000	**Rate of:** 10%
No. years: 25	**Mo. payment: $2,453.49***

(Monthly Payment × 12 = Yearly Gross Mortgage Debt)

$2,453.49 × 12 = **$29,441.88 (Yearly Gross Mortgage Debt)**

Yearly Gain or Loss

(Gross Income – Gross Expenses = Gain or Loss; Gain or Loss – Mortgage Debt = Yearly Gain or Loss)

$101,131 – $71,600 = $29,531; $29,531 – $29,441.88 = **$89.12 (Yearly Gain)**

Financial Summary

Yearly Gross Income $101,131 – Yearly Gross Expense $71,600 = Yearly Net Revenue $29,531. Yearly Net Revenue $29,531 ÷ 12 months = $2,460.92 per month. This is the maximum you can allow toward mortgage debt without putting finances in the red. A mortgage of $285,000, with $15,000 down, at 10 percent interest for 25 years = monthly mortgage payments of $2,453.49. In conclusion, receiving monthly net revenue of $2,460.92 per month will cover a mortgage payment of $2,453.49.

Check out the following figure to see how the mortgage payments (principal and interest) were calculated for this statement.

Figuring out Dominick's monthly and yearly mortgage payments could not be done without the guide of an amortized mortgage table (some banks will use their own). In our example, the monthly payments were calculated based on *Webster's 21st Century Personal Finance Amortization Guide* (Thomas Nelson Publishers, 1992).

Inn the Know

If you'll be doing some major work on your house, consider getting a construction loan. In this type of loan, the bank will release your money as levels of work are completed. For example, if you take out a loan for $50,000, they might release only $10,000 of that up front, depending on the scope of the work that needs to be done right away. This is different from a credit line, which is a set amount of funds (usually $50,000 or less) that you tap into whenever you need it (just like a credit card).

Here's an example of a mortgage table.

			MONTHLY PAYMENT			10%
			Needed to repay a loan			
TERM	15	20	25	30	35	40
AMOUNT	YEARS	YEARS	YEARS	YEARS	YEARS	YEARS
500	5.37	4.83	4.54	4.39	4.30	4.25
1000	10.75	9.65	9.09	8.78	8.60	8.49
2000	21.49	19.30	18.17	17.55	17.19	16.98
3000	32.24	28.95	27.26	26.33	25.79	25.47
4000	42.98	38.60	36.35	35.10	34.39	33.97
5000	53.73	48.25	45.44	43.88	42.98	42.46
6000	64.48	57.90	54.52	52.65	51.58	50.95
7000	75.22	67.55	63.61	61.43	60.18	59.44
8000	85.97	77.20	72.70	70.21	68.77	67.93
9000	96.71	86.85	81.78	78.98	77.37	76.42
10000	107.46	96.50	90.87	87.76	85.97	84.91
11000	118.21	106.15	99.96	96.53	94.56	93.41
12000	128.95	115.80	109.04	105.31	103.16	101.90
13000	139.70	125.45	118.13	114.08	111.76	110.39
14000	150.44	135.10	127.22	122.86	120.35	118.88
15000	161.19	144.75	136.31	131.64	128.95	127.37
16000	171.94	154.40	145.39	140.41	137.55	135.86
17000	182.68	164.05	154.48	149.19	146.14	144.35
18000	193.43	173.70	163.57	157.96	154.74	152.85
19000	204.17	183.35	172.65	166.74	163.34	161.34
20000	214.92	193.00	181.74	175.51	171.93	169.83
21000	225.67	202.65	190.83	184.29	180.53	178.32
22000	236.41	212.30	199.91	193.07	189.13	186.81
23000	247.16	221.95	209.00	201.84	197.72	195.30
24000	257.91	231.61	218.09	210.62	206.32	203.80
25000	268.65	241.26	227.18	219.39	214.92	212.29
30000	322.38	289.51	272.61	263.27	257.90	254.74
35000	376.11	337.76	318.05	307.15	300.89	297.20
40000	429.84	386.01	363.48	351.03	343.87	339.66
45000	483.57	434.26	408.92	394.91	386.85	382.12
50000	537.30	482.51	454.35	438.79	429.84	424.57
55000	591.03	530.76	499.79	482.66	472.82	467.03
60000	644.76	579.01	545.22	526.54	515.80	509.49
65000	698.49	627.26	590.66	570.42	558.79	551.94
70000	752.22	675.52	636.09	614.30	601.77	594.40
75000	805.95	723.77	681.53	658.18	644.75	636.86
80000	859.68	772.02	726.96	702.06	687.74	679.32
85000	913.41	820.27	772.40	745.94	730.72	721.77
90000	967.14	868.52	817.83	789.81	773.71	764.23
95000	1020.87	916.77	863.27	833.69	816.69	806.69
100000	1074.61	965.02	908.70	877.57	859.67	849.15
200000	2149.21	1930.04	1817.40	1755.14	1719.34	1698.29
300000	3223.82	2895.06	2726.10	2632.71	2579.02	2547.44
400000	4298.42	3860.09	3634.80	3510.29	3438.69	3396.58
500000	5373.03	4825.11	4543.50	4387.86	4298.36	4245.73

Estimating Income

On Dominick's income operating statement, he first estimated how much income each room would generate based on the room and season in the "Value Per Room and Season" column. He then calculated the "Estimated Income Per Season" to determine potential earnings for his high, mid, and low seasons. Since it may seem confusing to decipher from the income operating statement, we've broken down how Dominick estimated his potential earnings.

Estimating future income. When determining income, the lodging industry bases its projections on revenue generated per room and per room night. If your rooms are rented every night of the year, you would have a 100 percent occupancy rate. To estimate revenue generated from room bookings, you need to determine both occupancy rates and room rates. To calculate what you'll charge for your rooms, see Chapter 7, "All About Room Rates." Keep reading to find out how to calculate occupancy rates and, eventually, gross revenue.

➤ **Step 1: Determining rentable nights.** To determine how many rooms he "thinks" he can rent, Dominick needs to total the number of nights he'll be open during the year. For instance, Dominick's B&B is in a New England tourist town where there are low, mid, and high seasons. Based on the competition and his location, he can calculate room nights rented in the following way:

Dominick has decided to close the B&B Mondays through Thursdays in December, January, February, and March. The total number of nights available for these months is 52. Dominick will stay open every night from April to November with the exception of a one-week vacation in Bora Bora in April. (Fictional guys take the most exotic trips!). Dominick's total number of nights for these eight months is 244, minus one week, which makes 237. His total number of nights open for the year is 237 + 52, which equals 289.

Now, Dominick multiplies the available nights (289) by the number of units (5) to get 1,445; this is the total number of potentially, rentable nights for the year.

Note that Dominick had a potential of 1,825 rentable nights (365 days × 5 units) but due to lack of demand for mid-week in low season, he decides to close for 76 nights, or approximately 20 percent of the aggregate.

➤ **Step 2: Figure out your potential earnings.** Now Dominick is ready to project annual income. Having determined his room rates, he utilizes them as follows (all rates are per night):

Rooms 1–3 during low season	$75
Suites 4 and 5 during low season	$115
Rooms 1–3 during mid season	$105
Suites 4 and 5 during mid season	$145
Rooms 1–3 during high season	$140
Suites 4 and 5 during high season	$185

Now that Dominick knows what he'll charge per room, he needs to determine what he can get during each season. But what will constitute his high, mid, and low seasons? Dominick has estimated that he can achieve a 75 percent occupancy for high season; 50 percent for mid season; and 20 percent for low season. Here's how he figures out potential income from each of those seasons and what those seasons are …

101

Formula: Number of nights in season category × total dollar amount of all rooms × occupancy percentage = potential gross income.

High season: June 15 to September 22 inclusive (every night) = 100 nights; 100 × $790 × 75 percent = $59,250.

Mid season: May 1 to June 14 inclusive = 45 nights and September 23 to October 31 = 39 nights; 84 nights × $605 × 50 percent = $25,410.

Low season: Rest of nights = 181; 181 × $455 × 20 percent = $16,471.

Total projected gross income = $101,131.

To calculate the occupancy percentage, Dominick takes the number of nights he could be open in each season (100, 84, and 181) and multiplies each by the percentage of rooms that he expects to have filled in those seasons (75, 50, and 20 percent) to get the number of room nights he anticipates being full (80, 42, and 36.2). He then adds up these numbers (158.2), divides by 365 (total possible number of days that he could receive income in a year, or every day of the year), and gets a total annual occupancy percentage of 43.3 percent.

Even though you won't open your B&B every day of the year, the annual occupancy rate must be based on 365 days. Unless you want to set yourself up for a huge disappointment, calculate your *true* occupancy rate for the year, too; that is, instead of basing the occupancy percentage on 365, use the number of days you'll actually be open (for Dominick, 289) to see how you're really doing.

After calculating potential income in his operating statement, Dominick then lists how much of his profit will be eaten up by expenses. You guessed it—close to all of it. Start-up businesses cannot expect to generate huge profits, if any profit at all for the first year, and up to two or more years after that. Don't get discouraged, though. Your goal should be to ground the business and prepare it for the profit making years to come.

A B&B will have all the expenses of running both a house and business. Water bills, cable bills, food costs, taxes, electricity, insurance, and just about a gatrillion other things. In your business plan, you'll need to account for these expenses before they happen. Better to estimate how high your gas bill will be for the winter months than to be caught short when it arrives!

Dominick has estimated that if he can make a total gross income of $101,131, his yearly net revenue will be around $29,531 after expenses. His yearly mortgage payments total $29,441.88, which leaves Dominick a grand total yearly gain of $89.12. Discouraged? Don't be. Most businesses are in the hole for the first few years; it's just the nature of the beast.

At the end of your first year, work up the final numbers with your accountant to see how well you were able to predict your income and expenses. Once again, estimating your expenses high but looking for ways to cut costs (such as walking to the store on a nice day instead of wasting gas) will really add to your yearly gain. If you do make some profit in the first year, plan on paying down some loans. Look for the real profit in the years to come as word of mouth generates higher occupancy levels that correlate to a higher valued property, should you decide to sell.

The Least You Need to Know

➤ You need to have a business plan to get the real scoop on your business and to convince others that it's a good idea.

➤ Your plan should include your credentials, market research, marketing plan, financial projections, and a business timeline.

➤ When projecting your financial future, always underestimate your projected income and overestimate your anticipated expenses.

Chapter 9

Setting Up Your Business and Financial Structure

In This Chapter

➤ Choosing a business structure that works for you

➤ Financing your startup

➤ Setting up business bank accounts

➤ Learning how to keep financial records

➤ Looking good to Uncle Sam

Finances schminances! That's what most of you will think about all the accounting you have to do, and that's what we think, too. On the flip side, you won't have a business if you don't learn how to keep records, file taxes, and gauge incoming and outgoing funds. So get a good printing calculator, your reading glasses, your favorite drink, and a comfy spot. And try to stay awake: This is mega-important stuff.

How Much Cash Will You Need?

Wouldn't it be great if we could give you a dollar figure so you'd know exactly how much cash to scrape up? Well, because we can't do that, it might be helpful to know that most B&B owners will tell you "as much as you can get." Vague enough for you?

The ideal amount to have at your disposal would be a lump sum equal to one and a half years of estimated gross income, including start-up costs. Stop laughing! It sounds

Shoestring Solution

When feasible, paying an extra monthly payment on a mortgage will shrink that 30-year headache significantly. Even just paying down the principal a little more every month will reduce your interest over the long run.

like a lot of dough, and it is. The key words here are *at your disposal*. Renovations might take longer; they'll inevitably cost more; and you'll need something more to take to the grocery store than coupons. You might have to dip into savings or that $25,000 credit line from the bank that you've been holding back on—or maybe not. At the very least, having reserve money will be a great stress reliever.

Do the best that you can to estimate start-up costs (as we did in Chapter 8, "The Business Plan") separately from operating costs. You'll need to review your first year in business when you move on to the second year. The first year is a test case for what to do and what not to do after that. Keeping your finances straight and keeping good daily records will help set up your business for the future.

Determining Your B2B (Business to Be)

Setting up a legal structure for your business is fundamental. It will determine how you file taxes, manage your business, and divvy up income. In the following sections we give you the essentials of each structure, but there's more to it. Check with your attorney about which option would be the best one for you.

Sole Proprietorship

If you're a single person or couple who plans to own, manage, and live at the B&B, you'll be considered the sole proprietor unless you structure your business otherwise. Most B&Bs are under sole proprietorship because it's the easiest and least expensive business structure. Get licensed and register your name. That's pretty much it.

Here are the good and not-so-good aspects of operating as a sole proprietor:

➤ **Good:** Complete control of management and operations. You can be flexible in making "corporate" decisions and are the only one (or ones) to answer to.

➤ **Not-so-good:** Complete control of management and operations. All the liability is on your shoulders. This includes putting your personal assets on the line because, although the business operates separately, it is still primarily an extension of you. You also can be found personally liable for anything that goes wrong on the property.

➤ **Good:** You don't have to share income with partners.

➤ **Not-so-good:** You're limited when it comes to digging for more capital.

➤ **Good:** Less expensive to set up, little interference from the feds, and you're relieved of extra taxation.

➤ **Not-so-good:** Business stability is low, and you could fold in the event of your illness, death, or major debt. You'll also have a more difficult time selling the business if you don't have a good accounting system that separates your business finances from your personal funds. It's difficult (sometimes nearly impossible) to determine profit and loss when business expenses are mixed with personal ones.

Saddling Up a Partner

Going into this business with one or more partners could provide you with a little more stability. Depending on what kind of partner you choose, though, you'll have to give up some degree of independence in running your B&B.

If you have an active partner, you'll be expected to consult the person in everyday management and bigger decisions about the business. Having a silent or limited partner means that you run the show and the partner gets returns on whatever he or she invested. You might even have an arrangement in between these basic definitions. Consider having a buyout agreement made up ahead of time in case one partner decides to leave. Either way, have an agreement drawn up that is examined by attorneys for each party. When you all agree on it (and that could take a while), sign the document and have it notarized. This makes it officially witnessed; therefore close to written in stone.

Some of the elements you might want to include in a partnership agreement are type of partners, division of management duties, interests of each partner if the business is sold, actions taken if one partner dies, arrangement of salaries, and divisions of profits and losses. There will be a lot more to add to a partnership agreement that your attorney will fill you in on.

Here are the goods and not-so-goods:

➤ **Good:** More capital availability than as a sole proprietor.

➤ **Not-so-good:** Financing more difficult to obtain than for a corporation.

➤ **Good:** More expertise at your disposal.

➤ **Not-so-good:** More experts telling you what to do.

➤ **Good:** Less government control and special taxation than a corporation.

➤ **Not-so-good:** More hands-on interference by the feds than a sole proprietorship.

Going Corporate

Setting up the business as a corporation is a lot of work and hassle. The main reason that businesses small or large go corporate is to have the lowest liability possible and the greatest accessibility to funds. Of course, there are other reasons.

As a corporation the business will operate as a legal entity, separate from you as a person and from individual shareholders. Within this structure there are additional options to choose from. You can have a "subchapter S" corporation in which the property is owned by you and then leased to the corporation. In this case the shareholders act more like partners because liability and profit and loss extend to what they invest. A Limited Liability Company, or LLC, is very attractive to investors because of differences in the allocation of profit and loss. In an LLC, shareholders' personal funds will be protected from liability. Because of this protection, investors can be more active in operations.

Here's the lowdown on corporations:

Inn the Know

Check out the Small Business Administration's Web site at www.sbaonline.sba.gov. It's a great resource for loan information, how to obtain financing from the SBA, and where to find federal and state regulations on small businesses. You can even take online classes, check out property that might be for sale, and find a local SBA office. (There's even one in Guam!)

➤ **Good:** Business is, legally, the most stable because it exists as a separate entity from all persons involved.

➤ **Not-so-good:** The feds have a hand in everything you do.

➤ **Good:** Getting hold of funds from investors and banks can be a breeze compared to sole proprietorship and partnership.

➤ **Not-so-good:** Expenses are much greater in a corporation.

➤ **Good:** Feds are less concerned with private affairs of on-premises manager.

➤ **Not-so-good:** There are higher taxes on the corporation and profits made from the corporation.

➤ **Good:** Control of the business is delegated to one manager (usually the owner).

➤ **Not-so-good:** If the manager doesn't participate in profit sharing, the financial rewards are less direct.

Getting Start-Up Capital

Before you head to the bank or other lending institution (or Uncle Carl) to get the business off the ground, make sure that you know what questions they'll ask. If someone is investing in you, they'll want to be assured that they can get that money back, and then some. Develop a business plan (see Chapter 8) and be ready to answer these questions:

➤ What collateral can you provide as backup in case you can't make payments from the business income?

➤ How much money are you personally investing in the business? (If you're not willing to shell out clams for your own business, why would anyone else?)

Inn the Know

To consider funding for a B&B that is in operation when purchased, lenders will require tax returns, profit and loss statements, and other proof that the business is legal and has shown some profit for the past few years (or at least has the potential for profit). You might have to go back three to five years in the previous owner's records. Before you buy an inn, make sure that the records exist and that you have easy access to them.

➤ Can I trust you? Are you someone who has shown in the past that you can make good on your end of the bargain?

➤ Are you a hopeless case? Do you appear frantic on paper, trying to gather funds from any possible source? (Cashing in things like IRAs will make you look desperate and will cost you in penalties.)

➤ How will the recent (and local) economy affect this deal?

➤ When will you be able to start making payments? What happens if you have a negative cash flow system and can't make promised payments?

B&B-eware!

If you do decide to borrow from Uncle Carl, Aunt Sela, or even Mom, make sure you put specifics down in writing about when you can start repaying the loan. Keep in mind that promising to pay back private loans in the first year could get you into trouble.

When you climb up the legs of those who can prospectively loan you funds, put yourself in their heads. They'll want to know why they should choose to invest in you and what they're going to get out of it. Present your ideas, your financial forecasts, and your strategies so that they have a hard time saying no.

Setting Up Money Accounts

When you have the money you need and income starts flowing in, you'll need places to put it. Keep business checking and savings accounts separate from your personal ones. This is not an option: Having everything lumped under one account will make your life more difficult in every way, from filing taxes to determining how much you spend on the business.

There will be occasions when you buy business and personal items at the same time. Be consistent with your receipts; if you buy groceries for yourself and for the B&B, make notes on the receipt and tally up the amount that is applied to the business. Make a copy of the receipt for your personal finances and file the original with your business records.

Try to keep separate credit cards for business and personal use. If this isn't possible, review your monthly statements carefully. Make copies of statements, write notes about purchases made for the business, and file this copy with your expenses. If you use a business check to pay a credit card bill that includes some personal purchases, make sure you transfer money from your personal checking to the business account. Always pay the business back when you've covered personal expenses with business funds! Not doing so will mess up your accounting structure and how you look to the IRS.

Consider getting a ledger-style checkbook. You can make notes on the side about exactly where your money is going and it's easy to flip back and see your records.

Shoestring Solution

When you have a chunk of business funds to spare, think about a money market account. Its funds are liquid (meaning accessible), unlike IRA funds, which you can't access until retirement age without severe penalties. Some money markets require a minimum balance of $1,000 or $2,500. If you don't have the minimum to spare just yet, open a passbook savings account with what you do have. Once it reaches the level you need for a money market, transfer the funds. Putting this money away in little increments when you can and working up to an account with a higher interest rate will keep you motivated.

Online banking is fast becoming the wave of the future. You can check balances, transfer funds, and even schedule bills to be paid monthly right out of your account. This sounds like an easy option but do this only if you're completely on top of your finances. You might want to allocate only one bill to be paid directly online (one that you know you can pay on time). Whatever kind of banking you do on the Internet, make sure you keep written records. If you transfer funds, print out the confirmation for your files and, of course, write down any transaction in your check register.

Keeping Solid Records

Having an accountant help you out on a part-time or even full-time basis is a great option. Remember, though, that an accountant can only help you organize your finances. If you don't keep consistent records on your expenditures and income, an accountant can't help you. Set yourself up with a good system, either on the computer (recommended) or by hand, that will easily show the true state of your finances. Keeping your personal and business expenditures separate also will help at tax time and year-end review when you want to figure out exactly how much you spent and earned on the B&B.

Shoe Boxes Are for Shoes

If you set up a system for tracking money that comes in and goes out of your business, you'll be able to keep on top of it every day. Buy file folders for receipts (or keep them in large envelopes and then file); keep track of expenses by developing a chart of accounts (more on this to come); and follow your income closely by recording profits every month. Everyone will have his or her own system for accounting. You need to find what will work best for you and your accountant. A good basic guide to how to set up accounts is *The Complete Idiot's Guide to Finance and Accounting,* by Michael Muckian and Steve Pullara (Alpha Books, 1997).

Find a system that you'll follow such as using an accordion file that can be placed in plain view for receipts and notes. Make it a point to file receipts either as soon as you get them, at the end of the day, or the end of the week. Don't forget to make notes of items purchased online, or make copies of credit card bills when they arrive. If you really like the shoebox system, use it. You just might have to buy a lot of shoes!

Inn the Know

Charting and reviewing your expenditures on a routine basis (or somewhat routine basis) will help you keep costs down. It might not seem like you're doing much when you file those receipts but when you look over the totals you'll think, "Did I really need that?" or "Wow! That's expensive."

Inn the Know

Know how your money moves around. Investments and funds can be broken down into assets and liabilities; income and expenses. Mortgage payments are not listed as an expense in the chart of accounts because borrowed money is a liability, not an expense. When someone gives you money, it's not income, so paying it back cannot be recognized as an expense.

Choosing a system that is easiest for you to work with and stay on top of your finances is essential. One must-have item is a logbook, even if you track revenue and expenses on your computer. Having a place to make everyday notes on payments received from guests and trips to the grocery store is invaluable. Get into the habit of writing in the logbook at the end of the day, during a lunch break, or when you receive payment or buy something. If you get into a ritual things won't slip and your accountant will love you.

Charting Accounts

One of the best ways to keep track of how you spend your money is to break up each expense into subcategories. The same can be done with revenue, especially if you earn money in other ways additional to room rentals. Usually called a "chart of accounts," this system enables you to assign a number to each type of expense and income. You then can use these numbers in several different places such as in your check ledger and on reports.

Chart of Accounts

101	Food/beverages
102	Linens/towels/bedding
103	Nonfood supplies
104	Utilities
105	Phone
106	Postage
107	Office supplies
108	Legal fees
109	Accounting fees
110	Bank fees
111	Vehicle (leasing/maintenance/repair/fuel)
112	Business fees/taxes
113	Insurance
114	Advertising/promotion
115	Dues/subscriptions
117	External services
118	Travel and entertainment

Chart of Accounts

119	RSA fees
120	Miscellaneous
201	Room revenue
202	Renting out space for events
203	Consulting
204	Sales from crabapple jam (Grandma Ethel's famous recipe)

Notice that we started numbering expenses at 101 and income at 201. When you use these numbers on different forms and charts, that will make it clear that "108" next to something means "legal fees." If you jotted down "8" somewhere, you might later wonder, "8 what?" If you have new expenses or revenue to slot in, always put them at the end of your lists. We added a miscellaneous section for things that don't belong in any other category, but it's better to know exactly where your money is really going, so try to create specific categories to cover everything. Once you have your accounts neatly tucked into their own categories, creating income and expense reports will be a cinch.

Detailing Expenses

Recording expenses usually is done on a monthly basis. This doesn't mean that you should wait until the end of the month to log in everyday payments. As we mentioned earlier in the chapter, keeping track of expenses every day will only make your life easier now and later. If you can't get to logging your expenses every day, do it at least once a week. If you decide to record expenses at the end of the week or month, make sure you write notations on receipts and keep everything together, such as copies of bills that you might otherwise file after you've paid them.

Monthly Expense Report for: August 2001 [sample]

Property: 312 Village Hill

Date	To	Method	101 Food/ Beverages	102 Linens, etc.	103 Nonfood Supplies	104 Utilities
8/1	Gil's Shop & Save	Bus. check	$85.86			
	Disc. Warehouse	Bus. check			$54.67	
8/4	Bob's Bedding (online)	Credit card		$234.56		
8/6	Farmers' Market	Cash	$22.30			

continues

continued

Date	To	Method	101 Food/ Beverages	102 Linens, etc.	103 Nonfood Supplies	104 Utilities
8/8	North Gas Co.	Bus. check				$27.90
8/10	Fifth Street Liquors	Credit card	$125.45			

To log in routine daily payments, pick up an expense log, sometimes known as a "cash disbursement" journal, at an office supply store. Or, use your computer to create expense reports. If you use a computer program such as Microsoft Excel be sure to print your expense reports as a backup.

Recording Income

Find out how much gross income really has floated in through the door by tallying the numbers every month. Create an income report similar to the expense report, especially if you're receiving revenue from sources other than your rooms.

Monthly Income Report for: August 2001 [sample]

Property: 312 Village Hill

201: Room revenue

202: Renting out space for events

203: Consulting

204: Sales from crabapple jam

Date	From	Method	201	202	203	204
8/1	B. Edwards	Credit card	$195			
	Lillibridge	Credit card	$210			
	Seven Sisters B&B	Per. check			$250	
8/2	B. Edwards	Credit card	$195			
	Lillibridge	Credit card	$210			
	Aitken	Credit card	$225			
	Spoon Hangers Monthly Meeting	Bus. check		$75		
8/3	B. Edwards	Credit card	$195			
	C. Edwards	Cash	$195			
	Lillibridge	Credit card	$210			
	Aitken	Credit card	$225			

Date	From	Method	201	202	203	204
8/4	B. Edwards	Credit card	$195			
	C. Edwards	Cash	$195			
	Lillibridge	Credit card	$210			
	Aitken	Credit card	$225			
	Sunnyside Gift Shop	Bus. check				$55
8/5	Le Ny	Credit card	$195			
	Ilchert	Trav. check	$210			
	Aitken	Credit card	$225 (f)			
8/6	Pickett	Trav. check	$155 (d)			
	Le Ny	Credit card	$195			
	Ilchert	Trav. check	$210			
	Smeelay	Credit card	$275			
8/7	Pickett	Trav. check	$155 (d)			
	Le Ny	Credit card	$195			
	Ilchert	Trav. check	$210			
	Smeelay	Credit card	$275			
8/8	Pickett	Trav. check	$155 (d)			
	Le Ny	Credit card	$195			
	Ilchert	Trav. check	$210			
	Smeelay	Credit card	$275			
8/9	Pickett	Trav. check	$155 (d)			
	Pagan	Per. check	$195			
	Ilchert	Trav. check	$210			
	Smeelay	Credit card	$275			
8/10	Pickett	Trav. check	$155 (d)			
	Pagan	Per. check	$195			
	Howard	Credit card	$260 (t)			
	Hassell	Credit card	$225			

Key: (d) = discount (promo or returning guest); (f) = family/friend discount; (t) = third-person charge

Money Payments

Years ago, B&Bs had two choices for receiving payments: cash or check. Now, it's a little more complicated but more options mean more flexibility for guests and inn-keepers. If you don't accept credit cards, at least VISA and MasterCard, you'll lose out on revenue. People want to pay with a credit card because it's easy, and most impulse buys happen with plastic.

Always get some kind of deposit for your rooms; either with a credit card or, if time allows, by check. When using a credit card guests are less likely to cancel, and if they do you can refund the difference between the payment they made and the cancellation fee. Guests will understand this better than a "guarantee" hold (usually done by hotels). For a guarantee, the establishment tells the guest that they'll hold a room until a certain day or time. If the guest does not cancel and does not come up with a different form of payment, the charge is put through on the guest's credit card. Credit cards are very convenient but there is also that risk of a chargeback resulting from a cardholder winning a dispute over charges. You should make every attempt to resolve any disputes with your customers before they go to mediation.

We all hate the idea of giving money back. While getting money from a credit card purchase is immediate, it's not as easy to hold onto if there's a dispute. Although you'll have to wait longer to receive and process a check, the proceeds are in your control in the event of a dispute. This is not so in the case of plastic, where your customers "hold the cards." For more on cancellations see Chapter 17, "One Day at a Time."

When you order digital safes for the rooms, don't forget to get one for your office. Some guests will pay with cash and you'll need a secure place to hold that dough until you can get to the bank. Use the safe for checks and the office petty cash, too.

Here are the methods of payment that you can accept and how to accept them:

B&B-eware!

Don't accept a check as payment of a guest's remaining balance unless you have a credit card number and signed receipt (form with blank amount) to back it up. We suggest that you take a check only if you know the guest. If a guest gives you a bad check and then leaves for good, it might be almost impossible to get that money back.

➤ **Cash.** Cash is great on arrival but it doesn't travel well as a deposit. If a guest really wants to pay with cash, ask for a credit card or check deposit on making the reservation, with the remaining balance to be paid with cash on arrival.

➤ **Check.** Accept checks when takin a reservation if the booking is made at least three to four weeks before guests arrive. If you don't receive payment within ten business days of the arrival date, call them and tell them that they need to make a deposit with a credit card or they'll lose the room. Checks are almost as good as cash, except that they bounce. You need a couple of weeks to get the check, deposit it, and then wait for it to clear. In this era of credit cards, guests who say they want to send a check for the deposit are very often those who want to tie up the room while they continue to check around.

➤ **Credit cards.** You'll be charged fees for every transaction but accepting credit cards is well worth the money. Guests can make last-minute reservations and, once you put the payment through, the money goes into your account the same day (or close to it, depending on your bank). American Express charges the most (around 3.5 percent) but it is widely used by guests so it's a good one to accept. VISA and MasterCard charges can fluctuate from bank to bank (around 2 percent). Try shopping around for the bank that charges the lowest overall fee. Remember that, as credit card charges are automated, you don't have to make a trip to the bank for deposits, and with most banks you can check balances online. That means that you can set up a separate account for credit cards at a bank that you might never have to visit. Theft is virtually eliminated when you take credit cards. Be sure to ask for the card on arrival and check the signature, lest that card has been stolen!

➤ **Traveler's checks.** These work like cash, only better. Be sure to stamp the back of traveler's checks with your endorsement stamp.

Shoestring Solution

Punching in credit card numbers will cost you more than ½ of 1 percent more than swiping a card (in addition to the overall credit card fees charged by your bank or credit card company). Swiping the card on a credit card processor helps prove that the cardholder was present, provided that the signature on the receipt matches the one on the card.

Always, always, always track payments on paper. Get a receipt book for cash, checks, and traveler's check payments, and give one copy to the client. For credit cards, you'll have either an electronic processor, which prints out two copies of the transaction (one for the customer to sign and one for you to keep); or the manual kind, with a top copy that you keep and a carbon for the customer. Staple credit card receipts directly to your copy of the original reservation form (see Chapter 17), and use your reservation form as a permanent record. If a guest pays a balance in cash, write out in the "balance due" line how much the guest paid, the date, and your initials (or those of the staffer who received it). Give the guest your third carbon copy after you've noted the payment.

If you receive income from sources other than room rents, put original payment receipts together either in file folders or envelopes and group them monthly or weekly so they are ready to be recorded in your income reports. Make sure you have a final resting place for receipts that have been recorded. That way, at tax time, you can just pull out your file folder, accordion file, or shoebox and head to your accountant's office.

Taxes and More Taxes

As a home-based business, you'll need to prove to the IRS that you're engaged in a professional operation, and not just a hobby. If your B&B is more of a hobby because you rent rooms out only on weekends or at certain times of the year and you do not have areas reserved for guests only, understand that you will not be able to deduct as much. Plus, the feds might take more notice of you because, on paper, it could look as if you're hiding something (like money that belongs to them).

Inn the Know

The IRS will make its own decision about whether you're out to make a profit in your business or are just pursuing a hobby. If you operate in a businesslike manner, consult a professional with expertise (hire a CPA as opposed to your friend Lefty) to do your accounting, to help you show that the business is a professional operation.

B&B-eware!

Failing to record income and skimming cash off the top are good ways to get in trouble in the near future (with the IRS) and later on (if you plan to sell the business). Why would anyone want to buy your inn if you can't show true profit and loss? Don't skim, and make sure you report your earnings just as any other business does.

Keep accurate records on income, expenditures, and occupancy rates. Put your staff on the books and report everything. The more activity you can show in your business, the easier it will be to "expense" business-related items. Here are some more ways to look like a professional operation to the IRS:

➤ **Appear to be living at the B&B to run the business.** Having distinct private quarters will show that the B&B is primarily used for receiving guests. If you can, build a small kitchen area in your private quarters so that you can write off all expenses related to food and kitchen equipment used to serve guests. To determine how to expense parts of the house that belong to the business, do this in percentages. Figure out the square footage of your entire area and then the area that is used exclusively and regularly for the business. "Exclusively" means that the area is, at no time, used for private affairs; and "regularly" means that guests actively use an area that they have constant access to.

➤ **Appear financially responsible.** Have separate checking accounts for personal and business funds, and keep expenses separate. Carefully record revenue, particularly cash received from guests, so that you can show exactly how much your income was. Skimming is for milk and pools! Put yourself on the books with a salary.

➤ **Appear professional.** Have professional letterhead and business cards. Have a separate phone line for personal use (and don't deduct this expense) and at least one line for business.

➤ **Appear to be advancing your business.** Report the expense of seminars and classes to show that you're really serious about the business.

➤ **Appear consistent on your tax forms.** Be consistent with what you file with the feds, the state, and your local government. These branches do communicate with each other, especially the federal and state operations.

If you have employees, you'll find that payroll is a lot more complicated than just writing out checks and deducting for taxes. Get a local CPA or a national or local payroll company to do the work for you. This will cost you an extra $500 to $700 per year but it's well worth it to avoid the headache.

When Buying an Established B&B

The best advantage to buying a turnkey property is that you know that it's successful, or at least it appears to be. If you visit a B&B during a time when the house is full, you'll probably assume that the business is doing well. Don't: The current owners could just be having a good night, or might be entertaining a few friends.

If you're looking to buy a turnkey B&B it's imperative to get hold of financial records, tax returns, and anything else that proves profit and loss. If you plan to sell a turnkey operation, make sure you can prove that occupancy rates increased over the years, due not only to inn-keeping prowess, but to increased tourism in the area.

Coffee Talk

You might recall Jane Bertorelli, co-owner of the Union Street Inn in San Francisco, California, from an earlier chapter. She's back with more important questions you should ask before buying a B&B in operation: "Is the inn in a location where there is a reason for guests to visit? Remote spots are all very well, but is there enough business to support a mortgage? Has it proved 'impossible' to operate and make any money? What is the occupancy? If the owner does not have audited accounts ... beware! Make sure you carefully analyze operating costs against income. If you're not familiar with the local market, look at other inns in the area, ask questions, and compare room prices and facilities."

The Least You Need to Know

➤ Choosing sole proprietorship as a business structure is the easiest to set up, whereas partnership and corporate structures provide more stability.

➤ Keep accurate and consistent records to determine real profit and loss and prove to buyers and to the IRS that the business is legit.

➤ Separating your personal and business finances will keep you from being audited and will allow you to expense more business-related items.

➤ Make sure that you see the past financial records and tax returns of current owners before buying a B&B in operation.

Part 3

Getting the Word Out

Your B&B is the focus of your life, but your fellow residents and your soon-to-be guests across the country (and perhaps the world) know nothing about your favorite project. Before word of mouth can kick in, you need to create and implement a marketing plan that will put you on the map, take you through your first year, and possibly become the foundation of your marketing action plan for years to come. Learn how to sniff out networking opportunities and cross-promotions to get that word out without spending big bucks.

Chapter 10

Marketing 101

> **In This Chapter**
>
> ➤ Developing a marketing plan that you can pull off
>
> ➤ Working on local and global levels to promote your B&B
>
> ➤ Brainstorming cheap marketing tricks

When we first outlined the book, we had an entire chapter devoted to advertising. We soon realized that it didn't make sense. B&Bs do advertise, but mostly in magazines and newspapers, and usually only at the startup of a business. You won't be hiring an advertising firm to create a nifty national or even local television ad (unless you're a full-service inn with some extra cash flow). We do cover advertising in this chapter but only as a small part of the overall marketing plan. As Park has learned over the years and other B&B owners have told us, the best money you can spend is on your Web site and your brochure.

Attracting guests will be your first challenge as a new owner. Making a good impression on those guests so they'll spread the word is an even bigger challenge, but it comes later.

Before You Write That Brochure

You'll probably be tempted to write a brochure right away. Having one to hand out to people is a good thing, but don't make it your first project, especially if you don't have good photos yet or you think some vital information might change (such as the phone number). If you're itching to start promoting while renovations are still going on, work on the Web site. Changes can be made to a Web site within a day but a brochure will be around for a while. Put up pictures of your house in progress; get

Inn the Know

Before you spend money on a brochure that you might end up using as gift-wrap paper, spend some time researching your market and working on a plan. Then put those fancy photos and that snazzy verbiage into a brochure that you'll love!

people excited about the developments and what's to come. Give some thought to any promises you might want to make on your Web site about a completion date. If the house isn't ready when you thought it would be and you have rooms booked, you'll have to do some fancy dancing on the phone, and could even lose clientele altogether. Add a few weeks or even a month to your finish date and you'll spare yourself and everyone else some unnecessary anxiety.

Research: Not Just for Grad Students

Collecting market research is not done in an afternoon and it's not done solely for the marketing plan (a component of the business plan, covered in Chapter 8, "The Business Plan"). You may have already done some or most of your research to use in your marketing plan by determining your room rates (see Chapter 7, "All About Room Rates"), deciding on what amenities to offer (see Chapter 13, "Getting the Most from Your B&B"), and establishing what services will best suit your clientele (see Chapter 18, "Guest Services with a Smile"). All these things are part of market research and will help you focus in on your clientele; the first step in trying to reach them. Expending effort to reach all market sectors will be a waste of time and money. Be realistic. For example, if you're in a rural area that attracts mostly families because of Sal's Wacky, Wild Water Park, you won't have many older couples planning visits there.

Conversely, don't feel completely locked in to servicing only the typical clientele who visit your area. If there's a variety of lodging choices for travelers to choose from, you can target a more specific segment of the market—conducting market research before you open for business is even more critical in this case. You'll need to uncover the types of guests that other properties are targeting and then decide which area of the market you'll focus on. For example, if you're in an area of five-star hotels, don't feel as if you need to rise to their level to attract guests. Go for the spillover. Try to get the guests who want to come to your area but can't afford a full-service hotel. Just make sure that they don't expect five-star-hotel services! Be clear about what you do offer, and play up the fact that, because you're not a hotel, you can provide an informal, one-on-one atmosphere.

Word of Mouth: Promotion You Can't Buy

When we asked B&B owners and inn-keepers for their best advice on where to spend marketing money, they said, "put it into your house." That doesn't mean that you shouldn't do any marketing at all! If that were true this chapter would be very short.

What your faithful legion of B&B owners is saying is this: Make sure that guests leave with good stories to tell. Having guests spread the word for you is the best way to generate business. People who take trips to new destinations will ask friends and family who've been there what the best places are to roost. If a travel writer stays with you, give him or her the best room; it's a great payoff for what the writer may report on your inn. If your place is at the top of the list among guests and reviewers, you've reached potential clientele without spending any marketing dollars at all.

The Marketing Plan

As with almost every part of the B&B business, marketing is a never-ending project. As there are many different ways to get your name out there and lots of things to think about at once, marketing can seem overwhelming, especially at first. Break up the general project of marketing into pieces so you can accomplish them step by step. Think of each step you take as a layer of lasagna. As you layer each scrumptious piece you build a meal, a whole package. When you serve a portion of it, everything you put into it is there, even the stuff at the bottom. Marketing is the same way. You start out with a few projects and then keep adding more, but you retain those first few projects unless they turn out to be unsuccessful (the bottom burns).

Create a marketing plan that is realistic and will fit into your budget. The most difficult thing about beginning to market a product is that you'll be "guestimating." Even with all your research, you won't really know how well you've reached your market until guests start to show up at your door. As you go along it'll get easier because you'll be able to look back at what worked and what didn't work, and you'll know where to put your energy and money in future efforts.

Inn the Know

Your marketing plan will be part of the business plan that you hand out to consultants, potential investors, lending institutions, and others such as your insurance agent. Make sure that it's polished and realistic.

Put It on Paper

If you don't have a marketing background or any experience at all in marketing, don't panic. You might not know where to begin, but don't let that stop you. Marketing is as simple as writing down your goals, formulating a plan of action, and then sticking to it. Set reasonable goals and see them through.

Start out by listing your ideas for marketing and promotion. Don't go in any particular order; in fact, write down those ideas as they pop into your head or as you "borrow" them from other B&Bs, Web sites, and us. Don't think about cost or whether they're plausible or not just yet (we'll get to that). Here's an example list:

Design logo.

Have sign built and stationery printed.

Have photos taken of building and rooms.

Contact Chamber of Commerce and other local groups to gather info on area businesses and events for upcoming year.

Write out plans for connecting with local events.

Surf Web sites and homepages for promotional ideas and tricks that other B&Bs use to market to their clientele.

Develop layout ideas for Web site.

Hire Web site designer.

Assemble brochure and room rate info.

Decide on hiring a designer or work on computer for brochure and room rate card.

Have brochure and room rate card printed.

Create five ideas for an opening day promotion; develop plans for spreading the word about it locally and beyond.

Choose three main visitor attractions close by (such as a historical museum, hospital, or state park) and create ideas for spreading the word to their visitors.

Find 15 Web sites that you would like to be linked to or listed on.

Get advertising rates and lead time info from local publications.

Pick 10 guidebooks that you want to be listed in and develop a plan for reaching publishers.

Pick 8 to 10 periodicals (local and national) you'd like to be reviewed by and develop plans to entice them in your direction.

Create five ideas for slow season promotion; develop plans to spread the word about it locally and beyond.

Spend a couple of days coming up with ideas before you move on to the next steps: establishing goals for the year and then creating your marketing calendar. Writing out a list of ideas before you set your goals for the year probably seems a bit backward, but going backward actually will give you a better idea of what you want to accomplish as you go into your first year and beyond. You'll have a ton of marketing ideas that can't all happen in the first year. Writing them out, though, will give you a wider view of what you want to accomplish in the long term.

Marketing Calendar: 2001 to 2002 Season

Seasons

High season: mid-June to mid-September

Mid season: beginning of May to mid-June; mid-September to end of October

Low season: beginning of November to end of April

Goals for the Year

To generate local and national publicity before opening day through local advertising (and schmoozing) and the Web site

To continue local activities and exposure of your B&B by participating in events and meeting with local groups

To build national exposure through the Web site and inclusion of B&B into at least one guidebook or with a travel review

Month and Activities	Estimated Cost	Actual Cost
November 3: Assemble brochure and room rate info 5: Buy 10 guidebooks you'd like to be listed in 8: Surf B&B Web sites for promotional ideas and marketing tricks 10: Apply for Web domain name 12: Meet with graphic designer about needs (logo, stationery, rate card, brochure, and Web site) 15: Develop more layout ideas for Web site based on meeting with designer 19: Get advertising rates and lead time info from local publications 21: Follow up with designer to choose logo design/colors/fonts	$75: Books	$63: Books
December 4: Get disk from designer with stationery, rate card, and biz card art 5: Sign up for a toll-free number 6: Meet with printer to pick out paper and get schedule for printing stationery, rate card, and biz card	$350: Designer $1,500: Printer	$375: Designer $1,625: Printer

continues

continued

Month and Activities	Estimated Cost	Actual Cost
12: See proof from printer for all art (allow a few days for printer to make changes if necessary)		
18: Meet with sign maker		
20: Pick up stationery, rate cards, and biz cards from printer		
Yikes—Happy Holidays!		
January	$600: Sign	$450: Sign (found local artist to do)
3: Decide on sign design/have it created		
8: Query three publishers of guidebooks		
16: Find 15 Web sites that you would like to be linked to or listed on		
19: Work on content for Web site and brochure (have wordsmith friend review)		
23: Create five ideas for an opening day promotion and plans for spreading the word—locally and beyond		
27: Pick up sign		
30: Contact Chamber of Commerce and other local groups to gather info on area businesses and events for upcoming year		
February	$450: Designer $200: Webmaster $15: Film	$415: Designer $235: Webmaster $15: Film
5: Meet with designer and Webmaster to see designs-in-the-works of Web site and brochure		
12: Take photos of building and rooms		
15: Give photos to designer for Web site and brochure		
18: See revisions of Web site on the Internet; have trusted friends look over site and tell you what they really think		
20: Write out plans for connecting with local events in the spring		
25: Hire caterer for opening day event		
28: Choose three main visitor attractions close by and create ideas for spreading the word to their visitors		

Month and Activities	Estimated Cost	Actual Cost
March	$30: Flyers	$30: Flyers
3: Contact five online guidebooks to get listed on or linked to their sites		
5: Finalize brochure and get disk from designer		
7: Take disk to printer to pick out paper/ specs and decide on quantity and schedule		
9: Design and create flyer for opening day event		
10: Distribute flyers and spend day talking with local businesses and groups about opening day (get as many e-mails as possible)		
15: View finishing touches to Web site		
18: Web site goes live!; work on getting links to your site		
25: Pick 8 to 10 periodicals (local and national) you'd like to be reviewed by and develop plan for enticing them your way		
April	$1,200: Opening day $18: Invitations	$1,500: Opening day $18: Invitations
1: Invite local group to have an exclusive tour/tea on April 15, before opening day event festivities begin (only a fool would say no!) and personally invite local reviewer from your wish list created in March		
10: Make changes to Web site about upcoming opening day event		
12: Send e-mail reminding folks about opening day		
15: OPENING DAY!		
18: Take the day off!		
20: Create five ideas for slow season promotion and plans to spread the word—locally and beyond		

continues

continued

Month and Activities	Estimated Cost	Actual Cost
May	$150: Association $30: Printing of promo piece $25: Package materials $60: Festival materials/signage	$150: Association $30: Printing of promo piece $32: Package materials $48: Festival materials/signage
4: Update Web site (include one promotion idea created in April *and* report on opening day celebration) 7: Follow up with periodicals you queried in March by sending them clever package 11: Join regional association and get on Web site 15: Put cross-promotion with one visitor attraction (created in February) into place 25: Participate in local May festival 31: Get an update from friendly competition about their mid-season occupancy		
June	$55: Webmaster's magic	$75: Webmaster's magic
6: Check in with tourist attraction promotion to see if it's working 12: Query more guidebook publishers 17: Work on more Web site links to your site		
July		
15: Hook up with local group to create fall promotion 23: Create wish list of amenities and/or services to add in the coming year to attract guests 27: Check in with friendly competition once again, this time about high-season occupancy		

Month and Activities	Estimated Cost	Actual Cost
August	$25: Web designer	Free!: You learned how to make text changes on the site yourself!
8: Update calendar of events on Web site with brand-new, just-brainstormed ideas!		
16: Meet with local group to finalize details for fall promotion		
21: Contact Chamber of Commerce and other local groups again to gather info on area businesses and events for upcoming year		
September	Doc: ??? Free!: E-mail	Doc: $125 (double ouch!) Free!: E-mail
10: Review online guidebook listings—search for more if a few seem lame		
18: See doctor about recurring pain in arches		
23: Create plan for second cross-promotion with tourist attraction that garners most traffic in low season		
29: E-mail first year guests to offer low-season promotion and give calendar of events		
October	$30: Ad $170: Party	$30: Ad $220: Party
7: Put ad in local newspaper about fall promotion (now a Halloween event)		
12: Gather new rate card info		
16: Work on plan for upcoming year!		
31: Small ghoulish event for close friends and acquaintances—Happy Halloween!		

To determine your marketing budget for the year, look over your list and make notes about even the smallest costs (such as postage for letters and long-distance phone calls to contact publishers of guide books). Web site design and printing up the brochure and stationery will be some of your biggest costs for the first year but they're all imperative. If you look at your projected costs for marketing and decide that you can cover only your essential projects in the first year, you'll need to think of cost-free ideas to spread the word such as finding more places to leave your brochures and scouring the Web for free listings.

Working with the Locals

As your life will revolve more and more around the house and everyday operations, don't forget to keep your eyes peeled for local happenings. Make it a point to get out and talk to other business owners and attend events such as fundraisers and community celebrations. You won't be able to get out of the house as much as those nine-to-fivers, so be sure to read your local papers and stay in touch with people who know what happens in the town.

Being tuned in to the locals will help your business in more ways than one. You'll be in on the talk of the town, will learn how certain folks would like to see it grow (or not grow), and what new businesses are in the works. You'll have a better clue to the town's direction and whether it's actively reaching out to the tourist trade. You might have to get more involved in town politics than you expected. If your area could offer more to tourists than your town is promoting, it might be up to you and other businesses to bring it to the attention of town officials.

Seasonal Marketing

Paying attention to marketing your B&B in your highest season is important, as you'll be competing with others; but your biggest challenge will be getting clientele to come your way in the lowest season. Try out one project or promotion for that period that won't cost you that much, or work with other local businesses to create an event weekend. Plan ahead for it; if you don't have time to plan during your high season, plan a big event for the coming year. That way, you can tell more guests about it early and follow up later with a mailer or e-mail. Be sure you set aside funds for a low season event, as it will inevitably cut into your bank balance the closer you get to the big day. You'll need more money for food, Web site changes, and maybe a last-minute flyer.

B&B-eware!

If you don't have a property that's conducive to an event, don't kill yourself to come up with one. A cabin in the Ozarks wouldn't be the place for a festive, cabaret weekend. If your weather's lousy during low season, you'll have a hard time getting people to your door no matter what you do. Instead, use your slow time to work on local promotions, your Web site, and marketing plans for the coming mid season.

B&B Basics

As in our marketing calendar example, designing your logo and printing stationery, business cards, and the brochure should be the first things you do.

Don't Go Without a Logo

Even if you hire someone to design a logo for you, do some preliminary sketches of your own. Including your B&B's name as part of your logo is always preferable so that the two are connected. Many B&Bs use only the name as a logo, and that works well, too. A graphic designer will have a variety of fonts and styles, as will some basic computer software programs such as Microsoft Publisher.

Choose a logo that will look good everywhere—in large and small versions. Choose colors that suit your house, your theme (gold, black, and red for the "The Red Lion Inn"), and your tastes. Stick with clean lines and eye-popping but simple graphics. Create a logo that people will remember and that suits your style and the style of your house.

Try out a couple of designs and ask people who will give you honest opinions which ones they prefer. Make sure *you* like your logo—a lot—before you start spending money to have it plastered everywhere you look.

Stationery and Biz Cards

When you have a logo you love, head to a local printer for stationery. You'll be able to pick out text and colors that match your logo and the paper it's printed on. If you're computer-savvy, try out different fonts next to your logo and B&B name to see how they look. Take your best bets with you to the printer to have them matched up. If you're really handy with the computer, you can have your logo scanned in on disk and use it to create your own letterhead and business cards. You'll need a laser printer that will make your stationery look professional and card stock your printer can handle.

Inn the Know

You'd love an old sailing ship for your logo, but how will it look on a three-foot-wide sign? Draw it in different sizes and then enlarge your drawings on a copier. Thick lines will look great on a large sign but how will they look scaled down to an inch? That intricate design might look great on stationery but be incomprehensible on your sign.

Shoestring Solution

When you create your stationery and business cards, be sure the information won't change. Also, you might be tempted to order in bulk to save money but you probably should order the minimum quantity at first. You might like the design today and hate it next month.

Make sure you see what's called a "proof" of everything before it goes to print. Look over the proofs to make sure all the information is correct and the stationery or card looks the way you expected it to.

An Eye-Catching Sign

Check your local bylaws before you go out and order a six-foot neon yellow sign with flashing red letters. Okay, that's an unlikely choice for a B&B, but you get the idea. Some places will have limitations on the height of the sign from the ground or its dimensions; or you might not be permitted to have a roadside sign at all.

When you consider your sign's design and where to put it, take a good look at your property and the neighbors'. Do a couple of drive-bys to make sure that the sign can be seen from as far down the road as possible. If you're in a four-season area and you're having the sign created in the dead of winter, will it be covered with summer greenery in the spot you've chosen? Could the greenery be cut back? Take all the elements into account; if you're on a windy hill, pay the extra bucks for an ultra-sturdy sign.

The Brochure

Any brochure should be enticing, energetic, short and sweet, colorful, and up to date. Use language that gets your point across, is clear and concise, and gives potential guests a reason to take another trip so they can stay with you.

B&B-eware!

Stay away from cutesy language. Be careful not to oversell your property or what you offer. You'll want guests to arrive expecting what they saw and read about in the brochure. Write the text and then put it down for a few days. When you go back to it you might find that the language doesn't convey the feeling you thought it did.

Always have someone else read over your brochure for mistakes before you send it to the printer, and then again when you get the proof. Enlist as many editors as you can to cut down on the possibility of errors.

Here's a checklist of things to include in your brochure:

❑ All address and contact info, including e-mail and Web site

❑ Description of your place, type of breakfast served, any historical or interesting facts, and the best attributes of your location

❑ Directions to your place from all major highways or a local map

❑ Information on all of your rooms including amenities provided in every room and descriptions of each individual room

❑ Pictures of the front of the house and backyard sitting areas (if possible) and pictures of your rooms that will represent your B&B most accurately

Inn the Know

If you include photos of your rooms, make sure you show both your grandest room and your quaintest. Showing only your top-selling room will mislead guests. If you can't show a range, or if you're planning to change the rooms, keep room photos out of your brochure. Instead, put in photos of the exterior of the house, the back gardens, and the porches. Direct folks to your Web site for room photos.

Photos can lure guests to your B&B but they have to be true representations of it to make them glad they chose it. If you don't provide fresh flowers in the rooms, don't have them in a guest room photo; put them in the photo of a common room instead. You can spice up a guest room by draping a terry cloth robe over a bed or highlighting a cozy corner with a favorite chair. Just make sure that photos are not too dark or too light so that they'll reproduce well. If it goes with your gimmick (such as an Old West theme) choose black-and-white or sepia photos; even then, it's best to have some color photos, too. People want to see the true look of your place, which means color photos—and no pencil sketches.

The Next Level

If you're eager to place a national ad and have a Web site, too, but you don't have the green to do both, choose the Web site. One ad in a national magazine can cost as much, maybe more, than initial start-up costs of a Web site. One national ad might not bring you the extended exposure that a whole bunch of less expensive Web site links can bring.

Your Own Web Site

The Web site will be your biggest marketing weapon. You can update it regularly, provide lots of photos and room rate information, and accept reservations through e-mail. You can send potential guests to your Web site for more detail than you can give them over the phone. You can promote the site in your brochure and on your business card; and in stationery, flyers, mailers, invitations, listings in local event publications, and other printed materials.

Inn the Know

Having a Web site is not enough if no one knows it exists. Contact as many Web site hosts as you can about getting listed and cross-linked to their sites. Start with your area and state Web sites, and branch out from there to national sites (such as www.bandb.about.com). When you pay for listings, be sure to choose those that will reach your target market.

Shoestring Solution

Be sure to find out how your Webmaster and designer set their fees. They might charge a flat fee to get the site up and running and then hourly fees to make changes. Save yourself some dough and submit changes in bulk. If you call your Webmaster to make little changes here and there, you'll end up shelling out more.

If you're not sure where to start in designing a Web site, spend a good amount of time looking at what everyone else is doing. Print out pages from Web sites that you like and make notes on what would work for yours and what you would do differently. If you hire a Web designer, take the printouts along with your ideas for layout to your first meeting. Your designer will tell you what's possible within your budget. You then can decide what to incorporate and what to save for later on when you have more funds.

When you've settled on an official name for your B&B, it's a good idea to register your domain name right away. Some sites such as www.alldomain.com will let you search free for domain names to make sure that your chosen one has not been taken (and it most surely will be, so have backups and variations ready to go). Choose a name that's simple and memorable, and matches, as closely as possible, the name of your business.

If your budget doesn't allow for an expensive site, start with a homepage and work your way up. Find a reputable Web site designer who also is a Webmaster or knows a good one. The designer will create the pages of the Web site (and help write it if you like) and the Webmaster will get the site "live" on the Internet. Getting your site on the Internet is complicated. You'll want a Webmaster that knows how to get your site listed on all the major search engines. If someone types in the keywords "Connecticut B&B," you'll want to be at the top of the search results (that is, if your B&B is in Connecticut). A good Webmaster can make it happen.

In addition to the information that you'll include in your brochure, add the following to your Web site:

➤ Room rate info: Provide a range if you expect your rates to fluctuate depending on local events (such as concerts or conventions)

➤ Reservation form so that guests can check for availability through the site

➤ Photos of every room and details on what each has to offer

➤ Local map with area points of interest; pictures of downtown areas and most-visited sites are great

➤ Restaurant and entertainment suggestions

➤ Some other things such as gift certificates (sent via e-mail) and a monthly newsletter are items you can consider adding later on

Choose 100 to 150 words on your top page as your most important key words. When someone types in a broad search with key words such as "Connecticut B&B," their results won't come back with every B&B Web site in Connecticut. Computers are not that smart. A search finds Web sites that have the actual words "Connecticut" and "B&B" listed in the uppermost 20 percent of their top page. If your Web site is in Seattle and you don't have the words "Seattle" and "Bed and Breakfast" or "B&B" at the top, you'll be overlooked. Try to choose your 100 to 150 words carefully, putting the most important ones up front (location) and then following with descriptions of area events and attractions.

➤ Updated schedule of events. It's best to do this for several months in advance so you're not updating every week (it also will save you on Webmaster charges).

➤ Extras on a secondary or back page: photos of you, your staff, and pets; a brief background piece on how long you've owned the place and what you did before owning it (include things that relate to service and lodging); a "meet the staff" element if you have more than two staff members; and a longer description of the history of the house and the area (pictures of your place with previous owners are great for really old houses).

Make sure that visitors to your site are not tripping over the secondary information (photos of you, history of house, and so on) to get to more pertinent stuff, such as rates. Spend the extra money to have the Webmaster create buttons that lead to separate pages where people can click on each topic and quickly get to the information they're after. If they have to scroll down one continuous page to get to what they want, they'll go elsewhere. Have a professional-looking Web site that is easy to navigate so you grab attention instead of losing it.

Hometown Advertising

Just because you have a sign out front doesn't mean that everyone will know you exist. Spend some time reaching out to locals so they'll spread the word to out-of-towners.

> **B&B-eware!**
>
> Make sure you update your Web site info regularly, especially after a promotional event is past, you've changed your room rates, or redecorated a room. There's nothing worse than visiting a site with old information, or one that says "last updated September 1996." Guests will want to be sure that a place is still in business.

Advertising in a local paper is a great way to announce an opening day or event. Invite townfolk in for an open house tour and serve light refreshments. You won't get the whole town at your doorstep but you will get those who are active in town events (especially those who received your personal invitation as well; make sure you don't leave anyone out!).

Coffee Talk

"The very best thing that we did in the beginning was to invite the staff from the Rockford Area Convention and Visitor's Bureau for a breakfast. What rewards that produced within days!" recall Ken and Karen Sharp, owners of The Barn of Rockford Bed and Breakfast in Rockford, Illinois. "They have remained wonderful supporters and we still invite them over yearly for a big breakfast as our way of saying 'thank you.' Word of mouth is still the best advertisement! We have people who come out from Chicago who tell their relatives in New Mexico, and so on. It becomes a very small world! That's why it is so important to do your very best with everything. *You* are your best advertisement!"

Take an ad out in the Yellow Pages under accommodations, bed and breakfasts, inns, hotels, lodgings—whatever category works best. If you have a business telephone line you will likely get a free listing (not a display ad, which is costly and not cost-effective) in your local edition of the Yellow Pages. If you're located outside a city but within the same area code you might ask to be listed in the bigger county edition to obtain greater exposure to those looking for a weekend getaway. Larger areas may have separate listings for B&Bs, guesthouses, inns, and the like (or just "lodging") so make sure that your listing is in the desired section. Don't forget to include your toll-free number (keep reading for more on getting one). Continual advertising in a local publication is a waste of money. Concentrate instead on getting involved in local events and activities to increase your B&B's visibility in hometown circles.

Distribute your brochures around town where they'll get picked up by potential guests, not in places where they'll get picked up and tossed or just gather dust (such as in a local hangout that tourists wouldn't go near). First try to place them with travel agents who are geared toward bringing tourism to your area, rather than booking vacations for townies. Leave brochures at the Chamber of Commerce, tourist information centers, and trade shows; and take them to other local businesses whose business cards or brochures you'll want to display for your guests. For future planning, keep track of how fast the brochures disappear from each location.

Advertising Nationally

Advertising in *Travel & Leisure* or other national periodicals is fine for resorts and hotels (and maybe some large inns) but not worth your money. They are extremely expensive and you'll never know if you reached your target market.

To reach a national audience, your best bet is getting listed in guidebooks. Some will not cost you anything to get listed except the time and energy you spend to get noticed by the author. Others will ask for a fee that could range up to $500. You'll have to meet a certain criterion to get into any guidebook; this will vary for each publication. Getting into an independent publication (those not attached to an association) is a real coup and could generate future listings in other guidebooks. Authors of guidebooks watch their competition closely (just as you do) and sometimes will approach properties listed in other books to include them. If you do list in national publications, you'll definitely need a toll-free number.

Coffee Talk

Sam and Richard Corcoran, owners/inn-keepers of Hell's Blazes in Old Mystic, Connecticut, suggest spending advertising dollars on a toll-free number. Getting a catchy one like the one Hell's Blazes has—1-888-MY-DEVIL—is even better. "People who are looking to book their weekend while at work will call a toll-free number to avoid making long-distance calls on the company dime. You'll pay for each phone call but the lure of a toll-free number will pull in a lot more business than advertising will."

It's wise to contact guidebooks *before* you open for business. You might not get a response or a visit from the author for a few months anyway, and it could be a year before the publication hits stores. Guidebooks put out by associations can be considered paid advertising because paying members are automatically listed; they also enjoy access to their other perks. See Chapter 11, "Networking Works," for more on getting into guidebooks and joining associations.

There are a ton of elements to successful marketing, which include developing a useful plan, creating an eye-catching logo, and designing a Web site that really stands out. You don't need a degree in marketing to spread the word. Your primary goal as a new inn-keeper should be to find your core market—and then go get 'em!

The Least You Need to Know

➤ Develop a first-year marketing plan that fits your budget, and initiate projects you can successfully accomplish that year.

➤ Designing a logo and getting stationery printed are essential to a B&B startup.

➤ A good Web site is your best marketing tool because it can be updated regularly and can provide more information than a brochure.

➤ Getting listed in the right guidebooks is a great way to get your B&B on the map.

Networking Works

Just want to run your business in solitude without any interference from others? Living like a hermit is fine if you've been in business for years; however, if you're a novice hermit, you'll soon be an out-of-work hermit.

There are many types of resources available to B&B owners, and many organizations and fellow owners willing to help. When we solicited owners to contribute to this book, we had an overwhelming response! Because this business is so unique and complex, the advice of owners who've been through it all is invaluable. The more people you talk to, and the more you reach out to local and national organizations, the more successful your B&B will be.

You're Not Alone!

In this business there will be times when the house is full and you're stuck there, feeling like a total shut-in. You'll probably be so busy that you won't mind it that much, but if you run the B&B by yourself, there might be times when you feel alone in the world, and dealing with a sink drainage problem or an unhappy guest can seem overwhelming.

The best cure for feeling alone is to get connected. Join an organization or two, talk with other B&B owners (and other small business owners), take a class, take a trip, tunnel the Net … get out there!

Finding Networking Opportunities

Making personal contacts in this business can help you in every way. You'll develop friendships, find advisors, and possibly receive some referrals. Don't get nervous about approaching people. Most will be happy to answer questions and give you insight into the business. There's no need to be pushy; just talk casually and read the signals. If someone doesn't want to converse with you, move on.

Don't know where to start? Try starting with the opportunities that you already have. Maybe you're going to a cocktail party next week and you know that another B&B owner from across town will be there. Get your face out of the punch bowl and introduce yourself!

Talking with Other B&B Owners

Getting to know local B&B owners can be tricky or it can be a breeze; it all depends on your area. If yours is one of only two B&Bs in a small town that doesn't get truckloads of visitors, you might want to look elsewhere for support. If your B&B is in a bustling area where there are different levels of accommodations you'll have an easier time building a support network. Before you start reaching out indiscriminately to other owners, though, do some James Bond–style undercover work (no, it doesn't require a trip to Barbados on a chartered Lear jet).

Lay low and get a sense for how things work in your town before you make any moves.

Crank up your intuition meter to its highest level. Approach those B&B owners who are visible in town and seem to work well with other organizations. They're the ones who'll be most likely to see the benefit of joining forces with you or of at least getting to know you. Others will only view collaborating with the competition as a threat to their business. Again, you'll find more of this breed in towns with less activity. If you attempt to get to know an owner and you don't get a positive response, respect the person's wishes; you'll find others who are interested. (And remember, never, never put your drink down and look away; next thing you know you'll be trapped in an underground lair with only your wits to save you!)

Inn the Know

When Park gets a call from guests who, for any reason, he can't accommodate, he refers them to other B&Bs or inns that are a good match. Other houses do the same for him. Guests whom you help out that way will remember it; and so will the competitor you sent the business to, who will do the same for you when the opportunity arises.

Local Business Organizations

Tapping into your local network of other small businesses and organizations is a good place to start connecting.

Chamber of Commerce

Joining your local chapter of the Chamber of Commerce is worth every penny. If your town or area does not have a tourism office, the Chamber will get calls about accommodations. Even if you do have a nearby tourism office, the Chamber is a great resource for information about your area, your competition, visitors, and the local economy. Some Chambers even offer health insurance plans.

Local and State Tourism Offices

Most states and many localities (especially extra-touristy ones) publish tourism materials to generate out-of-state interest. Get listed in their brochures and pamphlets and on their Web sites. Just call their offices to find out their requirements and deadlines. Find an angle to sell yourself—for instance your B&B is located in a great area that is under-publicized or your early–nineteenth-century house would be an attraction during the town's upcoming 200-year celebration. Make sure you have some great color photos and a short description of your B&B ready to go.

Connecting with Other Small Businesses

Get to know owners of restaurants, small retail shops, parking facilities, gourmet food and gift shops, and guided tour companies. When guests are out and about, they'll get to talking with staff and owners of such establishments about their visit to the area. Inevitably, your guests will be asked, "So where are you staying?" If you're well known, what will follow is a nice conversation about what a good choice your guests made. This will make them feel good and it will spread the good word about your B&B. You, in turn, can recommend that friendly establishment to your guests.

Connecting with other small businesses also makes sense when it comes to staying in touch with town politics. Let's say that there's a new parking ban ordinance in the works that would be detrimental to your business. Joining forces with other small business owners who also would be affected could get town officials to give more serious thought to the impact the proposed ban would have on the local economy.

Joining a B&B Organization

Check out several different organizations before you start writing out checks to every one. Find out which ones will give you the best exposure on their Web sites and in their guidebooks (see Chapter 10, "Marketing 101," for more on guidebooks).

National Associations

Consider joining at least one of the three main national associations: American Bed and Breakfast Association, National Bed and Breakfast Association, and Professional Association of Innkeepers International (for complete contact information, see Appendix B, "National and Local Associations"). The greatest benefit of going national is that you'll be listed in the association's guidebook (and possibly other publications), which reaches thousands of potential B&B travelers. Almost all of the national organizations have a newsletter and a support system that includes information exchanges, start-up help, connections with vendors, marketing tips, and recipes.

Here are some details on the three major players:

➤ **American Bed and Breakfast Association (www.abba.com).** And you thought ABBA was a band of 1970s dancing queens! It will take more than funky hair to get into this ABBA. You must qualify to become a member, which means meeting their nationally set standards. An ABBA representative will inspect your property (and provide a consultation as well) and then rate it accordingly. You'll then be listed in their national directory and guidebook, and be connected to other services such as insurance plans.

➤ **National Bed and Breakfast Association (www.nbba.com).** To join the NBBA, you must be a privately owned B&B or inn and include breakfast in your room rate. As ABBA does, the NBBA reviews applications before granting membership. You'll get a visit from an NBBA rep and then be required to fill out some paperwork. Your B&B will be listed in its guidebook, *The Official Bed and Breakfast Guide, U.S., Canada, and the Caribbean.* The NBBA also can create an individual Web page for you on its main site.

➤ **Professional Association of Innkeepers International (www.paii.org).** PAII is the best known of the national associations for gathering industry research. Joining will get you access to PAII's research, member-only hotline, credit card processing at a low rate, discounts from vendors and on industry publications, and a special long-distance phone rate. If you don't want a full membership, you can also sign up for just the newsletter for about half the cost. PAII also organizes one of the biggest international conferences for aspiring and active innkeepers.

Regional Clubs

There probably are several different associations in your state and possibly a few in your region. Banding together with folks close to home has a lot of advantages.

Coffee Talk

Jane Bertorelli, co-owner of the Union Street Inn in San Francisco, California, and member of the California Association of Bed and Breakfast Inns, recommends joining an organization for many reasons. "Quite simply, for an inn-keeper, the greatest advantage of joining an organization like CABBI is to know that one is not alone. Along with the camaraderie of other inn-keepers, there is also the availability of legal and professional advice, group discounts for insurance and workers comp, access to vendors specializing in our industry, a Web site, an annual directory, and the wisdom and advice of both the executive office and member inn-keepers! It's also the opportunity to become more involved in the industry, broaden your perspective, and help promote the bed and breakfast experience."

Local support groups can exchange marketing ideas and information on legislation and politics. Most have Web sites linked to their respective state pages and larger tourist-oriented sites that help travelers find B&Bs according to area, type of property, and so on. Your local association also might be able to get group discounts from area suppliers of food and other products.

Most local associations have criteria for membership or limitations based on geographical location or business status (large inn with a restaurant versus a small B&B without one, for example). Local associations also can be narrowly based on a theme such as historical properties or family-friendly inns, but it's rare. Most small organizations want a fair amount of members to cover the cost of a Web site and to get group discounts.

Start Your Own Amalgamation!

Want to start your own little group of cohorts? Why not?! It might take a while to get people interested, and a while after that to get them officially on board. Before you buy a domain name for a Web site, ask yourself these questions:

➤ Are there enough B&Bs to form an association in your area? If not, branch out to a larger area or reach out to groups of B&Bs throughout your state that are similar in size and offer similar levels of service.

Inn the Know

Find a state or regional association through Bed and Breakfast Central Information at www.bbonline.com/bbci or the Professional Association of Innkeepers International (www.paii.org). We list local and state associations in Appendix B, but these two sites (especially PAII's) revise their lists regularly and will have the most up-to-date information.

➤ If there are enough area B&Bs, would they be interested, or are they from all different walks of B&B life? A large inn most likely will not want to be in the same camp as a homestay.

➤ Are there already associations in your area that others have joined? If it's working well for them (along with a national organization they belong to), they'll concentrate on those memberships.

➤ Will area B&Bs be able to put up enough dues money for a Web site? If the owners you're hoping to woo have their own Web sites and grumble about the expense, you'll have a hard time squeezing out more dough for another site.

➤ Can you spare the time to get this off the ground? If it's your idea, you'll have to do all the work. Enlisting members does not necessarily mean enlisting active members, so be prepared to bear the burden, at least at the beginning.

The biggest consideration when starting your own organization is whether the efforts are worth your time. If there are plenty of other associations in your area, why spend your limited time and resources on starting one that might never gather enough members? If you have ideas that would help other owners, bring them to an already up-and-running association.

In the guesthouse-rich community of Provincetown, Massachusetts, Park and seven other owners have formed a group to market their eight inns more effectively (and have lots of fun, as well). See their example at www.DistinctiveInnsofProvincetown. com. DIP is a close-knit group that meets monthly to discuss marketing and promotion strategies (which include entering in an annual carnival parade), swap ideas, and decide on plans for their Web site. They even created a visitors pamphlet with a points-of-interest map and descriptions and photos of each B&B.

Attending Seminars and Classes

Just do it. Set aside the funds and go to a conference or one-day seminar, and take classes in business, accounting, marketing, or cooking at a local college or university. The best way to keep up with industry changes is to stay ahead of them. When you're shopping around for a conference or seminar, make sure you get hold of an agenda or at least a detailed description of what you'll learn. Attending a start-up class will be a waste of money if you're a veteran (or nearly one).

Conferences and seminars are the best place to network. You get to converse with pros and others at your level. You'll share war stories, trade secrets, and pick each other's brains about everything. Connecting with others who are in the same business will, at the very least, help you keep your sanity.

In Appendix B we list a few conferences and seminars you can check into that are run by organizations and individual inn-keepers but the list is by no means comprehensive. Check with local and national associations, nearby universities, and favorite Web sites to find more.

Getting Listed in Guidebooks

There are a ton of guidebooks on accommodations published every year. You might be charged for listing your B&B in a guidebook, and you'll definitely need to pay up to join an association that publishes a guidebook (like ABBA or NBBA). Books published independently can be much more valuable because they'll (in most cases) describe a location and choose select properties to include. There also are lodging guidebooks for specific regions and general tourist guides, all of which can provide great exposure.

Some publications have specific hooks, such as B&Bs for hikers, that could be perfect for what you offer. The Professional Association of Innkeepers International (www.paii.org) publishes an annual *Guide to Inn Guidebooks,* which lists all guidebooks, their contact information, required fees, and deadlines. There are literally hundreds of national and regional guides published every year, so the PAII list will be a huge help in narrowing down the list of guidebooks you should contact.

The following are some of the major guidebooks covering B&Bs and inns across North America (see Appendix B for complete contact info):

➤ *AAA Guides* (American Automobile Association)

➤ *Mobil Travel Guides* (Mobil Corporation)

➤ *Bed and Breakfasts and Country Inns* (Deborah Edwards Sakach/American Historic Inns)

➤ *America's Best Bed and Breakfasts: Over 1600 Delightful Places to Stay in All 50 States* (Eugene Fodor, Caroline Haberfeld and Leslie Ruth Brown, Fodor's Best Bed and Breakfast Series)

➤ *Fodor's Bed and Breakfast and Country Inn Guides* (Fodor's Travel Publications)

➤ *Frommer's Bed and Breakfast Guides* (separate publications for certain North American regions) (Macmillan Travel)

➤ *The Complete Guide to Bed and Breakfasts, Inns, and Guesthouses: In the United States, Canada, and Worldwide* (Pamela Lanier and Richard Paoli, Ten Speed Press)

➤ *The Bed and Breakfast Encyclopedia* (Deborah Edwards Sakach, American Historic Inns)

➤ *The Annual Directory of American and Canadian Bed and Breakfasts* (Rutledge Hill Press)

➤ *Country Inns and Back Roads, North America* (HarperCollins Publishers)

➤ *The Official Bed and Breakfast Guide, USA, Canada, and Caribbean* (Phyllis Featherston and Barbara Ostler, National Bed and Breakfast Association)

➤ *Complete Guide to American Bed and Breakfasts* (Rik Barnes, Pelican Books)

➤ *America's Favorite Inns, B&Bs and Small Hotels: USA and Canada* (Sandra Soule, St. Martin's Press)

➤ *The Christian Bed and Breakfast Directory* (Barbour and Company)

➤ *The Good Bed and Breakfast Guide—Which Books Travel Guides* (Elsie Dillard and Susan Causin, Cimino Publishing Group)

➤ *Damron Travel Guides* for gay and lesbian travelers (The Damron Company)

➤ *Spartacus International Gay Guide* (Verlag)

Inn the Know

If your town or region isn't listed as a category, let the authors know that they're missing out on a well-traveled area; it's a good angle. Don't feel compelled to get into every guide there is, but try to get into the ones that you think will be the most effective in reaching your clientele.

Go to the library or a large bookstore and look at all kinds of guidebooks and travel guides (such as books on weekend getaways and regional guides), not just at those with listings solely for lodging. Read the sections about how the properties were chosen and how the publication rates them. (Note that even if the authors had the last say on who was listed, B&Bs still might have had to pay a fee; this won't be stated in the book.) Determine which books would be best for your B&B to get into, and consider going after those that don't list your competition—it's a great way to get noticed.

When you contact guidebook publishers, do your best to get the author, editor, or compiler on the phone, or get the name of someone you can write to. Ask for that person when you need to follow up on your written correspondence (which most likely will not be responded to right away if at all). Send a letter with a brochure and perhaps a photo. Always, always, always send a personal letter with any information about your B&B that that particular guidebook would find appealing. Be as accommodating as possible (pun intended) by including relevant information in your letter, directing the recipient to your Web site, and inviting the person to phone (using your toll-free number if you have one).

Remember that networking works best when you take advantage of opportunities when they arise. Don't think, "Well, I can talk to that business owner at another event." If a break presents itself, then take it! Not every avenue you take will work out but the more networking you do, the more your business will be in the spotlight.

The Least You Need to Know

➤ Networking will help you build a support system and will extend your market reach, locally and globally.

➤ Join a local association to get more exposure, exchange ideas, and have a voice in area politics.

➤ Joining a national association will cost you, but it's worth it. Your listing in the association's guide will reach potential guests across the country and beyond.

➤ Attending seminars and taking classes are among the best ways to get help with startup and stay current with what's happening in the industry.

Special Circumstances

Along with basic marketing strategies and networking, you can take other avenues that will help you stay visible. Think of this chapter as the potluck of the marketing section. Getting the word out is possible in so many ways—more ways than we could fit into just two chapters.

Sometimes it's easy to get caught up in running the business from day to day, especially during the busy times. Marketing usually is the first thing that slips. When times are good, your plans to generate exposure for the future might lose momentum. Try to stay out of those comfort zones by implementing promotions that reach potential clientele and by giving past guests a reason to return.

Events at Your Place

Promotions that revolve around events are always fun; they should be fun for you, too. Organizing an event in your backyard or living room will take a lot of work, so make sure you have the time, energy, and funds.

Before you check your savings account balance, take a good look at your house and grounds to determine whether creating an event on your property is feasible.

➤ Do you have enough seating and standing room for everyone? Uncomfortable space is made even more uncomfortable in unfamiliar territory. If your common areas are too small, don't force guests to cram themselves in. It's an unpleasant experience, and that's what they'll remember. Have an outside event, if possible, or think of another promotion.

➤ Do you have enough bathrooms for a large group? If you don't have any common bathrooms and you're fully rented during a promotional event, what facilities will your party guests use? Probably the bathroom in your private quarters. Consider hosting a smaller group to avoid bathroom congestion, or have the event when there's an open guest room.

➤ Is the area comfortable enough to encourage conversation in small groups? Work on room flow and motion before you invite people into the house for an event (see Chapter 13, "Getting the Most from Your B&B").

Inn the Know

New to town and afraid you'll have a bunch of no-shows? Build some personal relationships by calling groups such as the local Chamber of Commerce and the Business Guild, and work the "new kid in town" angle. Tell them what you're planning and that you'd like to get to know them better. They'll be flattered that you're throwing a get-together for them and they'll show up—and probably return the gesture. Who can resist when the new kid reaches out to make new friends?

➤ Will your house be fully functional on the date of the event? Schedule a promotional event to announce the opening of your B&B at least one to two months later than you expect to be finished with renovations. You don't want folks to remember stepping around sawhorses or seeing one of the "old" rooms and thinking that you've already refurbished it.

➤ Will folks have to park a mile away? If your parking situation is not the greatest, find neighbors who will let you use their lot (don't forget to invite them), even if it's a few blocks down. Don't forget to post big signs so that people will know where to park!

Events to Fit Your Style

When you're determining what kind of event to host, choose one that fits your house and your style. Maybe you have enough land for a small music concert under the stars; or maybe a Texas-style barbecue, complete with carnival games. Does your house have historical significance that you could tie into town celebrations? Is your living room perfect for eggnog and holiday carols? Maybe the house or yard can't hold a lot of people but your location is a great starting point for a hayride. Halloween is not just for kids anymore; if you have the space, throw a party for the guys and ghouls who can't get away with trick-or-treating anymore (a.k.a. adults).

Stick to things that make sense at your property and that you'll have fun at, too. Don't have a barbecue if you hate ribs. If you're worried about having a huge group of people in your dining and living room areas, make sure you have the event outside during a warmer season. Also, stay tuned to what other events are happening around town. Don't make people choose or you could lose out entirely.

Shoestring Solution

Maybe you're itching to have a garden party but your tulips and cattails are not up to snuff. Invite people over for the first annual Spring Seed Swapping event. Everyone brings baby bulbs or plants from their gardens (or the plant they picked up from a garden center on their way over) to swap with others in the group. Parties where people bring stuff to share are great icebreakers. If you don't have a garden (or just think this idea is for the worms), try swapping something else such as favorite desserts and the recipe to go with them.

"Open house" parties are a great way to spread the word. Chances are people have been curious about your place since you started renovating or hung a sign out. Having an informal gathering where you can open all the rooms and people can sneak peeks without having to be sneaky is a great way to get locals talking. The whole idea of an open house suggests that you're a welcoming host. Make sure you enlist the help of family and friends on the day of the party. If you can't be at the front door yourself, have a greeter there to hand out a refreshment or just direct people. Make people feel at home right away so they'll stay and have a good look around. If you're worried about having certain valuables on display, put them away. Chances are you'll be busy going from one person to the next to say hello (if all goes well), so have some helpers stationed on all levels to show people around and answer questions.

Tie in the theme of your B&B to any promotion you do. If you own the "Tiny Bubbles Inn," hand out little bottles of bubbles when people arrive, and serve champagne (or sparkling juice). Maybe you converted your house, now the "Jailbird Inn," from a building that once held prisoners. Your invitations or flyers could be "get out of jail free" cards, and your staff could dress up in black-and-white convict outfits and serve cider and gruel. Okay, forget the gruel.

Host a charity event in coordination with a local organization or the charity itself. Have a hundred-dollar-a-head dinner party or an art auction. Charity events are good because, well, you're doing a good thing for others and for yourself. It's okay to want some publicity for your B&B from a charity event. Even if you're spreading the word about your business, getting a tax write-off, and showing everyone what a really nice person you are, you're still doing a good deed.

The best promotional ideas are inspired by other events. Maybe a new restaurant in town is opening for business at the same time you are. They'd probably jump at the chance of a joint event. Their good food and your beautiful house—what better combination than that? (Just make sure their food is up to catering quality before you partner up.)

Getting People to Show Up

Partner with another small business, a local group, a circle of friends, a newspaper, and of course, your neighbors, and you'll share the burden of getting the word out. Be militant about promoting the event. Send out flyers or invitations, make phone calls, and mention the event to others when you see them in the supermarket. Do anything to get others to talk about it. Go above and beyond the call of an invitation and you'll get a full house.

If your event is open invitation, get it listed in town and newspaper event calendars and radio event announcements. Just don't forget to personally invite top town officials, local and regional newspaper people, and your neighbors.

The best way to get people to show up is to make your event fun. Make it unusual so they'll be intrigued. Encourage their curiosity about this new business of yours so they're itching to check out your house in person.

Inn the Know

Make sure you choose a date on the calendar that doesn't conflict with other events and likely will generate a sizeable crowd (Memorial Day weekend is not such a good idea and you'll be busy with guests anyway). Have an RSVP date that's at least two weeks before the party. You'll have stragglers who won't get back to you, but plan on them showing up. Make sure you call people who didn't respond right after your RSVP date so you'll know exactly how many to expect, and therefore how much chow and grog to buy.

Promising Promotions Elsewhere

When you're looking elsewhere for occasions that provide opportunities for promotion, try exposing yourself at public events (hey, not that kind of exposure!—although you would get noticed ...) already in the works. Enter a float in a parade, sell your homemade bread at a fair (don't forget your brochures), and contribute your jam to a pancake breakfast. Attend trade shows. Offer to speak at career day at your kid's school. Have a block party. All of these are suggestions that you can modify and adapt to your particular locale. Stay on top of events and happenings around you, and don't forget those you normally wouldn't know about (such as a school event when you don't have a kid in school, or a Catholic church bazaar if you're Jewish). You'll be surprised at the range of opportunities that will arise in unforeseen places.

Promotional Paper Chase

Get those creative juices flowing and then get things down on paper! A classy invite or catchy flyer can make all the difference in the world in getting people to notice your promotion.

You'll use some combination of the following to get people to come to your promotions:

Inn the Know

Start early to build a mailing list of people you meet in your region and at classes and seminars. Eventually, guests will account for most of your list. Be sure you get their e-mail addresses, too.

➤ **Invitations.** Printed invitations can be somewhat expensive, yet computer-generated ones can look cheesy. If your event is more casual, computer-generated invites probably will do just fine. If you're hosting an elegant wine and cheese party, look into getting nice postcards printed up on a decent (but cheap) card stock. You'll save money on postage and envelopes.

➤ **Flyers.** Best used for big, open-invitation events. Using flyers as invitations to small events will seem tacky and impersonal. Flyers can be done on a computer (if you're all thumbs, find a friend who's good at it) and then copied on a good color copier. Make sure your original printout is done on good paper (laser paper if a laser printer) and with a decent printer. Distribute your flyers to whatever shops, businesses, and town community boards allow it. Make sure your Chamber of Commerce and tourism center get a bunch.

➤ **E-mail.** A great way to reach past guests! Pick an e-vite from many of the free Web sites out there or send a personal e-mail.

➤ **Coupons.** A lot of touristy areas produce discount booklets for incoming travelers. This works well for motels or for guesthouses that are appealing to a cost-conscious group consisting mostly of elders and families. More upscale properties might choose to align themselves with a restaurant to offer a "stay two nights and receive a fabulous Sunday brunch at …" or "pay two, stay three" or "free whale watch tickets if you stay Monday, Tuesday, or Wednesday."

➤ **Gift certificates.** Spread the word that gift certificates are available, especially during holiday times. Gift certificates are a great option for locals looking to buy something unique for their out-of-town friends and relatives. You can sell gift certificates at set amounts of $50, $75, and $100 to be used toward a two-night minimum stay at your B&B, or allow folks to prepay for their lucky Aunt Stella and Uncle Frank's entire stay. Make the gift certificate good for at least a year so folks have options when booking, but make sure you include a "must be used by" date. If your rates change slightly, don't charge guests the difference! The best thing about gift certificates: Some recipients will either lose them or never get around to using them.

➤ **Sign boards.** Don't forget signage if you have an open house or any "come one, come all" kind of event. No cardboard tag sale signs! Paint stenciled letters on plywood that will be sturdy when standing up. Ask the town if you can put them in high-traffic areas and be sure to get them out there a few weeks before the event. Don't forget to have smaller "Today!" signs ready to add to the big signs on the day of the event.

➤ **Newsletters.** Have you built up quite a following of returning guests? Create a newsletter that you can send out once or twice a year or for an annual event that you've become famous for. They're a snap to create on the computer if you have the time to sit down and write them out. Newsletters usually are very personal and typically are sent out by the bigger inns. Let's face it: A larger place has more to talk about. It can include a recipe from its award-winning chef, give recaps of events, describe upcoming events in town and at the inn, and let guests know about rate specials.

Shoestring Solution

Instead of spending money on a newsletter, update your Web site regularly! When you have an upcoming event, send out postcards with the basic information and direct people to the Web site for details.

Niche Marketing

If your goal is to target a very specific market such as families or the gay-friendly, you'll need to find ways to reach these groups directly. Dig up publications and scout out Web sites specifically for these niche groups. Work on cross-promotions with other businesses that also are looking to bring the same groups to town.

You could offer discount coupons for local attractions that would appeal to your market. Also offer appropriate items at the house that you can promote on the Web site such as an outdoor play area for young kids.

Niche marketing also means finding clever and unusual ways to get your name out there. If you cater to gourmets, send your favorite recipe to the author of a B&B and inn cookbook or send it to a food magazine. Teach cooking classes or give local talks on running a B&B (more on this in Chapter 22, "Expanding the Business," as these are not solely marketing ideas; they're also money mak-

B&B-eware!

If you want to welcome kids of all ages (most B&Bs do accept kids over 12) make sure you announce it in all your advertising. Kid-less couples who show up looking for an extra-quiet weekend only to find small kids in the house will feel deceived, and why wouldn't they? Be clear about who you cater to on your Web site and in all marketing materials.

ers). If you have a gift for writing fiction, write a story set at your B&B and submit it to a magazine. Draw on your own unique talents and discover the best ways to exploit them! Start thinking about unconventional ways to gain exposure and you'll find some that make sense for you.

Cheap Marketing Tricks

Chances are you've skimmed the chapter just to get to this section. Everyone wants to save money and if you can cut back in the marketing department and still gain exposure for your business, more power to you. When you're searching for free or inexpensive ways to promote your B&B, don't compromise your marketing budget. Spend the money on your Web site (have we said this too often?) and other marketing fundamentals; then brainstorm for cheap tricks.

Here are some of ours:

➤ Get a vanity plate with your B&B's name (or part of it). If your B&B is "Grosvenor's House Bed & Breakfast Inn at Cape Tern on the Point," this might be a little tough.

➤ Look into cable access channels. Maybe you and other local businesses can do a bit together.

➤ Don't forget radio. Get on an interview program to talk about your latest promotion, and have it included in announcements about local events.

➤ Network with other businesses to cross-promote a local contest. Put an ad in the local newspaper announcing entries for "The best 30-word description of the town" or "Why your parents deserve a night off." Winners get a free night's stay at your inn and dinner at a local restaurant. The ad probably will cost you around $30 but you'll share this with the other business or businesses in the cross-promotion. Don't forget to get the local newspaper to do a write-up on the contest and the winners.

➤ Conduct your own contest through your Web site. Have entrants submit suggestions for a name for one of your rooms or the new house cat. The winner gets to stay at your B&B for one free night out of a minimum two-night stay or two free nights out of a minimum four night stay (or something similar).

➤ Drop hints or strong suggestions about event ideas. Start talking with local organizations about ideas such as a festival, art show, garden contest, or holiday house decorating contest. The art show could be a showcase for unknown artists. Think of ideas that are low budget (open houses are great for this) and generate publicity in a fun way. You could ask local celebs and glitterati to color Easter eggs, make masks, or donate a tie or scarf, which then could be auctioned off at your property for charity. Smells like a write-off!

➤ Participate in silent auctions at charity fund raising events. Offer a certificate for a free stay at your B&B. Attach a dollar amount to it such as $75, $100, or $150 (instead of "weekend for two"), and allow it to be used at any time. Require a "must be used by" date and "minimum stay over weekends" (or whenever).

When you're scouting out cheap marketing tricks, consider doing a bunch of small things that you can do for $1,000 instead of spending it all on one national magazine ad that might not generate its money's worth in exposure. Smaller ads here and there such as $50 Web site links and local promotions make it a lot more fun for you and will bring results from many different quarters.

The Least You Need to Know

➤ Events on the home front can be very successful if they're well promoted and are a good fit for your house.

➤ If you create the right kind of invitation for your event and spark curiosity with your language and presentation, people will come.

➤ You can succeed at niche marketing by finding unique ways to get the word out to your target market.

➤ To get more bang for your marketing buck, spend it on several small, cheap marketing tricks instead of one big ad.

Part 4
Making It Your Own

Like snowflakes, no two B&Bs are the same. Houses might share similar features or guest policies, but you are the one who will make your B&B unique. Choosing a decorating style and amenities that suit you and your clientele are key to building a list of returning guests. Deciding on guest policies you'll enforce also is fundamental to shaping your B&B and the clientele it will draw.

Chapter 13

Getting the Most from Your B&B

In This Chapter

➤ Finding your own style and creating a comfortable atmosphere

➤ Working with big and small spaces

➤ Determining what types of amenities to provide

If you feel a little lost when it comes to decorating, or even deciding where to put the coffee table, you're not alone. How many times have you said, "Does that really go?" If you're not confident in your decorating abilities or in getting the best use of your space, you will be after some practice and a little help from us.

Spend some time leafing through catalogues and magazines and roaming through furniture stores (or on the Internet if you can't get out of the house). Pay close attention to what you like and what gives you an immediate "not in my house" reaction. You can make your house more inviting in ways that won't break your bank; for example, by providing personal services and drawing on your own talents. Getting the most out of your B&B means creating little touches such as soft lighting to enhance an important space such as a cozy sitting area.

Just Say No to Decorative Ducks

Okay, there's nothing wrong with ducks. We're not suggesting that all you duck collectors toss your assembled fowl aside. We just don't want you to think that because you now own a B&B you need to run out and buy an antique spoon collection.

Antiques are lovely—in old homes and in newer ones—but they're not a requirement for owning a B&B. Find a style that matches your personality and the personality of your home.

Decorating Flair

One of the biggest tricks to having a flair for decorating is knowing what will make you happy, now and next year. Your house will evolve and guests will love to see the changes you make over the years, but it's best to find a basic style that you can build on. You might not have the money to spend to completely redecorate your house five years from now, so make sure you not only like those Egyptian art pieces, but they'll still go with the house and be a hit with the guests in 2006.

Inn the Know

If you're planning to build in a wall of fish tanks, take your interior design into account before you renovate. Have your decorator (if you're planning to hire one) sit down with your architect to make sure you're all on the same page. If you're rehabbing your entire house (or most of it) and you need to design things such as the heating ducts, pulling in contractors early on could be a benefit.

When you're hunting for room fixtures or furnishings, find things that will work well in several or all of your rooms. You might buy an antique blanket chest that you think will work well at the foot of the bed in a particular room and then remember—after lugging it home—that it has a fireplace only inches away. If it won't work in any of your other rooms, you could be stuck with it.

Even if you have theme rooms, having some common elements is nice and it might save you some money if you buy in bulk. You or your decorator might be able to get a better deal on ten sets of recessed lighting fixtures than on five. It all depends on how much work your decorator will be doing for you. If he or she is working as an hourly consultant or will buy all the furnishings for you there might be a discount, but the decorator will pocket the 10, 15, or 20 percent commission, and the savings won't be passed along to you. If you order some things directly (see Chapter 14, "Stocking Up on Supplies"), you'll save some money. Be careful when you buy items at discount or "off-price" stores. Items such as poorly made bed skirts or bedspreads may cheapen your rooms and cost you more because you'll have to replace them sooner.

If you can't afford to hire an interior decorator on a permanent or even part-time basis, consider consulting with one. A good one will listen to your likes and dislikes and help you develop a style that is uniquely yours and works well with your house.

Coffee Talk

Meredith Blakely of Cape Cod Interiors, Inc., in Orleans, Massachusetts, suggests choosing an interior decorator who'll work with your tastes and will see a project through completion. "When you hire a design firm, make sure that everything is guaranteed, so that when something needs fixing, they'll come back and do it. Don't be intimidated by anyone who calls him- or herself a decorator. If the person doesn't seem to listen and act on your requests, don't waste any more time with that decorator. Look for one who will listen to your suggestions. This *is your* vision."

You'll want each room to have its own charm. That's part of the reason guests will stay with you rather than at the Hilton down the street. Spend some time in each room and pick out focal points. Maybe you have hardwood floors in one room and a great view in another. One room could have great space, allowing you to buy that sleigh bed you've always wanted; another room is smaller but has a great spot for a window seat. Returning guests might have favorite rooms but they'll have fun discovering the charm of your other rooms, too.

Sensing Atmosphere

The first thing people will notice when they step into your house is how the place looks. Without even realizing it, they'll also sense your atmosphere. If it lacks warmth or it's too bright or smells like something that lives under your kitchen sink, that will hit guests at the door, too. If the mood in your house isn't comfortable, you might have some wonderful furnishings or lovely art that will go unnoticed.

Make sure that your house has a neutral smell all the time so that when you bake or burn candles, the scent won't have to compete with smoke or other strong aromas. You also don't want to cover up smells; it doesn't work. If you have a hankering for fried fish, make sure you crank open that window; or better yet, open a can of tuna! Have good ventilation in your kitchen for those times when you do cook for yourself. If your famous lasagna wafts into the living room where guests are thinking about how hungry they are, it might remind them that they could have stayed in a full-service hotel.

Having a good look to your rooms means having a bright, clean atmosphere. Unless your theme is medieval England, guests will want to see brightness and light, fresh flowers, and comfortable sitting areas. Bring your outside views inside by putting windows in all the right places and making sure they're open at the best times of the day.

Coffee Talk

Col. (ret.) John and Julie Rolsen, owners and inn-keepers of Garth Woodside Mansion Bed and Breakfast in Hannibal, Missouri, have learned a few tricks on breaking the ice with guests. "To make the guests comfortable we put them at ease when they arrive. We offer warm chocolate chip cookies (fresh from the oven), lemonade, hot tea, coffee, and soda. We also have a five dollar bill glued to the stairs. Many guests try to pick it up. When they ask about our little prank, I tell them a very famous man once said, 'A little nonsense, now and then, is cherished by the wisest men.' All of these little things help them settle into a comfortable mood right away."

When you're creating atmosphere, aim for the right degrees of light, sound, and motion in each room:

➤ **Light.** Your house will feel different at different times of the day. Open blinds to morning sunlight and then use soft lighting and candles to create a quieter mood in the evening. If you have guests checking into their rooms during evening hours when the sun is almost down, fix blinds so that they're partially closed, ready for nighttime but not shutting out the world just yet. Make sure blinds and drapes will shade light but not block it out completely. We all need some natural light to wake up or we'd turn into Rumplestilskins! The lighting in a room can set the perfect mood—or ruin it.

➤ **Sound.** A crackling fire in the winter or soft classical music during a storm are soothing sounds, unlike noise from trucks going by and the neighbor's crackpot dog. You'll get used to the noises in and around your house but any intruding or unpleasant sounds will be new to your guests. Spending time in each of your rooms at different times of the day is a good way to stay in tune with the different sounds that float in and out.

➤ **Motion.** No, we're not talking about a revolving restaurant on top of your B&B! The *motion* of a room refers to how everything in that room evokes movement. Adding a swivel or rocking chair to a corner encourages traffic flow. Not everything needs to be bunched against one wall just because it's there. If you create a resource center with brochures and information about your local area, make sure it's readily accessible. Put it on a table in a hallway or in a corner of a room where people don't have to cross busy areas to get to it. When you're thinking about room flow, zero in on how each room invites you in without making you feel cramped or lost in space.

Creating Theme Rooms

A lot of B&Bs use their own hobbies or personal interests to create a theme in the house or in individual rooms. Guests love this stuff. They eat it right up, particularly if you have some kind of connection to your themed ideas. Maybe you're a fan of western movie stars and have a ranch in North Dakota. Or, you love *film noir* and have a cliffside house in Maine. Don't feel compelled to have themes in every room; a little can go a long way. If you opt for a more mainstream B&B you can still add in bits of the unconventional. You might have one room dedicated to Marilyn Monroe, for example; it's a good way to introduce a theme and find out whether your clientele will think it's fun or find it off-putting. The chances are better that people will like your creativity.

Most B&Bs have "theme" rooms that don't have actual themes, but have names, such as the Raspberry Suite (because of the colors) or the Bill Gates Suite (the most elaborate). It makes it fun for guests to call back and request a room by name.

Inn the Know

Feng shui (*fung shway*) is the Chinese art of placement and balance. Most popularly used in the West to reconfigure space, it theorizes that positive energy in a room can be achieved through the placement of angles, corners, and furniture. People in the West find these concepts helpful in designing room flow. Check out *The Complete Idiot's Guide to Feng Shui* by Elizabeth Moran and Val Biktashev.

B&B-eware!

It's sad but true; there are thieves out there. Most guests who have an inclination to steal will take the oddest things, not because they need them but because they have the opportunity. If you're worried about valuable items or family heirlooms, don't put them out.

Small Touches Make a Big Difference

Guests might not tell you about the little things they notice but those little touches will affect their stay. A loveseat can look stiff without the right throw pillow; or crowded with too many. Providing coasters on a coffee table will let people know that it's okay to have food and drink in a sitting area, and it also will save your tabletops. Hiding electronics such as the television, VCR, and stereo in freestanding cabinets or in the walls can save space and provide a clean look when cabinet doors are shut. A quiet air conditioner or heater can be heaven-sent when guests are trying to sleep. As you go along you'll pick up little things that will make rooms more comfortable. Staying alert to what works and what doesn't work is the key.

Working with What You Have

You might have a house with some odd space and some rooms that don't work out as you'd imagined they would. Maybe you'll spend time working on fitting things into a smaller room, only to find that a larger room presents an even greater challenge.

Working with what you have means listening to what your rooms tell you. They might say, "hey, that might fit in here but it will make me look cramped!" or "what are you thinking?" Maybe your rooms will give more subtle hints, but paying attention to whatever they suggest will make them stand-outs.

The Small Room

You'd like to have a canopy bed in room 4 but you think it will make the room look too cramped; you're probably right. Don't think that you have to have that canopy bed or any other common B&B furnishing. If it doesn't work, bag it.

B&B-eware!

Glossy paint will make cracks and weird curves in walls pop right out. Use flat paint or wallpaper to hide imperfections.

There are many ways to make a small room comfortable. Think about minimizing those furnishings to rid the space of a cramped feeling. If a queen size bed will not fit in a room, use two twin beds or a twin and a day bed, possibly at different angles; you can offer it as a kids' room or a single if traveling companions want separate beds. Use an upholstered chair without arms or a small nightstand with shelves underneath for more storage.

Speaking of storage, how about that space under the bed? It's a great place for pull-out drawers. Just make sure to tell guests that they exist, as sometimes a hidden space such as this is overlooked.

Creating Little Havens in a Big Space

It's once again time to evaluate your space for its best and highest use (a real estate phrase meaning that your rooms will achieve their highest value). This means that, before you start buying furniture, determine the potential of the space based on the type of clientele you have: romantic couples, families, or business travelers. You won't be able to accommodate all three types in one room but you can usually meet the needs of two. Families need more convertible space (such as more sleeping areas or cribs) while business travelers need more work space or sitting areas. The romantics will look for a fireplace or cozy nooks. Once again, matching your clientele's criteria to what you can offer will only help market your rooms.

Big rooms can be a lot of fun to create because you have more options. If one of your rooms is big enough for a king size bed, don't feel as if you have to put one in. Maybe that space could be used for another chair or a small table. Or, if the space isn't too large, leave it alone. Most guests expect a queen size bed and will be happy enough with that, especially if it means more space in the room. If the space is large, but not large enough to break into two rooms, add in another bed to accommodate either a third guest or traveling companions who need separate sleeping areas. This will be a necessity for some guests and an attractive option for others.

If you have space to create a sitting area, even a small one, definitely go that way; a sitting area will allow you to bump up the room to "suite" status. People will always pay for more space; it's one of the best amenities you can offer.

When you're looking at a big room and what to do with it, concentrate on what will make the space most comfortable, not on how to fill it up. Buy a small settee or loveseat (don't forget the potential for third person income) that will work well with a chair or a tall plant. Make sure that guests can move around your furniture and spread out in that spacious room.

Odd Common Areas

Maybe you have low eaves near your stairs or a weird crawl space. Turn this space into storage or a library, with small stools and a basket of magazines. If the space is too small for functional use, consider decorating it with a large antique, for example, that will add a nice touch. But before you run out and buy a desk and chair, think about whether the space would really be utilized. A desk might be put to better use in a common area or in a guest room. Keep this thought in mind: have measuring tape, will travel.

Shoestring Solution

Don't like those cabinet doors in your kitchen or living room? Take them off! Paint the trim and use the open shelves to display dishes or books. It will save you the ton of money that new cabinet doors would have cost, and it'll look as if you did it on purpose!

Amenities for Every Room

There are industry standards that stretch across the board such as providing a comfortable bed, clean sheets and towels, and drawers or a closet. Then there are the industry standards at each level of service. At the highest level, the standards are a queen size bed, glass shower door, marble (somewhere in the bath), and a Jacuzzi tub. Standard at the lowest level of service are a clean but worn room with a shower curtain and a comfy bed. As the industry grows to meet guests' expectations, little bottles of shampoo and television/VCR equipment in rooms are becoming standards at every level of service.

There are some amenities that guests might expect everywhere they go (queen size bed and private bath) and some that will be appreciated (having binoculars available for bird watching). Guest expectations are increasing, and some will find it odd if they don't have a television or a clock radio in their room.

No matter what you provide, your amenities should always match the perceived value of the particular room. That might seem difficult at first, but finding out what comparable houses have done to match their rates with what they offer in a room (covered in Chapter 7, "All About Room Rates") is a good place to start.

When you compare your house with that of your competition, watch out for the "if I build it, they will come" thoughts that will tiptoe into your head. They'll lead to "amenity creep"; that is, houses competing to match one another in amenities. All things are relative. What's appreciated at the B&B down the street might not be appreciated at yours, and vice versa. You probably don't need a whirlpool tub in every room because it won't be the draw for every guest who chooses your B&B. Only honeymooners and other couples will get full use out of one, but it probably would be wasted on families, seniors, singles, and business travelers.

Basic Expectations

When you describe your rooms on your Web site or on the phone, make sure that you mention your basics. The longer the list of standard amenities you have in every room, the more you'll entice clientele by saying "every room comes with terry cloth robes, television/VCR equipment, and so on." Your standard amenities could include the following:

➤ **Queen size bed/high-quality mattresses.** A queen size bed is the lodging industry standard across the board. Good-quality mattresses are not negotiable. Full or twin size beds are fine but make sure you market these rooms to people who might not mind a single bed or twin beds. That would include older couples, friends, and kids. For example, if you have an eight-room inn that can accommodate all queen beds, who will be unhappy? Few people. Also keep in mind, however, that rooms with smaller double beds might be popular because you'll probably price them lower.

➤ **Private bath.** You might not be able to have a private bath in every room, but understand that guests will expect one unless they're told otherwise. If you have two rooms connected by a shared bath, you can get a family to take them, but it won't happen all the time. When you're prequalifying a guest who will take only one of these rooms, make sure they know the situation.

➤ **Television.** It's true; it's one of those expected things. If you don't have one for every room, consider buying one or two television/VCR combos (they're really cheap now) and a selection of movies that you can take to a guest room on request. Put VCRs in your best rooms, where they'll be expected; not in your smaller or least expensive rooms.

➤ **Telephone.** If you don't have phones in the rooms, have one or two phones for guest use only. Not having a phone solely for guest use will become annoying for them and a nuisance for you (count on getting requests to use your business line).

➤ **Ice bucket with ice and drinking glasses.** When you're considering the type of glasses to buy, know the levels of quality: Glass is preferable, next would be high-quality molded plastic, then disposable plastic (or an attractive plastic) or wax-coated paper. If you don't provide ice service in rooms, or allow guests access to the kitchen at night, or have an ice machine, you might want to consider getting an insulated chest or small fridge to store ice in a common area. Unless your clientele is older, you'll have late arrivals who will appreciate having ice and other amenities available in your absence.

➤ **Small appliances.** A hair dryer and an iron and ironing board available will be expected. If you don't install them in the rooms, have several on hand for guests to use.

B&B-eware!

Your most expensive room will get the most amenities, but don't throw all of them into that one. In a way, this will neutralize the quality of the house overall, even though you have one "fantastic" room.

Inn the Know

A voicemail system for you and guests can be a great way to go. Guests don't have to worry about missing calls and you don't have to worry about taking messages. Voicemail can be expensive in some areas, depending on what features you get. For business travelers and younger couples, though, it's a highly desirable amenity.

➤ **Clock radio.** Gotta have it! Some people prefer a wake-up call because they sleep through their alarms, but save yourself some time in calling rooms that do fine with alarm clocks. Make sure you get a decent radio/alarm clock with a CD player. Not everyone likes to wake to the sound of buzzing, and you've added a nice amenity without a great expenditure.

➤ **Ceiling fan.** A ceiling fan is a must, too. Not only will it instantly make the room more comfortable, it's the best way to help ventilate odd smells. We don't have to tell you that either heat or air conditioning is standard, depending on the climate. Having both is a luxury. After all, it can get cool in Key West and warm in Winnipeg (sometimes).

➤ **Soap/shampoo/lotion.** These items will not be a huge expense if bought in bulk and will be looked for by guests. Make sure to get well-known brands or brands that use mild ingredients. Guests who break out in rashes are not good for business! The quality range is as follows: lowest are recognizable brands; then those that have your name branded on them; and then, above that, boutique brands and botanicals. Overnight business travelers will be looking for Dial soap. Guests staying with you longer will look for something a little different such as a boutique brand. Botanicals are all the rage now!

Shoestring Solution

Some services such as nightly turndown and breakfast in bed can be just as appreciated as amenities. For more on guest services see Chapter 18, "Guest Services with a Smile."

Making Each Room a Stand-Out

Want to add more perks to rooms but don't have $30,000 to spend on whirlpool tubs? Try adding these first:

➤ **Mini-fridge.** Even if guests use them only to keep their spring water cold, they'll love this feature. You can buy very small fridges that fit neatly into cabinets and in small kitchen areas. Having a fridge also will keep people who are searching for ice out of your kitchen!

➤ **Coffee maker and supplies.** Great for early risers. Don't forget to include tea bags, nondairy creamer, and all variations of sweeteners. Also make sure that you get a sturdy brand that is easy to keep clean.

➤ **Digital safe.** Guests will feel secure about you and staff entering the room when they're gone if they have a small safe in which to hide their cash and valuables.

➤ **Heat-vent-light things.** We're not sure what they're called, but you know what we mean. Hotels have them installed in bathrooms so that guests can quickly heat up the room or ventilate the steam.

➤ **Bath salts and aromatherapy.** Guests will be surprised to find bath salts. Stay away from candles in the rooms; instead, provide a lovely spray scent that guests can use at will.

➤ **Towel warmer.** It doesn't take up that much space and is so very nice. These could be either the hard-wired or plug-in type.

➤ **Night lights.** Having a night light in the bath will save energy and is just the perfect amount of light when someone gets up in the night. It's also a nice alternative to candles (honeymooners usually attempt to sneak in their own).

➤ **Bedside reading lamps.** Again, a low wattage bulb in a small lamp could save energy and is a nice option. Just make sure that the lamps are not too close to sheets or drapes, as some can get extremely hot when left on a long time. (It also is a good idea to forewarn guests that lamps will get hot.)

➤ **Dimmer lights.** Having one set of dimmer lights in a room might be all you need. If you're doing a full rehab to your house, dimmer lights, along with recessed lighting, is easier to install. If you can't afford dimmer lights, you can get lamps with dimmers or different levels of light.

➤ **Extra-nice bedding.** Down or feather comforters and pillows and chenille or flannel throws make sleeping areas super comfy, particularly if the weather is cool in your area. Make sure that you have nonfeathered items on hand (having both feathered and non-feathered pillows in the room is a nice option) for those plagued with allergies.

Only have $100 to make rooms nice? Here are our picks for finishing off a room on a low budget: deck of cards, coffee maker and supplies, Bible or "feel good about yourself book," a few videotapes (especially if you haven't built up a collection in the common room yet), some classic paperbacks, and a night light. It's the little things, you know?

Working Up to Jacuzzi

What if you can't afford to install a pool or Jacuzzi now, as you had hoped? No biggie. Working up to bigger amenities can be a better way to go. Installing a swimming pool that gets no use from your business traveling clientele is just, well, useless. What a waste of hard-earned money! Stay in business by slowly adding amenities every year and seeing how they do. Pay attention to what guests inquire about when they call to make reservations, what they comment on when they leave, and what your competition is providing.

If you want to have resort-style amenities and you can spare the change, don't hold back. Guests with money to burn are staying with B&Bs that suit their lifestyle. Why not yours? The following are some of the amenities that will raise you to resort-style status:

➤ **Jacuzzi and/or sauna.** If your clientele are singles and couples—minus the kids—this will be well used.

➤ **Deck or patio.** Outdoor sitting areas off rooms or common areas can be a great way to gain more living space and they'll allow you to bump up those rates.

➤ **Swimming pool.** This is a really nice feature to add if you have the space, money, and can get the town's approval for it. Make sure to follow all safety regulations, and caution guests who use it at night to not disturb your neighbors and your other guests. Otherwise, count on some sleepless nights.

B&B-eware!

Big amenity equals big liability. If you plan to have a pool, you might need to have a sign that says "No lifeguard on duty," and staff that has CPR training. Regulations will differ in every locale. If having a pool or Jacuzzi on premises will make you shudder in fear of an accident don't go this route. Check out Chapter 6, "Legalities and Liabilities," for more on liability and getting good insurance.

➤ **Fireplaces.** Even if guests don't use them, they love knowing that they could. If you decide to have working fireplaces that burn wood, your insurance company will consider it a big liability, which it is. Having an ornamental fireplace can be fine, but be careful to not represent it as a working fireplace. If your fireplace uses gas or propane, we suggest that you don't try to save money by using a timer on it. If you're going to provide a fireplace as an amenity, up your room rates accordingly.

➤ **Bathrobes.** They're especially appreciated if you have a Jacuzzi or sauna that guests will have to traipse back and forth to.

➤ **Whirlpool tub.** Great not only because it's shooting aerated water at you; don't we all sleep better after a nice hot bath?

➤ **Kitchen.** If you have a cottage or a big room with a sitting area, a kitchen will be a big incentive for guests to stay with you longer than a few days.

➤ **Data ports.** A great option for business travelers. For more on amenities you can provide for suits on the move, see Chapter 18.

➤ **Magazines and books.** Having them in a common room or on a hallway table is cheap—and a nice invitation for guests to make themselves at home. Do keep magazines and books out of bathrooms. Enough said.

Building on Your Talents

Everyone can do something. Everyone is special. Maybe your special talent is playing the saw or shoveling a fry in your nose and out your mouth.

These talents might not be put to their best use at your B&B (except on those rainy days) so you might want to learn how to upholster furniture or take good photographs. Other talents that you can build on, such as sewing and doing your own repairs, will save you more than just some pocket money.

If you're an art school dropout or have a hidden talent for painting, why not exploit it? Paint a small mural of a historical spot in town, or stencil away. Someone we know, not a B&B owner, once painted an "antique brass" headboard behind a bed. Most people who saw it thought it was the real thing!

You don't need the talents of Monet to add appeal to your B&B. Maybe you sew well, and can make your own duvet covers. Good at building models? Work on some to display in the house. Restoring old furniture is pretty easy and there are some great techniques out there to make newer pieces look old—and vice versa. If your real talent is cooking, definitely concentrate on it. Consider serving a full breakfast or have afternoon tea. Maybe send guests home with goodie bags of your favorite bread, or offer packed lunches.

Any way that you can build on your personal talents will make you and the atmosphere of your B&B stand out. Guests will know that you truly love being their host and that you're going out of your way for them.

The Least You Need to Know

➤ Owning a B&B doesn't mean you need traditional or old-fashioned looks. Your decorating flair should come from your own personal style and what works in the house.

➤ Create atmosphere and add small touches to put guests at ease.

➤ Work with the space you have to create a cozy atmosphere in big and small rooms.

➤ Guests will expect standard amenities such as phones and welcome the possibility of staying in a room with a luxurious amenity such as a fireplace.

Chapter 14

Stocking Up on Supplies

In This Chapter

➤ Getting a handle on what you need in each room

➤ Learning the smart way to buy and stock up on perishables

➤ Using your own resources to have some fun and save some clams

---

If you feel as if you spend half your life at the grocery store now, just wait until you're up and running! Already open for business? Reading this chapter will help you streamline costs and save time that you normally spend scurrying around store aisles. Those of you who love to shop will love running a B&B, but if shopping isn't your bag, you'll find ways to make it less taxing in this chapter.

Stocking Up on Goods

Obviously, most of your shopping will be for meals and cleaning and bathroom supplies. Just as in your own home, keeping on top of what's in your pantry and closets will keep you from running out. There will be times when you need to "run out" for milk or juice for yourself, but planning ahead will keep these last-minute trips to a minimum.

Shopping doesn't end at the grocery store. The B&B is a business within your home (for most of you), which means that you'll need to shop for the kitchen (meals and supplies), guest bedrooms, guest bathrooms, guest kitchen areas, common bathrooms and living areas, lawn and garden, and the office. On top of gathering provisions for each area of the house, you'll need cleaning and maintenance supplies (paper towels, light bulbs, and so on) and accessories for special circumstances (such as buckets to chill wine bought by guests).

Inn the Know

Some of the decorative items for a room, such as throw pillows, can be bought through your designer (if you hire one); but you should still write down what each room needs and then make notes (or different lists) on how many you'll buy and where.

At startup, shopping will be a huge undertaking. You'll need to determine which items should be bought well before you open (office supplies), just before you open (pantry items), and what can wait until after you're in business (hair dryers in every room as opposed to keeping a few on hand).

Writing Out the "A" Lists

If you're starting the business from scratch, buying everything at once will be overwhelming but it will be fun, too. To keep it fun, make sure you're efficient in your shopping excursions. There's nothing worse than driving an hour to a warehouse supply store only to come home and realize that you forgot toilet paper.

Before you head to the store for any item, from sugar substitute to pillow protectors, make lists for everything. Start by going from room to room and listing the accessories and necessities needed for each one. With the exception of furniture and items such as carpet and drapes, your list might include items such as these:

➤ **Kitchen** (excluding food and appliances and depending on the type of breakfast served). Potholders (keep some clean ones to use when carrying items to the table); pots and pans (variety of iron skillets and stainless steel for everything else—no aluminum!); griddle, crock pot, and cooking utensils (ladles, wooden spoons, spatulas, and so on); baking utensils (large measuring cup and individual measuring cups); serving utensils and can openers (manual and electric); large canisters (for flour, sugar, and other baking ingredients); bottle opener with corkscrew; cookie sheets; heavy duty and lint-free dish towels; and serving trays.

➤ **Dining area.** If you'll be serving your breakfast buffet style, you'll need to set aside a small area where guests can deposit dirty dishes and garbage. A rolling cart with bus tubs (available from American Hotel Register or restaurant supply firms) can do the trick nicely. You'll also need different sets of complementary china, glassware and flatware, dozens of cloth napkins and very high quality throwaways, tablecloths, serving dishes, juice containers, carafes for hot beverages, a couple of salt-and-pepper sets, sugar containers, and hot plates.

➤ **Guest rooms.** Bed pillows; one or two throw pillows; linens including pillow cases, sheets, mattress pads, duvets (comforters) and covers; throws for bed or comfy chair; pillows for daybed; terry cloth robes; drinking glasses; ice bucket; tissues; light bulbs for each fixture; non-skid material for area rugs; and hangers for closets (no wire hangers).

Shoestring Solution

Make sure to buy dish sets, flatware, and glassware with patterns that complement one another. Dishes and glasses will break and silverware can get thrown out so make sure to buy from well-known companies so they can easily be replaced! Even so, a company might discontinue a popular pattern, so keep an eye on it (have their mail-order catalogue sent to you), and if they do discontinue your favorites, buy extra pieces. Items planned for discontinuation sometimes are discounted, so this could be a good thing!

➤ **Guest bathrooms.** Towels; toilet paper; complimentary toiletries (shampoo, soap, hand lotion); nightlight; toilet brush (concealed in attractive container); hair dryer; shower curtains; throw-away shower caps; smaller drinking glasses; spray scents; shaving or cosmetic mirror; and waste basket.

➤ **Guest kitchen.** Coffee maker and supplies, flatware and tray, small set of dishes, mugs, glassware, dish towels, garbage pail and plastic liners, sponges, scrubbing pads, dish soap, bottle opener, and paper napkins.

➤ **Common bathrooms.** Hand soap, hand towels or disposable towels for drying hands, spray scents, and waste basket.

➤ **Common living areas.** Coasters, book and video library (buy a few at the get-go and then add on whenever you can), magazine and newspaper subscriptions, nonskid material for area rugs, candles, and small lights for evening.

➤ **Lawn and garden.** Sand buckets for smokers, potting soil, gardening gloves, garden implements, standalone lighting for summer evenings, citronella buckets, fertilizer, edger, and edge cutter.

➤ **Office.** Reservation materials (booking calendar, reservation forms, and so on), receipt booklet, calculator with printout, small pocket-size calculator, Post-its, stapler, tape, lined notepads, small pocket-sized notepads (for you and staff), graph paper, printer paper, dry-erase board with markers, waste basket, ample supply of pens and permanent markers, and files and file folders.

➤ **Cleaning.** Multi-purpose cleaner in concentrate formula (see Chapter 19, "Housekeeping Basics," for more on this subject); spray bottles (for cleaners and misting plants—make sure you keep them labeled); cleaning rags (buy sturdy cloth and make your own or buy in bulk); scrub brushes, sponges for the kitchen buckets or baskets to hold cleaning supplies, tub and tile cleaner, bleach, wood cleaner, floor cleaner, dusting spray, brooms, and a dust pan set. You'll want a heavy-duty vacuum as well as a small hand-held electric or battery-operated one for quick clean-ups.

Inn the Know

If you're buying a B&B already in business, make sure you get details from the owner on quantities bought during different seasons and the complete list of suppliers and vendors that products were purchased from. Contact the vendors and find out whether all of their accounts have been paid up—before the owners are out of your life for good. If there are any outstanding bills, the vendors will definitely let you know.

➤ **Extras.** Light bulbs, paper towels, various baskets and decorative containers (to hold everything from tourist information to kindling wood), matches, heavy-duty plastic storage containers of all sizes (they can hold extra linens and things bought in bulk), flashlights, first-aid kit, batteries of all sizes, flower vases of different sizes, baskets or other containers for large plants, a couple of sturdy pairs of scissors (to cut everything from paper to peonies), extra night lights, and door mats.

Work from this general list of items to create individual shopping lists or make notes on where items will be purchased and in what quantities. You'll have different lists for ordering from catalogues, on the Internet, your interior decorator, discount warehouses, and local stores. Hunting around for the best bargains is always worth the time. Keep track of all receipts and credit card bills so you'll know when you're going overboard!

Pesky Perishables

You'll get the hang of shopping—what to buy and when—after you've been in business a while and have made some mistakes. To plan for breakfasts that you hope people will eat (as usually is the case), you'll need to have one part intuition and one part common sense. Sometimes you won't be able to predict what will be consumed at all; one day your guests will eat all of your breakfast and the next day they might not touch much of anything—or even show up!

Coffee Talk

Rainer Horn and Jürgen Herzog, owners of the Carpe Diem Guesthouse in Provincetown, Massachusetts, suggest depriving guests of the satisfaction of the midnight munchies if you want to be able to serve the breakfast you planned for the next day. "Our favorite stories are of coming into the kitchen in the morning and finding the cake that had been pre-pared the day before for the morning's breakfast, taken out of a zip lock bag or other kind of container, and eaten, halfway or entirely. Great way to start a morning! Now we 'hide' from our guests all the goodies that are baked and meant for the next day!"

Overestimating your groceries is common. When you're at the market, you might think "those Gala apples aren't on my list but they look nice" or "maybe I should get a gallon of milk because I had a few guests this morning drink more than the usual." Getting carried away at the store is easy. How many times have you gone shopping for yourself without a list and come home with fudge cookies, gourmet olives, and beer? Resisting the temptation to pick up the wrong things or to buy things that aren't on your list is difficult but not impossible. Control the urge to overbuy food that might go to waste by making complete and realistic lists. Stay on top of those ex-piration dates so you're not pouring those savings down the drain. Juice and creamer can last a month; milk maybe only a couple of weeks. You'll save a lot of money.

Many B&Bs offer the same selection of dishes every day. Sticking to a handful of dishes doesn't mean that the innkeeper lacks creativity; it's a smart way to do business. Crea-ting new meals requires shopping for extra ingredients and guessing at what guests might consume. As most guest stays are under a week, hosts are able to rotate a few dishes and still provide variety. You'll save money in the long run because you'll know exactly what to buy and how much to make for the number of guests you have. Even if a guest stays with you for a long time and gets a few of the same meals twice, they won't complain, especially if the dishes have become favorites!

Along with ingredients you need for making breakfasts and ready-to-go breakfast items (such as juices), don't forget …

➤ Lots of coffee, assorted teas (including decaf versions), and instant cocoa; coffee filters and individual coffee packets for rooms with coffee makers.

➤ Nondairy creamer.

➤ Sugar, sugar substitute packets, and honey.

181

➤ Paper lunch bags, hot and cold disposable cups, plastic ware and paper napkins for quick breakfasts or snacks for guest on the go.

➤ Drinking straws.

➤ Toothpicks.

➤ Snack foods that you can offer to late arrivals.

➤ Sparkling juice or wine to give as gifts to guests celebrating a special occasion.

➤ Chocolates for nightly turndown service.

➤ Hard candy for the reception area.

B&B-eware!

Make lists that make sense. If you have only two guests in the house, why would you buy the same number of eggs that you'd buy for six? If the same two guests didn't touch your cranberry-raspberry smoothie, don't buy more cranberry juice. It's difficult to judge what new guests will and won't eat before they show up, but pay attention to their eating habits during their stay and plan accordingly.

Getting produce vendors who'll deliver right to your door can be a great time saver and delivery will cost you little (if anything at all). Give vendors precise details on exactly what brands, quantities, and sizes you want; do the same with staff when you send them out shopping.

You might need to (or want to) send staffers out regularly for supplies, so start out by taking them on a shopping excursion that ends with a light lunch. Show them exactly how to find the items and quality that you prefer. They'll learn the quickest route to your staples, how to choose produce and dairy for freshness, and you can build on your employee/owner relationship.

Provisions You Can't Eat

The best way to keep on top of your nonperishable inventory is to keep track of your stock on a regular basis. After you get into the swing of things, you'll know when you need to go on a big wholesale shopping trip or go to the office supply store before you run out of computer paper.

If your staff generally cleans guest rooms, make it part of their job to alert you when supplies are running low. There are some great discount "odd job" stores out there that sell everything from Cheerios to lawn gnomes. Frequenting these stores (as brands and quantities can change weekly) can save you some money. You don't have to buy your paper towels at the grocery store. Why would you when they're cheaper at a discount place? Just make sure that the quality is up to snuff and that the quantity matches the deal. A roll of paper towels with 80 sheets for 80 cents is no deal compared to a roll of 125 sheets for 95 cents. Sniff out those bargains the best you can but don't kill yourself over it. If something is a deal, buy it and move on.

What to Buy in Bulk

Wholesale places can be great places to get stuff in bulk. The biggest dangers in going wholesale are getting things you don't need such as 30 bottles of maple syrup (only 96 cents per bottle!), and not always getting a good deal. Buying perishables in bulk is rarely an option either because, well, they're perishable. The best thing about buying from wholesale stores is that you'll save shopping time by stocking up. Things that are good to buy in bulk are office supplies, paper products (including coffee filters), dish detergent and most cleaning supplies, and tea and coffee. Note that tea and coffee quality can diminish after several weeks, so as with all dry goods, store it in a cool, dry place.

The other difficulty in buying things in bulk is storage. Having under-the-sink storage in guest rooms will help. You can spread out your stock of tissues and toilet paper among the rooms. Having a pantry or a dry cellar with a storage area will be a great advantage. If you're short on storage space, don't buy a huge quantity of toilet paper. You might have saved money but do you really want to stare at it under the coffee table for a few weeks?

Here's a good rule of thumb to follow when choosing brands: Try to purchase brand name foods for anything that will appear on your table, and use the "no-names" for cooking and baking. At whatever level you buy, always choose quality products.

Online and Catalogue Shopping

The Internet and catalogues are great places to shop. Clicking on a few icons or ordering over the phone and then having boxes show up at your door saves a lot of time. You'll have to venture out for most things, but items such as linens, towels, laundry bags, bathroom fixtures, and plaques and signs can be bought through distributors specializing in the hotel and lodging industry. You also can order insignia robes, staff shirts, branded soaps, and even mattresses!

Check out these distributors on the Web:

➤ **www.americanhotel.com.** This is the site for American Hotel Registry (1-800-323-5686), one of the biggest and best distributors for the lodging industry.

➤ www.lodgemart.com. Lodging merchandise at a discount.

➤ www.e-hospitality.com. A really big site focused primarily on hotels and big business but worth a look. In addition to merchandise, they have hospitality industry news, a career center, and software you can download.

➤ www.paii.org. PAII has a vendor marketplace where vendors advertise their wares. Most are small-time, but it's worth checking out for unique items.

➤ www.staples.com. Ordering supplies online is a snap.

When you choose items on the Net or from a catalogue, make sure you know exactly what you're getting. If you order the wrong item, size, or color, you'll have to spend money to send it back (in most cases), and wait for the replacement. A good way to shop is to look in stores for what you want and then head to catalogues or online distributors to see if you can get a better deal. Watch out for delivery charges; the bigger the object, the more it will cost you to have it delivered.

Big Equipment Must-Haves

Do yourself a favor and get good quality equipment that will last for several years. Check out *Consumer Reports* (www.consumerreports.org) for ratings on brands, the durability of models, and price and quality comparisons. Online subscribers have access to their current reports but you can purchase their buying guides, subscribe to the print magazine, and obtain individual reports for a fee on the Web site.

Laundry Facilities

If you don't use a laundry service, consider getting a highly rated, large capacity, heavy-duty washer. Front loaders wash better and save water. Dryers tend to be a little more straightforward, and having a second one does become helpful if you have more than six rooms. Get a long table in your laundry center so you have a place for folding, folding, and folding again. Commercial washers and dryers will last longer and be more efficient, but also consider upfront costs, space required, and the potentially higher cost of repair. We suggest that, if you have more than four guest rooms, you seriously consider sending out the bulk of your laundry. You might save some money doing it yourself—then again you might not. Consider the money spent on energy, water, detergent, fabric softeners, and bleach, not to mention your time and your aching back. Think about it: With a full house you (or staff) might spend hours dragging dirty laundry around, putting loads in, and folding everything. Professional laundries iron and press sheets and pillow cases for a crisp effect. Most laundries charge by the pound; be certain that your laundry charges are based on the weight of the clean and dry product. For more on laundry services, see Chapter 19.

Inn the Know

No matter who does your laundry (you or a service) you still need to make the bed and replace the towels with clean, dry stock. In most instances you won't be able to wait until the first set is clean and dry, so you'll need extra linens. Keep in mind, however, that you might have to wait even longer for a service to return your laundry than you would if you do it yourself. That means if you use a service you'll probably need to have more than two sets of linens for each room, but only two sets if you do your own laundry.

In the Kitchen

Shopping for kitchen appliances and accessories can be a lot of fun. There are so many gadgets out there, you might be tempted to pick up all of them, "just in case." Start with the big guns, then move on to salad spinners and knives that cut through cans. If you already have enough basics such as decent pots and pans, wait to replace them until you really need to. If guests won't see your toaster oven and it works fine, why spend $60 on a new one? For items you do need, consider these tips:

➤ **Fridge.** Stay away from the side-by-sides. Great for a residence and people who have dogs that can open the fridge door (can't get their paws in a side-by-side) but for a B&B, it just isn't the best use of space. The freezer is a tight fit and doesn't accommodate big bags and boxes well.

➤ **Freezer.** Get an extra freezer and stick it in the basement. You'll be glad you did. You can buy bacon and other meats in bulk and keep them nicely tucked away until you need them. Also a must if you don't get an ice machine or a fridge with icemaker.

➤ **Convection oven.** These are great. They're expensive, but if you cook a full breakfast and want that breakfast to be raved about, consider getting one (or a stove with a double oven if you have a bigger B&B). Convection ovens cook food more quickly and evenly and, depending on the size and type of operation you have, your health regulations might require you to purchase one anyway (see Chapter 6 for more on local regulations).

➤ **Dishwasher.** No, don't hire your neighbor's kid! We mean a real dishwasher; one that doesn't require you to rinse the dishes beforehand and is ultra-quiet. A commercial under-the-counter dishwasher with glass racks will be more durable and time-saving than a conventional residential unit but can have the same drawbacks as buying a commercial washer and dryer.

➤ **Microwave.** Remember when they first came out, how huge they were? Microwaves aren't clunky anymore. You can find one that will fit just about anywhere in your kitchen. Make sure that it's not a micro-mini, though, and get one with a rotating plate.

➤ **Icemaker.** Having an icemaker for guest use depends on the number of rooms you have and whether you have a full turndown service that includes rechecking the ice buckets. Keep in mind that some light-duty ice machines don't require drains, but most commercial units will need them. One other thing to consider is that icemakers can be noisy! If you get one that is separate from the fridge, try to place it in an accessible area, but far from any guest rooms.

➤ **Essential accessories.** Toaster and microwave for guest use if you serve continental breakfast, two coffee pots (get the kind made for commercial use that keeps water in reserve so that you just pour in fresh water and out comes your coffee), wooden and plastic cutting boards, blender, juicer, mixer, food processor, and coffee grinder.

Cleaning Essentials

Get a big vacuum with good attachments and a small handheld cleaner for stairs and quick spots. Upright vacuums are easier to tote around and store but the canister kind can be more versatile. If you have a property with more than four rooms, we suggest that you buy two vacuums. Try an upright and a canister and you'll find out which one you like best.

You'll need a floor polisher for waxed floors. You can use a carpet cleaner for small jobs, but having the professionals take care of your wall-to-wall carpets at least once a year can be worth it.

Inn the Know

If you have a really small yard, consider landscaping with a garden and wildflowers so you don't have to worry about the grass getting away from you.

Have a couple of brooms on hand and get a commercial mop and bucket (you know, the kind that first mates use to swab decks in old war movies). There are some broom-like dusters out on the market that are great for reaching high ceilings.

The Great Outdoors (a.k.a. Your Lawn)

If you've already owned a house with a yard or are converting your house into a B&B, chances are you'll have all the equipment you need. If not, depending on your area, you'll need a ride-on mower if you have a large yard (even if you hire someone), a weed trimmer, snow blower, back-saving shovels, salt or sand to melt ice, rakes, wheelbarrow, and a nice-looking shed to put all this stuff in.

Using Your Own Resources

Let's face it. We're living in a time when convenience is king. We even have "convenience stores," designed just for the purpose of saving people from the hassle of going out of their way. Convenience stores, prepared foods, and "all in ones" make our lives easier—but not cheaper. If you have the time and resources to prepare things at home during your off or low season, you'll get a lot of satisfaction out of doing the inconvenient thing. You'll save some money, too, for those busy times when you'll have to go the convenience route.

➤ **Grow stuff.** Growing and drying your own herbs is easy (as long as you can keep them going until they're cut and dried) and they make your kitchen look and smell wonderful. Grow your own chives to throw into omelets. Have a vegetable garden just for your own use. Grow things that are hearty, easy to take care of, and can be used in a variety of dishes.

➤ **Stock up for the cold months.** Grow your own zucchini for batches of zucchini bread that you can freeze. If you attempt to grow fruit such as blueberries (they'll take a few seasons before they get going), you can make preserves for the winter and beyond. Have a great recipe for plain tomato sauce? It can keep for weeks. Make up batches and then pour it into heavy-duty freezer bags. Flatten and squeeze the air out of them so they're easy to thaw.

Inn the Know

If you have acreage that could be put to good use, try moving to the next level in growing stuff. Put in a pumpkin patch or fruit trees. It's a good way to expand the business because you can attract "pickers," weekend drivers looking for something seasonal and fun to do (see Chapter 22, "Expanding the Business," for more on the subject).

Even the smallest attempt to draw on your own resources will help you save some dough and will make you feel extra good in the warm-fuzzy area.

The Least You Need to Know

➤ Organizing your items and streamlining your shopping sprees can save you money and time.

➤ Online and catalogue shopping have broadened your options for buying supplies, large and small.

➤ Save money in the kitchen by waiting to replace equipment that guests won't see.

➤ Using your own resources isn't convenient but can be satisfying and save you money.

Chapter 15

Setting Guest Policies

In This Chapter

➤ Instituting basic guest policies for a smooth operation

➤ Creating house rules for the safety and serenity of *all* guests

➤ Dealing with rule breakers

➤ Changing a policy or rule

Policies schmolicies—who needs them, right? You do! Policies on both ends of the business—for guests and for staff—are a must. Setting policies might seem restrictive but actually has the opposite effect. Guests prefer to have clear boundaries, and employees need policies that clearly define their jobs and responsibilities (see more about staff policies in Chapter 20, "Help Wanted"). Whenever you've stayed at a B&B, chances are you wanted to know three things up front: the rate of your room, check-in and check-out times, and when breakfast is served. These policies are staples; and depending on the type of B&B you run, other policies can be just as important.

Making Policy a Priority

Before you open for business, try to have as many policies in place as possible. Head off potential problems with guests and avoid confusion by telling guests what the policies are and putting them in writing. You can fill in some details, such as the location of guest common areas, during your tour of the house.

When you institute policies do your best to strike a balance; don't go crazy with too many written policies. There's an owner of a small B&B (who shall remain nameless) in a very nice touristy town who uses index card labels for everything. "Please put dirty dishes here." "Please use a plate to keep crumbs off the floor." "Shut the door when sitting on patio to keep out bugs." How can guests relax when they're constantly being told what to do? They can't; the atmosphere at this B&B is very tense, and so are the guests.

You can reduce the number of signs by eliminating petty rules and by making the rules intuitive (instead of a "Don't park here" sign, for example, put flower pots in the space. That way guests naturally do the right thing without feeling that they were lectured).

Coffee Talk

Stephen Mascilo and partner Trevor Pinker of Beaconlight Guesthouse and The Oxford, both in Provincetown, Massachusetts, had a policy of locking the kitchen after 9 P.M. simply because they'd inherited it from the previous owner. When Mascilo and Pinker found that guests were annoyed that they couldn't access the kitchen at night to get ice they asked the previous owner why he'd instituted the rule. He said he'd done it years before, after a guest had helped himself to a midnight treat of fried eggs. When they heard that the rule had been made as a result of just one incident, Mascilo and Pinker abandoned it. Now the kitchen is open at all times and they have yet to smell fried eggs or any other late-night snack.

Whether you inherit policies from a previous owner or you make them yourself, don't be afraid to change them; particularly if there's been a change in your business or your clientele. Just remember to first take a deep breath and think about how the policy change will affect your guests and the business.

Check-In and Check-Out

Some policies might not be necessary for your type of B&B but there are some standard ones that you can't run a B&B without. If you're not strict with any other policy, do yourself a favor and stick to your check-in and check-out times. Keeping control of when your guests come and go will help you to have a smoothly run business and happier guests.

Give yourself enough time to give your departing guests a gracious send-off and your "inn-coming" guests a warm welcome. The absolute worst thing you can do to arriving guests is to make them wait for their room while you or your staff cleans it! Weary travelers don't care that you had a late checkout so you didn't have time to clean the room. They're tired and they want to shower; waiting to check in will give them an attitude that you'll have to work hard to overcome.

Most B&Bs use a check-in time of 2 or 3 P.M. and an 11 A.M. checkout. The 3 P.M. check-in is popular with most establishments because it gives them more time to clean up rooms, which is crucial when there are many check-outs on the same day. If you require a check-in time later than 3 P.M., be prepared to have very few guests— a 4 or 5 P.M. check-in time is just unheard of.

Office Hours

When you're in the business of accommodating strangers, it's a good idea to specify fixed hours during which you're available. You will receive some after-hours calls, but most guests will leave you alone late at night and early in the morning.

Consider starting your office hours at 8 or 9 A.M. and ending them at 9 or 10 P.M., when most guests are in for the night. Having set hours will cut down on early and late calls but it's a good idea to answer the phone during off hours in case of an emergency. If you use an answering machine or voicemail, be sure to check it frequently.

When guests arrive tell them when and how they can reach you and when they'll get your answering machine or voice mail. If you have a Web site, list the hours next to your phone number. We strongly advise you to not include your hours of operation in your brochure or other printed material because your specific hours probably will fluctuate with the seasons.

Inn the Know

If you can swing it, an earlier check-in time is preferable to most guests because it allows them more flexibility. It also will give you more time to make dinner reservations for them and to help them get acquainted with the area.

Breakfast Rules

Your breakfast policies will depend on what kind of breakfast you serve. If you serve a full breakfast, chances are you'll be cooking eggs, toast, and so on—restaurant-style—for one guest at a time unless you specify one or two fixed sittings.

If you offer a buffet-style breakfast where guests can grab coffee and a muffin on their own, definitely keep food out for a designated range of hours. If you have a lot of business travelers, try to accommodate these early risers by having breakfast ready by 7:00 or 7:30 A.M. Vacationers sleep in, so have breakfast available for them until 11:00 A.M.

B&B-eware!

Fight the urge to turn the ringer down on your phone at night unless you have a foolproof way (such as a hot pink neon sign) of reminding yourself to turn it up again the next morning. You might daydream until lunchtime, wondering why it's so quiet, and miss an entire morning of calls!

Always tell guests at check-in time when breakfast will be served. This is one policy that should be written on a card in their rooms as well. You also might consider having a small sign near the breakfast serving area. Having breakfast times posted will cut down on repeating your policy to forgetful guests.

Methods of Payment

These days, most guests pay with plastic, so you might as well use it to your advantage. Avoid no-shows by taking credit card numbers when guests make reservations and charging them right away for 50 percent of the total rate. Charge guests the remaining 50 percent when they check in; don't wait for check-out or you'll be hunting them down—and you could miss a few. Depending on your accounting methods, you can take a 50 percent deposit that includes the room tax (if this applies to you) or just charge the guest for tax upon arrival.

Inn the Know

You'll pay a small premium for charging the deposit rather than just getting an authorization. However, guests are less likely to cancel after they've seen a charge on their card.

Cancellation Policy

A good cancellation policy is the best insurance there is against loss of income. If you don't have a penalty in place and a guest cancels at the last minute, you'll be scrambling to fill that vacancy, and chances are you won't be able to do it. In the course of running your business you can count on losing some anticipated income along the way, but having a good cancellation policy will prevent you from losing your shirt.

Set a strict policy and make sure it's stated on your reservation confirmation sheet (see Chapter 17, "One Day at a Time"). We suggest that you give a full refund only if guests cancel 10 to 14 days before their arrival date and if you're able to re-rent the room for the same dates. If you grant a full refund apply a 5 or 10 percent service charge (based on the total room rate) to cover the time spent handling the cancellation.

If a guest calls to cancel a day or two before arrival, saying that there's been a death in the family, put your client on hold for a minute while you strategize. What are your chances of reselling all or part of the stay? The claim might be valid, so should you be lenient if you're likely to see this guest again? Have a three-part policy that 1) makes the guest responsible for the entire stay, 2) has a cancellation charge (percentage or dollar amount), and 3) requires resale of the space. If these are all on your reservation confirmation, you'll be able to eliminate or modify any one of them. In addition to a penalty (and if you're not sure the truth is being told), consider holding on to the deposit for a future stay.

B&B-eware!

Watch out for SGDS (sudden grandma death syndrome). Funny thing about grandmas: They tend to kick the bucket only during bad weather. There will be a few guests who will try to weasel out of paying a no-show reservation by using a family death. Obviously, sometimes it's true, so you'll need to use that old B&B owner intuition. Guests who know your policy but call and try to bargain with you are more than likely telling the truth about dear old Grandma Heddy's demise. Those who don't think they owe you anything most likely have succumbed to SGDS, and will do anything to get out of paying you. If you're really pretty sure they're lying, ask for the name of the deceased and of the funeral parlor. If you're not sure the truth is being told, tell the guest you will hold on to the deposit for a future stay.

If there is no time to send a confirmation of a reservation in writing, be sure to state your policy clearly over the phone. Ask for an e-mail address (or fax number) so you can send a message about the reservation and the cancellation policy. Print out the e-mail or fax and attach it to the guest's reservation form for your records.

Late Arrival

Greeting guests who arrive late can be tricky so you'll need to develop a system that works for you. If you can't greet them in person you've missed your five-minute opportunity to connect with them and show them around the house. Those five minutes can be valuable in getting guests settled and making them feel at home.

If you can't greet guests, do your best to compensate. Leave a note and their key near the door. Have copies of a typewritten note that has a standard spiel ("Welcome … because you are checking in after hours …"). If there are special instructions about parking or special amenities that might need explanation, leave a handwritten note in the room. If guests arrive very late in the evening, leave a little snack in their room or a take-out menu and another note telling them that you look forward to meeting them in the morning. Small gestures such as this will compensate for not meeting them in person. When you meet them on the following day make it a point to talk with them a little longer than usual about their journey and how they slept, and then let them ask questions about the area or things to do.

Tipping the Staff

If you have staff that guests come in contact with, such as housecleaners, the protocol or "unwritten rule" usually is that guests should be given subtle hints that tipping is allowed. If *you* are "the staff," tipping should not be expected, as is the case with the owner of a hair salon, for example.

On the day before a guest's departure have your staff write a note on an envelope (with your B&B's address printed on it) in plain sight in the room. Notes left by staff in guest rooms can be handwritten ("I hope you've enjoyed your stay" or "Come back and visit soon!"); or printed reminders, such as "Please check the room carefully for your possessions" and "You may leave your key here or at the front desk." You'll have fewer keys to replace, and it's a graceful way for your staff to encourage a gratuity. While you're at it add the names of the staff to the envelope you print out. People will know what the envelope is for and very few will leave without putting something in it. Your staff will get stiffed some of the time but that's to be expected (more on this in Chapter 20).

When Guests Phone a Few Friends

The phone situation can be tricky, especially for smaller B&Bs. Hotels and larger inns can be equipped to handle phone charges placed on the guests' final bill. Most B&Bs can't afford to install a computer/phone system that will track every room's calls. Some will put blocks on the phones so that only calling cards can be used to make long distance calls. Others don't have phones in the rooms at all, but do place a block on the common use phone.

Avoid letting guests make long distance calls you'll have to bill them for after they've been long gone. More likely than not, you won't be reimbursed. If a guest needs to make a call for a minute or less, offer your phone; but stay in the room while the guest calls. For longer calls, point guests to your (blocked) house phone. Print up the toll free numbers for several long distance carriers and place them by the phone. Make it easy on yourself and institute a policy that works best for guests and doesn't hit you in the pocket. For more on phone systems see Chapter 18, "Guest Services with a Smile."

House Rules

House rules differ from the policies in the preceding section in that the primary concern of house rules is, well, the house. Most of these rules should be written down and all should be strictly enforced.

Let's say that you don't allow pets, and you cave in to one guest who brings Fluffy (a.k.a. "No Trouble at All"). Gentle Fluffy turns out to be an ornery shih tzu who bites one of your staff. Now you have two problems: a nasty dog on your property and an injured staff member with the law on his or her side.

Just remember that you established rules for a reason. Breaking your rules will only hurt you in the long run.

The "No" Rules (Pets, Smoking, and Others)

Rules prohibiting pets and smoking are the most common ones because pets and smoking are the most bothersome to other guests.

➤ **No pets allowed.** If you're not equipped to handle pets of all kinds—mess and play areas for dogs, cat houses and litter boxes, extra cages for birds and other creatures—don't accept any at all. One guest might bring everything to maintain Sparky the pet turtle but another might not bring a dog cage for Cosmo, the German Shepard. And what if you don't have an area for Cosmo to run around in? Or the owners go off for the day leaving the pup cooped up in their room where it chews your throw pillows?

If you are getting a lot of requests to take pets, it might be a good idea to find a kennel nearby that you can refer guests to. Visit the kennel (find one that's been recommended to you by a pet owner) and talk to the owner about working out a deal for your guests to receive a 10 percent discount or something similar. Most kennels will be happy to do business with owners who will refer customers to them. Remember, however, that the exception to this rule is accepting a dog for the hearing- or sight-impaired.

Shoestring Solution

If some people with pets don't want to use a kennel, work out an arrangement with a like-quality B&B that's pet friendly. They are just as likely to need a good place to send guests who might be allergic.

➤ **No kids allowed.** Having a "no kids" policy is quite common among B&Bs, especially in very touristy areas where families can rent a cottage or stay in a hotel. Some B&Bs allow kids over a certain age or during the week or during slower seasons. Kids are not allowed mainly because guests don't want to listen to babies crying!

If your B&B is close to an amusement park, beach, or any family-oriented magnet, you'd be wise to at least allow school-age children. Singles and couples shy away from areas that are kid-oriented anyway, so families might be your main clientele.

If you do allow kids, make sure you have play areas for them outside and in the house. Your rooms will have to have flexible sleeping arrangements to allow for the varying needs—and you'll need to have an iron fist when it comes to enforcing some of your house rules.

➤ **Smokers.** Now that smokers are in the minority, most B&Bs prohibit smoking in some or all of the guest rooms and particularly in indoor common areas. In addition to being the ultimate fire hazard, smoking stinks; furniture, drapes … just about anything in a room used by smokers develops a stench that is difficult if not impossible to remove. If you do allow guests to smoke in outdoor common areas, provide a bucket of sand for their use (much nicer than a stinky ash tray) so you're not forever picking up cigarette butts you find on your patio or lawn. Place tactful reminders of this rule around the house and in guest rooms.

Enforcing no-smoking rules can be difficult if you, too, are a smoker. A smoker friend once stayed at a small B&B where smoking was not allowed in the house or even in the outside areas. She decided to sneak a smoke by hanging her cigarette out of her open room window. After a few puffs she looked down to find that she had been shaking ashes on the owner, who was beneath her window doing the same thing! It might be easier to enforce a no-smoking rule if you allow smokers an area, inside or outside, where they can smoke.

Fire Safety First

If you've read Chapter 6, "Legalities and Liabilities," you know that safety measures such as smoke detectors and proper exits are required. What can be nerve-wracking for a lot of owners is learning to trust their guests. Don't fret; there are ways to encourage fire safety in guests' private quarters without sounding like a Smokey the Bear commercial. You can gently remind guests at check-in that smoking and candles are not allowed. If you allow smoking in some rooms, it will be hard to enforce a ban on candles so if you become aware that a guest is burning candles offer a safe container for them.

Placing aromatherapy candles in rooms has become a trend among owners, but we don't recommend it. Most guests won't bring their own candles, so why encourage a fire hazard? You can create a relaxing mood with soft lighting, gentle spray scents, classical music, and fresh flowers.

Uninvited Guests

Some sneaky guests might try to stow away an extra person or two in their room. Instead of getting into an awkward confrontation, blame it on the law. Tell guests that if they add extra bodies to their room, you'll be in violation of town safety codes. It's a bit of a stretch of local ordinances (or maybe not, depending on where you live) but it works better than just saying no, and you don't make yourself look like the bad guy.

This is a good rule to state on a policy card. Use something like: "For the safety and consideration of other guests in the house, we must ask that you do not invite others back to the house. Because there are maximum occupancy limits in every room, non-guests will not be allowed in these areas." You won't always be able to catch unwanted guests in the rooms but if you suspect that some extra bodies are floating around, talk to your guests right away. If these uninvited guests cause problems in your house or with other guests, you will be liable.

If your location is near nightspots, you might expect a single man or woman to bring home a guest. Determine your policy on uninvited friends in advance so you don't have to get up bleary-eyed at 3 A.M. to throw unregistered strangers out of your house.

No Curfew, or Wicked Stepmother Syndrome

B&Bs used to have curfews so that everyone could feel safe and secure late at night behind locked doors. As an added precaution, guests were not given house keys that they could give to late-night visitors, or worse, duplicate for the purposes of burglarizing the house.

For the most part, curfews have fallen by the wayside and would not sit well with today's guests. If you do decide to impose a curfew, make sure it's not earlier than 11 P.M.; preferably midnight. When guests call to make reservations, tell them what your policy is up front. You'll find that a few guests will decide to not stay in your establishment, whereas others might not mind abiding by a curfew. Either way, guests should be told about it before they arrive.

Inn the Know

If you have a lot of honeymooners and singles, a curfew might not be a good idea, but families and older folk might not mind it.

Base your decision on how a curfew will affect your business. The majority of your guests can be trusted and why shouldn't you take your chances with the rest? After all, there's more than one way to break into a house!

Posting House Rules

There are two good reasons to post the house rules:

➤ Guests can refer to the written rules, preventing a lot of repetitive questions.

➤ If you fail to tell every guest about every rule, you're covered anyway.

As we've said before, not every rule needs to be written down; some don't even need to be stated. It will depend on how your business operates.

Inn the Know

When you're talking to your guests about house rules, keep it light. Avoid using "must not" and "cannot" altogether. As the old saying goes: You attract more flies with honey than you do with vinegar.

197

In a small B&B where you are the host and primary staff you might find it more comfortable to tell guests about the rules when they check in; you could find that you can dispense with posting many if not all of them. For bigger operations in which you have staff checking in guests it might be wise to post the main rules in each room. Even well-trained staff (and even you) can miss a few things when running a busy operation.

During your stay, please observe the following:

🚭 Smoking is allowed on all patios and outdoor areas. Guest rooms and other indoor areas are always smoke-free.

🍽 A continental breakfast will be served buffet-style from 8 to 11 A.M. in the downstairs common room. Feel free to bring breakfast back to your room.

☎ For your convenience, each room has a phone with voicemail capability. Instructions for recording an outgoing message, picking up messages left for you, and emergency contacts are near the phone.

🚑 Dial "0" to reach us during our regular hours, 8 A.M. until 10 P.M. If you need assistance after hours, use one of our emergency numbers listed near the phone.

🗝 Please keep your room and house keys with you at all times.

☺ Because water is one of our most important natural resources, we ask that you use it responsibly.

🎧 Our quiet hours are from 11 P.M. until 8 A.M. If you enter the house between these hours, please be mindful of other guests who are sleeping.

✔ Checkout time is 11 A.M. Let us know in advance if you'd like to have luggage stored during your last day in town.

☏ Most of all, call on us for anything that might make your stay more enjoyable!

Village Hill Bed and Breakfast
312 Village Hill Road
Inntown, USA 06066

It is a common practice to post the rules on the door inside guest rooms. If you have a portfolio that contains other items such as brochures and event listings (see more on this in Chapter 10, "Marketing 101") add your rules to the folder. Wherever you decide to post the rules, make sure that they're visible and easy to read. Keep the language friendly and colorful, and use a computer printer or a typewriter. Handwritten rules look unprofessional (unless you do calligraphy for a hobby). Also keep your rules short and sweet, sticking to the important elements. Too long a list means that many guests won't read any of it.

What to Do with Rule Breakers

How you react when someone breaks a rule will depend on the crime that the person committed. Take a deep breath, then wait a few minutes before you pounce on the couple in room 3 who you know have been burning incense late at night. Then, approach room 3 with a smile and suggest that, even though the aroma from their room is lovely, it's creeping into the house and bothering other guests. To put them at their ease, joke about it, or even about something else. If they use incense again, speak to them again, only this time more firmly. If they ignore your requests and other guests continue to complain, you'll have to ask room 3 to either abide by the rules or leave the house.

If you suspect that an illegal activity such as drug dealing or even prostitution is going on, call the authorities right away. Remember that you will be liable for any illegal activity occurring on your property. Before you call the cops, though, be sure you have solid grounds for suspecting that a guest is committing a crime.

Inn the Know

Always try to approach a rule breaker in person. Don't dance around the issue or apologize in any way. Be firm, say what you have to say, and then put the person at ease with light conversation. This will work with most people, particularly those who didn't even know they were breaking a rule.

Changing a Policy or Rule

Changes that take place in your business or in your perspective over the years will lead you to find policies that work better for you. Definitely change a policy if it's not working.

When you change a rule, make sure that all your staff is aware of the change and that any written material is updated. An important policy such as check-out time should not affect guests' staying with you when it goes into effect. Phase in a new policy with new guests, and be sure to tell returning guests about the change.

Above all, use your best judgment. If you have to change five policies or remove seven, don't hesitate to do so for fear of looking wishy-washy. If something doesn't work, get rid of it. The only factor guiding your decisions should be the success of your business.

The Least You Need to Know

➤ Institute policies and house rules that work for your guests and for your business.

➤ Some rules can be related orally; others, such as check-out time, should be posted for guests' reference.

➤ Enforce house rules for the benefit of all your guests; but always do so graciously.

➤ Be flexible; if a policy doesn't work, change it or get rid of it.

Part 5

Getting Down to Business

The everyday business of a B&B ranges from making breakfast to running the office. Organizing and scheduling your day will keep the business running smoothly and keep you sane. Learn how to keep on top of housekeeping and the services you offer to guests, and when to hire staff to help you carry out your daily responsibilities and keep your business growing in the right direction.

Chapter 16

Start with a Good Breakfast

You won't find two B&B owners with the same idea of what kind of breakfast to serve. If you've checked out your local zoning regulations you know the type of breakfast—continental or full—you're allowed to serve (for more on zoning, see Chapter 6, "Legalities and Liabilities"). Variations on that continental or full breakfast theme, however, are entirely up to you.

Keep in mind that most guests will be looking for comfort food. Even people who never touch breakfast in their normal routine usually will expect some kind of home-style fare at your B&B. After all, breakfast is included in the rate. Don't disappoint them; a well-fed guest might well be a returning guest!

Breakfast Types

Before you decide what to serve your guests, think about your own breakfast tastes. Do you go for cereal or ham and eggs? More important, can you cook ham and eggs? If you're not a whiz in the kitchen, try to stick with what you know. Get used to preparing and serving breakfast to your guests; then try to experiment.

If your license limits you to a continental-style breakfast, don't fret about being limited in what you serve your guests. There are lots of ways to present a yummy breakfast without serving diner-style plates of hot chow. Your guests won't feel cheated if you serve lighter fare as long as you do it right.

Shoestring Solution

Stephen Mascilo and Trevor Pinker, owners of the Beaconlight and The Oxford guesthouses in Provincetown, Massachusetts, have received accolades for their own cereal, the "Beaconlight Blend." They offered to share their secret recipe with our readers: "When you have a few boxes of store-bought cereal that are running low, combine them. Voilà! You have the famous Beaconlight Blend!"

Inn the Know

Describe the type of breakfast you offer on your Web site, in your brochure, and to guests making reservations. Highlight your best breakfast feature such as home-baked muffins or scones from scratch.

A full breakfast can be quite a crowd pleaser, particularly in retreat areas or out-of-the-way places where restaurants are scarce. People staying at a B&B are hoping to get a memorable meal, especially if they can't get one at home!

Continental Divine

If you've ever been to a cheesy hotel or business conference (usually held at cheesy hotels), you've had their version of a continental breakfast: stale croissants, warm OJ, cold coffee, and maybe a few grapes. Most of your guests have had that experience, too.

Because a continental breakfast has a stigma attached to it, a lot of B&Bs brighten theirs up with extras such as instant hot cereals, yogurt, cheeses, and a wide selection of fruits. Offering a wider selection without adding hot dishes is commonly called "continental-plus" or "expanded continental."

Offering the freshest foods and paying attention to details of your continental or continental-plus breakfast will leave guests feeling satisfied. Make sure all your breads and cereals are fresh, the milk isn't old, the coffee isn't stale, and your juice is ice cold. Offer a basket of fresh fruit. Try varying the menu a bit, particularly when you have guests staying for more than two or three nights. One day, offer blueberries for cereal; the next day, oatmeal in a crock pot with brown sugar. Guests will appreciate the little variations and feel as if they're getting their money's worth.

The Full Menu

Mmmmmm … thick-style French toast, honey-smoked bacon, eggs Florentine, hot apple cider, homemade coffee cake … sounds good, doesn't it? Well, you'd better get cracking—guests will be coming down looking for that hearty meal any minute! Such is the pressure of serving a full meal every morning. If you've promised a full breakfast, you can count on guests to be looking for their fill.

Food preparation rules will vary from place to place, depending on the strictness of your state health department. Dishes may need to be washed at a certain temperature; food may need to be placed in certain containers, and so on. If you run a small operation, don't worry about unexpected visits from the state. They'll be busy with the big boys. Do yourself and your guests a favor, however, and get hold of a good, basic book on food preparation and sanitization. You'll learn things such as how to properly thaw frozen items, and that you shouldn't put hot quiches in a fridge because it will speed up the bacterial growth on other foods. Your health department may also have pamphlets on food preparation and the proper procedure for cleaning food areas.

To a guest, "full" breakfast indicates a meal with some kind of hot dish (eggs, meat, pancakes, waffles); some accessories (sweet bread or toast, fruit); and a nonstop supply of beverages (coffee, tea, juices, milk). Variations on a full breakfast are endless and many B&Bs have become known for their one-of-a-kind meals. Get hold of some books of recipes from B&Bs and inns (see Appendix C, "More Resources," for further reading). Some include tips on entertaining and food preparation, both of which can be just as important as the meal itself.

The trend in full breakfasts is to stay away from cholesterol-packed meals such as the one we described. For some, getting lean and fit has become a priority—at home. As vacationers we all tend to loosen our belts a bit more. The trick is to offer a meal that will give guests full, satisfied bellies without that post–Thanksgiving-turkey feeling.

Use lots of fresh fruit and ingredients. Lighten up your pancakes by using whole-wheat flour and 2 percent milk. Instead of oil in your muffins, use applesauce. Get low-fat scallion or veggie cream cheese for bagels. Pay the extra bucks and get extra-lean bacon from the butcher. Guests will leave your table satisfied and ready for the day instead of sluggish and ready for a nap!

Guests love to get a real "taste" of the area they're visiting, so why not bring it to breakfast? Find locally made jams, honey, and other items that guests might not get at home such as Portuguese sweet bread. You might be able to help promote local businesses and your guests will feel as if they've savored the region.

Traditional bacon and eggs have fallen by the wayside a bit as food trends creep toward the exotic. Some B&Bs are experimenting with Asian and Latino foods and cooking practices to spice up their menus. Getting creative with dishes is fun for guests (as long as you don't stray into bizarre, unheard-of fare or un-breakfast-like food such as lasagna) and it will keep you interested, too!

Breakfast in Bed

Coffee, juice, muffins, and fruit delivered right to your door … sounds divine, doesn't it? A lot of guests, especially honeymooners and the lone traveler, will appreciate this extra service. If you have set times for serving breakfast, offering breakfast in bed allows guests more flexibility.

Inn the Know

If you wish to serve breakfast in bed, buy some elegant trays or sturdy baskets for serving. Make sure guests know when breakfast will be placed outside their door so that everything is fresh; the cold things stay cold and the warm things stay warm. Wrap up hot goodies in cloth napkins or keep them under covered plates; put coffee and hot water in carafes and juice in a glass container from the fridge. Include plates, silverware, napkins, mugs, juice glasses, and every condiment your guests will need.

Before you decide to offer this treat, consider all the reasons not to. The major one is more clean-up. Muffin squished into carpet and spilled coffee can be impossible to get rid of completely, not to mention ruined sheets. One way to combat extra messes is to provide small tables and chairs in your rooms (if you have the space). Most often, people will opt for the table rather than balancing food on their knees.

Another reason to not serve breakfast in guest rooms is time and hassle. Imagine serving breakfast in bed to one or two guests while four others wait for a sit-down meal. Now, imagine yourself carrying trays of food up to other guests and having to pass by those hungry guests waiting at your dining room table. If your breakfast is buffet-style, consider suggesting that guests take food back to their rooms, particularly if you offer bathrobes and can provide individual trays with handles.

If you'd like to offer breakfast in the rooms, take it for a test drive. Try doing it as a special for honeymooners only, on weekdays, or as a last-night treat before checkout.

The Back-Up Breakfast

No matter how good you are, you won't always get breakfast right. Stan your Siamese cat might get into your ready-to-serve oatmeal or you'll forget to buy eggs. Something might fall out of place once in a while, and you'll be stuck with hungry and perturbed guests.

Coffee Talk

Here's a suggestion from Rainer Horn and Jürgen Herzog of Carpe Diem Guesthouse, Provincetown, Massachusetts, for something you can always keep on hand: "Prepare plain muffin dough and keep it refrigerated. In the morning just add whatever fruit or other extras you have on hand and bake fresh. You can make and keep plain dough three or four days in the fridge; this makes it very easy to prepare wonderful muffins in the morning."

For those last-minute, no-turning-back mishaps, make sure you have back-ups. Serve plain or vanilla yogurt with anything you have on hand—granola, Grape Nuts, shredded coconut, chopped almonds—for guests to add in themselves. Make a fruit salad. Freeze leftover fresh bagels and then serve them (within a couple of weeks) toasted with brie. Oatmeal or grits are always a good staple. Once you get into the groove of shopping and serving breakfast for guests, you'll be less likely to have a screw-up; having extra meal ideas on hand will cover up any unforeseeable mishaps, and guests will be none the wiser!

Guests with Dietary Concerns

Milk, wheat, food additives, and nuts are just some of the allergies people suffer from. Other guests might be on special diets such as vegetarian, no dairy, low salt, no sugar, and low cholesterol. If you serve a full breakfast, it's wise to have recipes on hand for guests with these special needs.

When your guests arrive, describe the breakfast you serve when you tell them about your other policies. Most people will take this opportunity to let you know if they have severe allergies.

Bare Breakfast Essentials

Whether you serve a continental or a full sit-down breakfast, don't forget about the bare essentials such as milk for coffee and butter for breads.

Inn the Know

If you serve a full sit-down breakfast and you have a chef and more than ten rooms, consider posting a weekly menu. For a smaller B&B, detail your meals on your Web site; then guests can alert you to their dietary concerns—and your menu will get their mouths watering, too!

The more variety you have in the meal, the more accessories you'll need. Depending on the breakfast you're serving, essentials might include milk and cream, sugar, sugar substitutes, honey, lemon, salt and pepper, butter, jam, syrup, and a jug of ice water.

Most people are either coffee or tea drinkers so make sure that your breakfast has plenty of both. Flavored coffees are popular, but not with everyone. Many people will look forward to a good ole cup of regular Joe. And don't skimp here—buy the good stuff. Also offer a selection of herbal and decaf teas. Although the barest of continental breakfasts might include only coffee, tea, and muffins, we strongly urge you to provide juice as well. Premium, not-from-concentrate orange juice is readily available and will create greater guest satisfaction.

Before your guests arrive for breakfast, make sure that any bare necessity they possibly could ask for is already there. Running around to get sugar substitute for one guest and honey for another will take you away from the kitchen.

How Much to Make

You probably know from your own experiences that recipes in cookbooks seem to exaggerate how many people will benefit from a meal. Ever read, "Serves eight" and think, "Eight what? Chihuahuas?"

As you go along you'll get a better sense of how much to make for your guests. As with anything, especially if you're not used to cooking for a lot of other people, have a rehearsal before you open for business. Throw a dinner party or cook for your extended family. Pay attention to how much food you make and what's left over.

Although cooking for people you know is easy because you know who'll show up (and they'll all tell you it's fabulous!), cooking for guests is more unpredictable. When they check in try to get a sense of whether they'll be joining you for breakfast or seeking sustenance elsewhere. Some might oversleep or decide in the morning to skip it, but that's just one of those things you can't control. What you can control is having enough food for each guest, and that's the most important thing.

Hiring a Chef

If you're useless in the kitchen and have enough revenue to hire a cook, that might be the way to go. Most B&Bs hire chefs with the aim of providing four-star meals. Gourmet chefs do not come cheap but you might find someone who works at a local restaurant whose schedule would enable him or her to cook for you as well.

Look for someone who has had some hotel, B&B, or catering experience. You're hiring a chef to save you the time of planning and preparing consistent, perhaps gourmet, meals. You'll want someone who's used to preparing at least as many meals as you'll need in an allotted time. A cook who has catering experience and puts out 50 meals at once might not be well suited to preparing only a few meals at a time. Reliability also is key. If your chef is late or doesn't show up at all, you're sunk. Talk to past employers about your prospect's reliability. If you do hire someone, spend some time in the kitchen with your chef so you can learn the ropes. That way, if the chef gets sick and can't come to work, you'll at least have some idea of what to do with those pots!

Breakfast Is Served

Serving the meal—how it's presented and where—needs some planning, too. When you do it right your presentation of the meal and the setting in which it's consumed will be taken for granted. It's only if you *don't* pay attention to these details that guests will take notice.

It's All in the Presentation

We don't have to tell you that dirty dishes and old tablecloths are unacceptable. You already know that if a meal looks good enough to eat that's what will happen.

There are some subtle details—and some obvious ones—that will make the meal an even better event for your guests. Using crystal glasses and fine china is one way; having serving dishes and utensils that coordinate is another. If you offer a sit-down breakfast, try to dress up the plates with a slice of orange twist on the side or powdered sugar dusted on the rim of a dark-colored plate. Try to direct some of the pleasant aromas from the kitchen into the dining area. Place fresh flowers on the tables or at least in the dining area. Don't forget yourself: Make sure that your sleeves aren't covered in muffin batter when you present the main event.

If you're not sure where to start creating a super-elegant affair, pay a visit to some fancy restaurants. See how the pros do it and then steal, steal, steal!

Sit-Down or Buffet

Continental and continental-plus breakfasts typically are served buffet-style. Think about your guests sitting down to eat and a host "serving up" bagels and coffee—it just doesn't feel right. Of course you can give that personal touch to your breakfasts by doing things such as pouring additional coffee for seated guests. It's a nice way to have a momentary chat but to not tie up either the guests or yourself for too long. Buffet-style breakfasts are an attractive option for business travelers and vacationers who can "eat on the fly." It can also be a benefit for you if space is limited. The plus side of hosting a sit-down breakfast is that you can control portion size and be more creative in the kind of fare you serve.

209

Coffee Talk

When (or if) you sit down to eat with your guests, try to be conscious of their personal space. Reonn Rabon, innkeeper of Green Gables Guest House in Seattle, Washington, suggests: "Don't dominate conversations with your guests. After serving breakfast, stand back and let your guests talk and ask questions. If you try to take over the conversation you will be seen as pesky rather than personable. Let the guests talk among themselves freely. One of the best places for my guests to learn about Seattle is over the breakfast table from their fellow tourists. They share those things that either they miserably hated or enjoyed immensely."

A full breakfast can be either sit-down or buffet style. Buffets are an especially nice option for places without a large area where everyone can sit. Buffets encourage social interaction, whereas a few guests sitting around a big table might not have a lot to say to each other. They also might feel trapped into conversation when they'd really prefer to eat quietly, go back to their room, or get on the road. Guests might enjoy each other's company, but there's no guarantee. If you have the space, try having tables of various sizes so that guests have more options.

B&B-eware!

Beware the pushy traveler! Don't take requests for breakfast at un-scheduled times. For special situations, such as a guest who needs to catch an early flight or leave sooner than expected, offer to pack up something to go.

When Do We Eat?

When you're determining your breakfast schedule, consider three things: what makes sense for your guests, what makes sense for you, and what makes sense for the breakfast itself.

If you have a lot of business travelers, serve breakfast early. Vacationers will want to sleep in. If you have a mixed clientele, consider serving very light fare (coffee and breads) at 7:30 A.M. and a larger breakfast at 9:00. A sit-down meal might appeal to you as the owner, but we believe that today's sophisticated traveler prefers a less formal setup. Unless you have an all-inclusive resort location, most people will want a quick breakfast to get them going—and then they'll just want to go.

Also consider your own habits. If you aren't fast in the kitchen or you need more time to prepare a full breakfast, schedule accordingly. Don't promise service at 8 A.M. if you don't get out of bed until 7.

Finally, and most important, think about the type of breakfast you serve before you fix your schedule. As continental and continental-plus breakfasts are primarily buffet-style, they're usually offered over a range of time such as 8 A.M. to 10 A.M. That will require you to tend to the food itself—check on the coffee, make sure food stays wrapped and fresh for the next guest, remove dirty plates—during the entire breakfast period.

A full sit-down breakfast should be offered at one designated time (or two if you run a large B&B). Otherwise, you'll find yourself operating like a restaurant. Not only will you run yourself ragged, a quiche that is fresh at 8:30 A.M. will be flat at 10:00 A.M. Now that real men do eat quiche, it must remain palatable. Even if your full breakfast is served buffet style, consider setting a designated time for it rather than a range of hours.

Creating Breakfast Areas

Don't make your guests eat on their laps. Throw those TV tables in the garage! If need be, create space in a common area of the house that can be used year-round and can accommodate all the guests at once. Use the dining room, part of the living room, an enclosed porch, or even a break-fast nook off the kitchen. Using the kitchen itself is not a great idea; unless you're super-organized and are prepared to be "on stage" throughout service, don't attempt it. Guests will see all the behind-the-scenes work that you want to hide!

Whatever space you create, make sure it's cozy, comfortable, and that it encourages socializing. You'll want your guests to be talking among themselves so you can whiz around and concentrate on preparing and serving the meal. If you have the space, use small round tables that fit three or four chairs. Small areas (as opposed to one large dining room table) work very well to encourage interaction among guests.

Inn the Know

Before you officially open to the public, spend some time in the eating areas. Does the sun shine in too brightly at 9:30 A.M.? Are there drafts? Can people easily move around the furniture and get to the food without spilling someone's coffee? Guests might not pipe up and complain about these little annoyances so you'll need to head them off before they're noticed.

During weekdays, have the daily newspaper handy and maybe even tune the radio to NPR or turn to a 24-hour news station on television. And don't forget the coasters!

Serving Other Treats

Lots of inns and some B&Bs offer other meals and nibbles as an enticing extra. Afternoon tea is very popular, especially at B&Bs and country inns in rural areas. Packing a lunch for guests going on hiking adventures or long drives also is a welcome option. Evening wine and cheese or cocktail hours often are found at B&Bs that don't cater to families.

Common practice among most B&Bs is not to charge for these extras. If you offer a picnic-basket-size lunch for day trippers, bump up your rates, and highlight this feature on your Web site and when taking reservations. These bonus treats won't cost you that much more and they might even please guests more than the breakfast, which they *did* expect to pay for.

Keep in mind, though, that serving these extra delights will take up more of your preparation and serving time when guests might expect you to socialize with them, make dinner reservations for them, or answer questions about the area.

As they say, breakfast is the most important meal of the day. At a B&B it's not only expected; a satisfying breakfast will leave a lasting impression on guests, particularly when it's the last experience they have on check-out day.

The Least You Need to Know

➤ You might not have a choice in the type of breakfast you serve—continental or full—because some zoning laws will make the decision for you.

➤ If you plan to serve a full breakfast, create meals that you can handle and that you'll have enough time to prepare.

➤ Don't forget to stock the basic essentials for any meal, and always have a back-up in case of mishaps.

➤ Deciding when to serve breakfast will depend on you, your clientele, and the type of breakfast you serve. Where and how you present it should be carefully planned; guests will notice only if it wasn't.

Chapter 17

One Day at a Time

In This Chapter

➤ Scheduling a daily routine

➤ Taking reservations

➤ Working with reservationists

Devoting an entire chapter to daily duties makes sense because the B&B business is pretty predictable. Every day you'll make breakfast, meet and say goodbye to guests, make beds, take reservations, do laundry, do dishes, and do paperwork. These are just the basics. Throw in extra guest services such as nightly turndown and your day is already planned for you.

Try to stay in control of your daily schedule instead of letting it control you. If writing out an hourly schedule is the only way you can stay organized, do it. Sometimes the day will get away from you no matter how much scheduling you do. This happens to everyone. Don't beat yourself up about it; keep your eye on the big stuff such as keeping your guests happy.

Schedule a Daily Routine

As we noted in Chapter 3, "What It's Really Like," your daily activities will be a combination of the routine and the unexpected; mostly the routine. Think about setting up your day before it begins. Evenings are a calm time to write out a to-do list for the next day. It will not only save you time in the morning, it can relieve that "I have so much to do I don't know where to start" panic that can kick in at the start of a new day.

Here are some scheduling tips:

➤ **Work around breakfast.** The good thing about offering breakfast at your establishment is that this part of your day is already planned for you. Ever wonder why some B&Bs that serve a full breakfast schedule it so early? You will, too (unless you serve a continental-style breakfast), so you can have the rest of the morning to concentrate on other guest services such as cleaning up after breakfast and checking out guests. If you find that most guests are sleeping in on you, move your schedule around a bit. Consider serving your breakfast a little later—not so late that it cuts into the day—but keep getting up at the usual time. Do something in the morning that you'd normally do in the afternoon—but not laundry; you'll deplete the hot water for the guests' morning showers!

Coffee Talk

Consider this quick tip on how to handle everyday B&B life from Dr. Daniel and Evelyn Shirbroun, owners of the Joshua Tree Inn, Joshua Tree, California: "Do Fast. Be Fast. Go Fast."

Inn the Know

Lock boxes are extremely popular now and a great way for guests to pick up their keys. The boxes are locked with a code that guests have to punch in. Just be sure to give guests the code before they arrive!

➤ **Don't check out during check-out.** Try not to leave the house when guests check out or check in. The first and last thing guests will want to see at your B&B is your smiling face. If you can't be there for guests when they arrive or depart, leave them a personal note with your apologies. As we've already mentioned, if they're checking in, leave their key (determine a secure area with the guest before arrival) with instructions about the house, the breakfast schedule, and anything else they'll need for the evening. If they're checking out, leave them instructions on where to leave their key, a set of directions just in case, and maybe even something for the road (sweets or fruit, not hooch!).

➤ **Keep on top of housekeeping.** The chore of housekeeping is endless. When you finish cleaning a room or the kitchen there's no time to enjoy your sense of accomplishment; you'll need to start working on something else. As much as possible, break up housekeeping with other chores so it doesn't seem as if it's never-ending. It won't be easy, though, because housekeeping in a B&B tends to schedule itself. If guests get up late and go out for a bit, you have to stop what you're doing to ready their room for the day.

The best way to schedule cleaning is to jump at the chance to do it whenever you can. If you have fifteen minutes, tidy up the common areas. If a guest checks out early and you have a spare hour, don't save cleaning the room for later; finish it up when you have the time. You never know what else will come up during the day but you can always count on something getting dirty and there is always potential for money coming through the door in the form of a walk-in. Staying on top of housekeeping will make a lasting impression on your guests and will help your business grow. No room at the inn for complacency!

➤ **Penciling in personal errands.** When it comes to taking care of personal business you might find yourself playing "catch me if you can." Try to piggy-back your personal stuff with business-related errands or spend some extra money to get things delivered. If you need medications, have the prescriptions filled at a market that has a pharmacy so you can pick them up when you go out to shop. Do your banking and buy your stamps online. Consider paying the extra to have the B&B wash done by a laundry service; most services will pick up and deliver. Walk the dog with a purpose: Take Shortie, your Great Dane, to the mailbox, the store, the bank, or wherever you can go on foot. There will be many times when you'll have to put your personal errands aside to take care of the B&B. Expect it; it goes with the territory, so learn to be flexible about when your personal stuff gets done.

Reservation Paperwork

The phone rings; it's your first reservation. You're so excited that you grab your lip liner and some junk mail to write on. After you hang up you realize that you forgot to ask a few questions—including the caller's phone number! That won't happen if you're prepared with reservation forms, a booking calendar, and a good filing system. And don't forget the pens and pencils (lip liner can get very smooshy).

Reservation Form

Using a reservation form enables you to accomplish many things. Here are a few:

Inn the Know

When you take a reservation, collect all the information you need and tell the guest as much as possible about the house policies and so on. Better still, ask the caller if he or she would like to check out your Web site. You'll save time on the phone and at check-in.

➤ You get vital information about your guests down on paper right away such as the amount paid, arrival and departure times, reason for the visit, and any food allergies they might have.

➤ You have a cheat sheet to follow when taking a reservation. Having a fill-in-the-blank form prompts you to record and pass on all accurate information.

➤ It provides a written record for other staff to follow.

➤ It allows for easy record keeping and guest tracking.

➤ It guarantees fewer mistakes such as double bookings, unrecorded cancellations, and incorrect arrival or departure dates.

As you can see from Park's reservation form later in the chapter in the section called "Over the Phone," the following details are covered: guest name and contact information, date the reservation was made, payment information, arrival and departure dates (including means of transportation), directions, and important policies.

Using a preprinted form on standard (8½ × 11) size paper such as Park's, with two carbon copies, is an unbelievably easy way to track guests. You keep the top copy for current and future records, along with the second copy to present to the guest upon arrival. If you're using a credit card for a deposit, you can affix the carbon copies to the first two sheets of the form. The last copy can be sent to the guest along with a promotion piece such as a brochure or a small map of your area.

Other ways to record reservations include using large (4 × 6) index cards that you can easily file upright next to the phone, and using a reservation form created with computer software (be sure to make a copy for the guest's confirmation). Some B&Bs make notes on index cards and then have a "fill in the blanks" letter to send as confirmation. Others use postcards to confirm a guest's stay.

B&B-eware!

Using a postcard for reservation confirmation will save you money on postage but you won't be able to write in payment information or enclose your brochure (or other items that confirm a guest's wisdom in choosing your B&B).

Booking Calendar

Keep track of arrivals, departures, and important dates on a single calendar. You won't be able to keep track of who came and went after a week has gone by, much less a month, so be sure to keep accurate records of guest stays.

When you write in a reservation, write down the name of the guest who made the reservation, the date it was taken, and whether a deposit was received or is on its way. Determine your own system for pending reservations by penciling them or writing them in a different color.

Use a yearly calendar (buy or create your own as we show you here) or a one-sheet erasable one that can be used month to month.

August 2001	Room 1	Room 2	Suite 3	Suite 4
8/1 Wednesday	B. Edwards (C) 7/11/00		Lillibridge (A) 5/24/00	
8/2 Thursday	B. Edwards		Lillibridge	Aitken (C) 6/30/00
8/3 Friday	B. Edwards	C. Edwards (C, 1) 7/11/00	Lillibridge	Aitken
8/4 Saturday	B. Edwards	C. Edwards	Lillibridge	Aitken
8/5 Sunday		Le Ny (C) 5/19/00	Ilchert (T) 5/19/00	Aitken
8/6 Monday	Pickett (A, 1)* 3/23/00	Le Ny	Ilchert	Smeelay (A, 3)** 7/20/00
8/7 Tuesday	Pickett	Le Ny	Ilchert	Smeelay
8/8 Wednesday	Pickett	Le Ny	Ilchert	Smeelay
8/9 Thursday	Pickett	Pagan (C) 7/10/00	Ilchert	Smeelay
8/10 Friday	Pickett	Pagan	Howard (T, 3)** 2/28/00	Hassell (T) 4/9/00
8/11 Saturday	Pickett	Pagan	Howard	Hassell
8/12 Sunday		Pagan	Howard	Hassell
8/13 Monday	Sanchez (C) 3/19/00		Howard	Hassell
8/14 Tuesday	Sanchez		Howard	
8/15 Wednesday	Sanchez	Cone (C) 4/17/00	Howard	
8/16 Thursday	Sanchez	Cone		Moore (B) 8/1/00
8/17 Friday	Sanchez	Cone	Cerio (A) 4/11/00	Moore
8/18 Saturday	Sanchez	Cone	Cerio	Moore
8/19 Sunday		Hamm (T) 6/27/00	Cerio	Zavatto (C)* 7/12/00
8/20 Monday		Hamm	Cerio	Zavatto

continues

continued

August 2001	Room 1	Room 2	Suite 3	Suite 4
8/21 Tuesday	Gobena (C) 3/15/00	Hamm	Cerio	Zavatto
8/22 Wednesday	Gobena	Hamm	Cerio	Zavatto
8/23 Thursday	Gobena	Hamm	Cerio	Zavatto
8/24 Friday	Gobena	Hamm	Cerio	McSorley (A, 3)** 8/20/00
8/25 Saturday	Gobena	Hamm	Cerio	McSorley
8/26 Sunday	Gobena		Sobiski (T) 5/1/00	McSorley
8/27 Monday	Gobena	Phinney (T,1) 8/10/00	Sobiski	Berkowitz (C) 6/2/00
8/28 Tuesday		Phinney	Sobiski	Berkowitz
8/29 Wednesday		Phinney	Sobiski	Berkowitz
8/30 Thursday	Smith (C) 1/3/00	Phinney	Abbruzzi (C) 2/17/00	Berkowitz
8/31 Friday	Smith	Phinney	Abbruzzi	Berkowitz

Last name = person who made the reservation/contact person.
All rates are double-occupancy unless otherwise noted with (1) or (3).
Date = date booking was taken
Mode of Transportation: C = car; T = train; B = bus; A = airplane
* = Family discount
** = Charged for extra guest

You can get hold of reservation booking calendars at an office supply store or create your own on a computer. Make sure the calendar is compact but has enough space to write in guest names and brief notes. See to it that staff members review the calendar often, whether they take reservations or not.

Using a Computer

Computer software for the lodging industry has come a long way. There are dozens of programs to choose from and they can run into thousands of dollars. Some programs offer fairly complicated interfacing of guest service fees for items such as valet parking, dry cleaning, meals, and phone usage. Look for a program that handles properties with fewer than 50 rooms.

Inn the Know

Most software programs are all-inclusive. They have calendars, different types of reservation forms, letter styles, wait lists, guest name searches, and amenities searches. Several companies offer high-quality software products for properties with fewer than 50 rooms that include all the preceding options and more. TCS Systems Guest Tracker has a solid reputation and is a popular option with the 10- to 30-room set. Park swears by—not at—their property management software. Other options worth investigating include Easy Innkeeping by Grace Software and GuestAll by Applied Technologies. Check PAII's Web site for the latest developments in software.

You'll want to buy from a company that has a proven track record. There's been a lot of consolidation among these companies so be sure to get software that has a good chance of offering a support system down the road. Before you commit to a program, try to use one on a trial basis or get one with a money-back guarantee in case you absolutely can't stand it.

When you shop for a computer system that you plan to use to the fullest, invest wisely. Get a good one with lots of free disk space and make sure it's fast and can handle your heavy-duty reservation program. Skip the laptops; they're great for people who travel and you might think they're great because they take up less space, but laptops are not as reliable as desktop computer systems. If you plan to make good use of a computer for the business it pays to shell out the bucks. And don't forget to save that receipt for tax time!

Filing Reservations

So, you've taken a reservation and sent out a confirmation. What do you do with your own record of the reservation from now until the guests arrive? What do you do with it afterward? We all have our own filing systems. Figure out what's best for you by how you organize things. If you buy a filing system, make sure it's one you'll really use and that it can be accessed easily within your office area.

When you take a reservation on paper, put your copy of the confirmation where you can see it. Post it on the wall (use clips; one for each room) or in an upright file. There are a lot of options in files now. Probably the easiest to use are the all-in-one collapsible folders, with sections for each month and slots for the days in each month. With this type of folder you can sort reservation confirmations by arrival date. Wherever you put information on a reservation, make sure that you and the staff can get to it easily and quickly in case the guest calls back or you need to double-check information on the form.

After the guest has left, remove the form from your active files. Make any notes on it that will be helpful if the guest stays with you again, such as any food allergies you weren't aware of before the visit. Now you're ready to store it in its final resting place—no, not the circular file! Develop a good filing system for quickly retrieving information on a past guest who might phone soon after departing.

You'll need to let your records age like a fine wine. Store in a cool, dry place for seven years in case of an IRS or state tax audit.

Taking Reservations

Save yourself some headaches and practice your reservation spiel before you do it for real. When that first guest calls, you need to sound confident, easygoing, informative, and ready to take down information the guest gives you.

Over the Phone

E-mail is an easy option these days for those who have it but most reservations will still be taken over the phone. Even people who've checked out your Web site and have e-mail probably will have questions or will want to book a room without waiting for an e-mail response.

Coffee Talk

"Learn as much as you can about customer service," suggest Sabrina Riddle and Lynette Molnar, owners of The Fairbanks Inn in Provincetown, Massachusetts. "Be friendly on the phone, greet guests with a smile, address them by name, make eye contact, respond to complaints, right any wrong, go the extra mile, and ask for feedback. These are small, simple gestures that go a long way toward establishing a strong, loyal following of satisfied guests. Remember that no matter how busy you are, you have only one chance to make a first impression—whether that impression is on the phone, through e-mail, or in person."

Referred by _Search Web_   E-Mail: _GAYLE @ GAYLE. COM_

RESERVATION CONFIRMATION

Name: _GAYLE + MARK THESPOT / SHEILA TORGESON + SANDY WALLOP_

Address: _321 YOURVILLE RD. BESTOWN. N.Y 10000_

Home Phone: _(914) 555-1017_ _____ Work Phone: (___) _____

Arrival Time: _5 PM_ _____ Car? _Yes, 2_ _____

Date of Reservation: _5/27/01_   By: _PARK_

Room #: _P1 + 7_ ___ for _2 + 2_ _____ person(s) has been reserved for you starting not before

2:00 pm on _Wednesday, 5 June 2001_ You are responsible for the entire period reserved. A deposit

in the amount of $ _548 50_ ____ form: _4321 0000 0000 0000 - 11/04_ is acknowledged and
represents half of the period reserved. Your deposit is nonrefundable, unless (1) there is at least a ten day notice of
cancellation, and (2) the room is re-rented for the same dates. If these two conditions are met the deposit, less ten
percent (10%) service charge based on the total room rate, will be refunded. The balance is due in full upon arrival in cash,
money order, traveler's check or major credit card. We cannot accept personal or business checks except for advance
deposits. All payments must be in U.S. funds made payable to the property at which you have reserved room(s). There
are no refunds on room charges. We regret that we cannot accept pets. No more than two guests are allowed per room
except by prior arrangement. We ask that you respect our quiet hours from 11:00 pm to 9:00 am.

Rate per night: _250_	x _4_	
Total Room Rate	$ _1000 —_	Arrive _Wed. 5 June, 2001_
Room Tax 9.7%	$ _97 00_	Depart _Sun 9 June, 2001_
Sub Total:	$ _1097 —_	
Less Deposit Received: (Date _5/27_	$ _548 50_	Remarks _Staying with_
Balance due upon arrival:	$ _549 50_	_Sheila + Sandy - rm 7_

Please Note: Travel time by car from Boston or Providence is approximately 2.5 hours. From N.Y.C. bridges, approximately 5.5 hours. Please advise us if you are delayed or your travel plans change. We look forward to seeing you!

☑ **Benchmark Inn**
6 Dyer Street
Provincetown, MA 02657
     (Directions below, as for Central.)

(508) 487-7440 Reservations and guest line

*The reservation form that Park uses for his properties. Use this as a guide and compare it with
other reservation forms so you can decide what will work best for you.*

What better way to get an idea of how to take a reservation than to listen in on one?
Let's have a listen as Park works his magic on a guest we'll call Gayle:

Park: Good afternoon, Benchmark Inn, this is Park.

Gayle: Hi there. I'm looking to book a couple of rooms with you next week.

Park: I can do that for you. Can I put you on hold for just a second?

Gayle: Sure.

B&B-eware!

Watch out for tricky language! The word "through" can be very dangerous indeed. If a guest says, "I am looking to stay with you from June 5 through June 9," does this mean they'll check out on June 9, or leave on June 10? Confirm arrival and departure dates by clearly stating the day of the week and the date (Wednesday, June 5, for example).

Inn the Know

Always ask guests how they heard about your place. Write that information on the reservation form whether it was a referral, your Web site, or a guidebook. Knowing where your clientele is finding out about you is extremely valuable in determining where to place your marketing dollars.

Park: And your name?

Gayle: It's Gayle.

Park: Okay, Gayle, I'll be right with you.

Park quickly finds a pen, reservation form, calculator, and the booking calendar. He also takes a two-second glance at what's available next week so he's ready to discuss Gayle's options.

Park: Okay. What days were you planning on next week?

Gayle: Wednesday through Sunday. I actually will need two rooms; one for me and my husband and one for another couple.

Park: Great. May I ask how you heard about us?

Gayle: We did a search online and found your site. I looked at just about everything on the site; your place looks lovely.

Park: Thank you. (Knowing that this guest has viewed the Web site, Park has a better idea of how to proceed.) Well, I have three rooms available at the Benchmark Inn. Two units, Penthouse 1 and Room 7 are right next to each other. Both have bay and harbor views from a deck that connects them. Room 7 is our coziest room and has great views, and Penthouse 1 is a suite that also has a kitchenette and a whirlpool tub in the bath. I also have room 1 available; a sunny, first-floor room with pine flooring and a private balcony with garden view. These rooms all come with fireplaces, terry cloth robes, fresh flowers, refrigerators, coffee makers, daily housekeeping, and an evening turndown service.

Gayle: Hmmmmm. We'd like to be next to each other but I know that the other couple will want a suite as well ….

Park: We have a couple more suites. Unfortunately, they're booked for much of your stay. Are you flexible with your dates?

Gayle: No. We've already arranged our days off from work.

Park: Well, I'm sure you'll enjoy these rooms; we'll try to show you the other suites when you're here for future reference.

Inn the Know

When you start taking a reservation, clients most likely will want to know what you have available for specific dates. If you have a lot of open rooms, it's not just a matter of picking a bed for them to sleep in (unless all your rooms are comparable). This is an open opportunity to talk up your place. Describe the rooms you have and what's available in each one. Depending on how the person responds, you might ask whether they're looking for a certain rate or a specific amenity.

Gayle: That sounds great. We'll take the smaller room this time.

Park: Perfect. Gayle, will the deposit for both rooms be paid by you?

Gayle: No, I'll have Sheila or her girlfriend Sandy call you.

Park: Will you be able to contact one of them soon? We're nearly full and I'll be able to hold their room only for another hour.

Gayle: I'll get on the phone with her after hanging up with you.

Park: Okay, is Gayle, G-A-I-L?

Gayle: Actually it's G-A-Y-L-E. And the last name is T-H-E-S-P-O-T. My husband's name is Mark, and that's with a "k."

Park: Does he have the same last name?

Gayle: Yes.

Park: And both couples will arrive on Wednesday, June 5th and leave on Sunday, June 9th.

Gayle: That's right.

Park: Okay, Gayle, may I have your address? (Gayle gives address, including zip code.)

Park: Will you be driving in?

Gayle: Yes, in two separate cars.

Park: That's fine. Our normal check-in is 2:00 P.M. Do you know approximately when you'll arrive?

B&B-eware!

Always ask guests to spell out names and unusual words in addresses. It seems trivial but misspellings can come back to haunt you later on, especially if you get someone's address wrong.

Gayle: Around 5:00 in the evening.

Park: That's no problem. Do you need directions?

Gayle: No, I'll print out the map on your Web site.

Park: Okay, great. Let me calculate your rate. The rate for your room will be $250 per night for a total of four nights. The total for your room is $1,000. Rooms tax at 9.7 percent brings the total to $1,097, and we require a 50 percent deposit which is $548.50. The balance of $548.50 will be due on arrival. We don't have time to process a check (eliminating the option), so which credit card would you like to use?

Gayle: I'll put it on my VISA card. Let me get that info for you. (Gayle gives card number, name on card [which happens to bear her first and middle names, different from what she gave Park] and the expiration date.)

Park: Gayle, have you been to town before?

Gayle: No, but I believe Sheila has.

Park: Well, I'll ask Sheila when she calls if she's familiar with the restaurants and if I can put reservations in for one or more nights during your stay.

Gayle: Oh, how nice.

Park: Terrific. You're all set for Room 7, Gayle. Would you like to hear our cancellation policy?

Gayle: It's unlikely that we'll cancel; our bags are practically packed but I did glance at your policy on the Web site.

Park goes over arrival and departure information and mentions the amount discussed. He also tells Gayle that the deposit will be placed on her VISA later that day and that she'll receive confirmation within a few days.

Park: I look forward to hearing from Sheila and to meeting you on Wednesday the 5th.

Gayle: Same here, Park. Thank you.

Via E-Mail

E-mail will be a little less wordy than our phone example because no one wants to write that much down! You should have a checklist of points; or even better, a fill-in-the-blanks e-mail that you can alter for each reservation. Make sure that you ask as many questions as possible in that first go-round to cut down on back-and-forth e-mails. It will save time and, on the return, you will have most of the information in one e-mail.

Consider writing out a reservation confirmation form and sending it by snail mail. That way, you have a formal record that you can file with the e-mail or fax so you're doubly sure that the reservation is confirmed.

Handling Cancellations

Make sure that all guests have your cancellation policy in writing. Even if they don't read it, you can refer to it if they call to cancel. Stick to your guns as much as you can on this. Losing money on a cancellation can be like losing money on that room twice: the money from the guest who cancelled and the money from a guest that you could have locked in if the cancellation had been made earlier.

After a guest cancels, send a letter confirming the details. Have a form letter ready to go so that you can quickly fill in the blanks. Attach a copy of the cancellation letter to the original reservation form and file it under cancellations. Be sure to write the reason for the cancellation on your copy of the form for future reference.

Inn the Know

Try to sound as personable as you can in your e-mail, but don't get too cute. Things can be misconstrued when you have just words to go by instead of a laugh or tone of voice to accompany a comment on the phone.

Reservation Services

A reservation service agency (RSA) is great because it can take care of the legwork for you. RSAs advertise your place, take guest information, send the guest all the information they need about your place, and contact you with all the details.

You'll need to pay for that legwork in the form of a commission per referral (usually 20 percent) and sometimes an additional flat membership fee. Check with your RSA regarding cancellation fees, if any. There are local RSAs (city- or town-based, mostly only in high tourist areas); regional ones (statewide, within a group of states, or in part of a state); and national RSAs. You might need to shop around a bit before finding a fit. Some RSAs will limit the number of hosts that they'll refer guests to in a given area, especially one overcrowded with B&Bs. Once again, talk to your B&B brothers and sisters to find out what has worked for them.

Before you sign up with an RSA, determine what's best for your business. The costs might not be worth it to you if your room rates are low or if you can handle the reservation paperwork yourself. However, if your marketing plans and word-of-mouth recommendations haven't done their job yet, RSAs do help you get guests. The good ones also get more information on guests than you might be able to (such as age and reason for travel), which you can use in your marketing plan. You might have an option to try out an RSA before signing a contract. This policy varies among agencies.

Working with Travel Agents

You won't need to sign a contract with a travel agent and usually they will find you first. Most will call you looking for a room for a client and you'll start a relationship that way. The agent might ask about specific amenities, room rates, payment, cancellation policies, and commissions. The agent might be hesitant to give you the client's address but it's always appropriate to get the guests' home or business phone number.

Sometimes you'll get the initial booking through an agent, pay the commission, and then deal directly with the guest for confirmation, finalizing details and payment. However, it is more likely that you'll go through the agent for all the details, including confirmation. The commission usually is around 10 to 15 percent—less than an RSA because agents usually do less legwork; and generally is paid after a guest's stay. Many agents have been charging their clients service fees to compensate for recent cuts in commission rates, so some agents might not expect a commission at all from a small property.

Due to the repetitiveness of your daily tasks—this bears repeating—organization is key. In time you'll establish your own pattern of communicating with guests during the reservation process, but good record-keeping is a pattern you'll want to establish at the start.

> **Inn the Know**
>
> Direct booking capability, otherwise known as "real time booking," is coming to a small B&B near you. Now guests can book accommodations directly, online, with hotels and larger inn operations. Direct booking capability requires compatibility with your reservation software and looks to be the wave of the future.

The Least You Need to Know

➤ Schedule a daily routine that fits into your prearranged duties such as serving breakfast and doing household chores.

➤ Give and get as much information as you can when scheduling a reservation.

➤ Using a reservation service agency or a travel agent will cost you in commission fees but it can be worth it if they help you get guests.

Chapter 18

Guest Services with a Smile

In This Chapter

➤ Exploring the different levels of service you can provide

➤ Learning the ways of a concierge

➤ Tailoring your services to your guests' needs

The services you provide can be just as pleasing as some of your amenities. Picture this: A young, married couple decide to celebrate their anniversary with a weekend getaway at your place, which is in a resort town they've never visited. They plan to arrive at 6 P.M. but get stuck in traffic and call you to say they're going to be a few hours late. You ask if they'd like late dinner reservations and they tell you not to bother. After getting lost a few times in a downpour they finally arrive at your doorstep at around 8:30 P.M., weary and soaking wet. You show them to their room, where there's champagne on ice, take-out menus, and a small plate of cheese, crackers, and fruit for them to nibble on. Who wouldn't want to be greeted like this on a cold, wet night after spending several miserable hours stuck in a car?

Guests will appreciate your efforts to take care of them this way and, depending on what you charge, some might even expect a certain level of service. Don't worry if you can't afford to add a lot of amenities; the thoughtful little services will go a long way.

Trends in Guest Services

B&Bs that compete with other B&Bs, large inns, and hotels for business are starting to provide more of the concierge-type services that used to be associated only with hotels. The homey atmosphere of a B&B and hotel-type services is a great combination. Guests who like having a host they can connect with but also like services such as having theater tickets reserved will go back to a B&B that has both—and they'll tell their friends about it.

Services Guests Can't Live Without

We've said this before, but it bears repeating: Providing fresh towels and sheets and clean rooms and baths during a guest's stay is not an option; it's a necessity. Even if you have only one guest room and you rent it out for only a few months of the year (or whenever the mood strikes you), you still need to offer these basic services that guests can't live without.

After clean linens and rooms, the services that are considered basic and are expected will depend on the quality level of your B&B. You wouldn't provide an on-site masseuse if your average room night charge is only $100. On the other hand, if your average room rate is $275 and you provide amenities such as a hot tub, of course you'd also provide the smallest types of services such as a wake-up call. Once again, what you offer must match the rates you charge. The following are some basic services that would be offered at different quality levels, with level 5 representing the highest quality:

➤ **Level 1.** Should include comfortable beds, attractive furnishings in good repair including at least two light sources; alarm clock; good linens; clean linoleum or tile-floored shared or private bathrooms with wrapped soap and plastic cups, facial tissues, sanitary bags, and a back-up roll of toilet paper (you'll also want to provide air freshener and a toilet brush in shared baths); bed making; towel exchange; and full cleaning of shared bathrooms daily. Breakfast can be simple; consisting of juice, tea, coffee, and muffins. You should have a television in the living room and a phone available to guests on the property. Guests should be able to access the owner or manager in the morning and late afternoon or early evening with an emergency number thereafter. Outside grounds should be attractive and tidy.

➤ **Level 2.** Similar to level 1, but with better towels and linens (180 thread count minimum), clock radio, television in the room or 24-hour access to a room with one, shampoo and conditioner in 1- or 1½-ounce bottles, hairdryer, and an iron with ironing board available to all guests. Private baths should be cleaned daily. Add two items to breakfast (fresh fruit, yogurt, granola, cold cereal, for example). There should be a telephone with a data port available in the common room along with a selection of games and puzzles, umbrellas, and expanded information about area attractions. Your property should have some indoor plants and upgraded landscaping.

➤ **Level 3.** Includes everything in the first two levels and more: Most rooms feature queen-size beds and all have closets, upgraded furnishings, television in the room, bedside reading lamps, in-room phone with data port, and simple outgoing service. Some rooms have wonderful views and air conditioning (should climatic conditions require). All baths should be *en suite* (private) and in excellent repair; with small bottles of shampoo, conditioner, and hand and body lotion. Breakfast can be either an appealing and nutritious sit-down or an expanded continental with two more items than in level 2, and a greater selection of baked goods. A VCR or DVD with a small selection of videos or discs in the living room or separate viewing lounge should be provided. A fax machine and refrigerator should be available to guests morning through evening; as should you, your spouse or significant other, or your manager. Offer wake-up calls and restaurant reservations as needed. Sport some fresh flowers in your common room and be certain that your grounds are lovely.

➤ **Level 4.** Everything that applies for the first three levels, with the addition of excellent quality furnishings and mattresses and fluffy towels and linens (200 thread count is ideal). All rooms should have phones with dataport and voicemail, a CD or radio alarm clock, television with VCR or DVD, and air conditioning (where necessary). Some rooms will offer luxurious features such as a balcony, fireplace, wet bar, king-size bed, whirlpool tub, or an excellent view. Baths are tiled and feature boutique bath amenities including bath gel (don't forget bath salts for tubs), upgraded lighting, fan vent, and hairdryer. Common room should have a video or DVD library with 75 or so titles and excellent reference materials on area attractions. A fruit basket or snack item should be available outside of breakfast hours; ice and washable plastic tumblers should be available after hours. Courteous assistance from you or your staff should be available from 7 or 8 A.M. until 9, 10, or 11 P.M. daily. Binoculars should be available for sightseeing. Concierge duties should include dinner and entertainment suggestions and subsequent reservations on request. Your property will have special characteristics: location, views, or amenities (such as an outdoor hot tub or pool; don't forget the towels) that enhance its value to guests.

➤ **Level 5.** At this level of service, your amenities and property must shine. Rooms feature individual climate control (heating and cooling); down comforters; safes; soundproofing;

Inn the Know

When guests book a room with you over the phone or through e-mail, let them know you can make reservations for them. Some will be surprised that you offer this service and delighted that you'll provide it before they even arrive!

direct dial phone service; flat screen televisions (okay, we think they'll be afford-able around 2005); expanded cable or satellite offerings; bar setup that includes wine key, filled ice bucket, and glassware; in-room plants or fresh flowers; and umbrellas. Also consider variable-speed ceiling fans and dimmer lighting. Most rooms will feature two (preferably more) of the level 4 luxuries. Bathrooms might have deluxe fixtures, marble trim or floors, glass shower and tub enclo-sures, terry robes, lighted mirrors, and vanity packs. Guest laundry services can be provided at additional cost. Guests will expect superb breakfast offerings and flexible dining arrangements that allow them to eat when and where they choose. Common areas might include a small business center offering fax, Internet access, and laser printer. Build your DVD collection and consider hav-ing compact discs (or whatever format is *de riguer*) available for guests to sign out. Service hinges on excellent housekeeping (full turndown service) and a knowledgeable and responsive concierge for all entertainment including horse-back riding, spa treatments, golf, tennis, or watersports (lucky guests if any are on site!) The person who handles services also arranges for pickup and drop-off to local airports, piers, and train or bus depots. Your property has much to offer in the way of location and amenities and probably has some killer views. Wow!

These are just basic guidelines. Instituting services gradually is the way to go. That way, you can keep close tabs on a new service and decide whether it's really being used. If it isn't, try something else!

B&B-eware!

Having high-end services avail-able that don't get used (such as shoe shining) might seem impres-sive, but you won't be able to justify rate increases based on these alone. You can bump up your rates for providing services (some don't cost anything but time) only if your guests take ad-vantage of them.

Catering to Clientele

The services you provide will depend on your location and your clientele. If you're in a seaside town, some of the reservations you make might include things like whale watches. If there are breathtaking views from some of your suites, offer breakfast in bed. If your B&B is within walking distance of a lake, provide an out-side shower with extra beach towels and a sunning area (this will keep sand out of your house, too). It might take a while to develop your services, but that's fine. Take note of which services are used most by your guests and which ones can be found at your competition's property. If a competitor offers a service that your guests would use, too, consider adding it in.

Take into consideration that some of your clientele might be staying with you to get away from it all—including you! When that's clearly the case, it's best to let guests know what you can do for them in a short conversation over the phone or on arrival; then get out of their way.

Turndown Service

This probably is one of the nicest—and cheapest—services you can offer. It can work really well if you're in a bustling area where guests will be out shopping and sightseeing all day. The atmosphere you can create with turndown will relax guests more than they might have imagined it could.

Here are the basics of providing turndown service:

➤ Tidy up guests' things in room and bathroom; replace towels if necessary; remove garbage if overflowing; clean up kitchen area.

➤ Make bed with precision: Remove wrinkles, turn back the sheets and blankets, straighten pillows so they have defined corners, place throw pillows on a nearby chair or stow beneath the bed or in a closet, place chocolates or your treat of choice (nothing crumbly like cookies) on top of the turned-back sheets (placing them on upright pillows will cause them to fall down or be overlooked when guests go to bed).

➤ Turn bedside lamp or dim overhead lights on to a romantic glow (not so dim that guests can't see their way); keep a nightlight on in the bathroom.

➤ Turn music on at low level to a classical station.

Inn the Know

Adding your own touches will make your turndown service unique. Consider a tent card on the bed that offers a nightly proverb (or words of nondenominational spirituality), or a carafe of hot cider and mugs. You can use this time to tie into the theme of your B&B as well. Let's say you own the Spotted Owl Inn. You could get a CD of the rain forest to play continuously instead of classical musical. Want to include fireplaces as amenities but can't afford it? Buy *The Amazing Fireplace* video from Light Rain Entertainment (www.lightrain.net). They have a cool aquarium video, too.

Plan to spend 20 to 30 minutes in each room for turndown. It might be shorter, depending on how clean the room is, but it shouldn't take you any longer. As in your everyday cleaning of rooms, you'll have to juggle to get turndown accomplished. You might have some guests who leave for an entire evening and some who get a quick bite and realize that they really just want to relax in their room. For this reason, it's best to take care of turndown as soon as guests go out. If you're planning on providing something quirky such as hot cider, make sure that it's still good enough to drink late in the evening. If you have a lot of younger clientele who will spend more time at a restaurant or bar hopping, consider leaving something else that will still be fresh at midnight (such as bottles of spring water).

You'll be handling this service in the evenings when you'll be dead tired, so we suggest doing it only if you have staff. Do it yourself only if you have a very small number of rooms—three or fewer; maybe four at the most. If you have six rooms and no staff, this means you will spend an average of two to three hours every evening (when your house is full) doing turndown. You'll end up hating it, and the service itself might slip in quality. Take on this service only if you or staff are equipped to cover it every night.

Creating a Guest Portfolio

A guest portfolio is a binder or folder left in guest rooms that has information about your place and the surrounding area. Don't cram the portfolio with too much information, but consider the following items:

➤ Brochures for area events that you recommend (don't just grab brochures from a tourist center for events that you haven't checked out personally).

➤ List of your guest policies (see Chapter 15, "Setting Guest Policies").

➤ If you serve a full breakfast, a menu list of breakfasts served for the current week.

➤ A list of your guest services.

➤ How you can be reached or how to find a staff member if you're away from the house.

➤ How to operate the phone system (if long-distance calls are blocked) or where a guest phone is located if they're not provided in the rooms.

➤ Blank paper (with letterhead if possible), a pen, and envelopes (again, with your property's logo). A Benchmark Inn (Park's B&B) signature touch is stamping the top envelope with first-class postage.

Find some nice leather, good-looking vinyl, or cloth-covered portfolio folders at an office supply store or through accommodation supply catalogs (see Chapter 14, "Stocking Up on Supplies"). Make sure you place the portfolio where guests will see it right away when they go to their room.

Concierge-at-Large

Probably the best concierge-type service you can provide is being available. You might get some odd requests from guests at odd hours; and whether you can fulfill them or not, guests will be frustrated if they can't get hold of you. Some guests will expect you to be at their beck and call at all times; others will appreciate any extra service you provide; still others won't bother you at all, or want to be bothered themselves. However, at the very least they all want to know you're around if they choose to call on you.

What are the top 10 ways to take care of guests, you ask? Check out this top 10 list from Warren Lefkowich, owner of the West End Inn in Provincetown, Massachusetts:

➤ Eye contact and a smile go a long way. A friendly demeanor and a sense of humor should always be a part of your "stage presence."

➤ Treat guests the way you would like to be treated. They are, like us, individuals with special needs and wants.

➤ Anticipate the needs and wants of your guests and act to solve any problems they might have.

➤ Have a can-do attitude and never say, "It's not my job."

➤ Anyone who receives a guest complaint owns that complaint until it's resolved. React quickly and resolve the problem immediately.

➤ Leave personal problems in your room.

➤ Be a team player.

➤ Show interest in what a guest is saying. Listen carefully and be able to answer any questions the guest might have.

➤ Always introduce yourself and acknowledge each guest by name; frequently, formally, and professionally.

➤ Take pride in your work. A positive attitude is the key to success.

The Concierge Personality

If you don't have your hosting smile down, start practicing. Find a mirror and look like a goofball for a few minutes while you try out faces (best to wait until you're alone). This doesn't mean you should come up with the biggest, fakest, cheesiest grin. Just know how your face looks and what kind of signals your body language sends. Do you shrink your shoulders when someone talks to you? Fold your arms? Do you walk with your head up or stare at the ground? What does your normal gaze look like? We're serious here! Some people have a look that makes others think, "Is she all right? Is something bothering him?" You must know someone like this. If *you* are someone like this, you'll need to find ways to ease back a smile or at least have a game face on when talking with guests.

Coffee Talk

Hosting requires strength, resilience, and a certain amount of skill in the performing arts. Rick and Ruth-Anne Broad, owners of Anne's Oceanfront Hideaway B&B in Salt Spring Island, B.C., Canada, agree. "Be prepared to cook, clean, shop, greet guests, and be a concierge every day with a smile on your face. You might be tired, ill, or feeling blue, but your guests don't want to know that. For them you *will* smile and be cheerful."

Now that you can face the public (pun intended), keep in mind the traits of a good concierge (and all-around good host):

➤ **Speed.** You take care of reservations and requests right away.

➤ **Follow-through.** You make sure that guests have the information as soon as you can gather it. If you can't speak to guests directly, you follow up to make sure they found your note or retrieved their voicemail message.

➤ **Efficiency and accuracy.** You get all the information you need from guests to make reservations and take care of other services and you provide them with all the information they need.

➤ **You're pleasant but not gushy.** You take time to explain or discuss things with guests without going overboard. Don't give them your life   story, what happened to you that day, or why you're so dang tired. Talk about what relates to their stay and let them ask the questions. Be brief, funny, and sweet, and you'll always win your guests' hearts and patronage.

As the owner or manager of a B&B, you'll be regarded in the same light as the B&B itself. If guests find your inn inviting and comfortable, they'll expect you to have these same traits—and you should. The B&B is an extension of you; there's really no getting away from it!

Making Reservations for Guests

When you book something for a guest, make sure you get it right the first time. This is a great service that guests will appreciate but only if you don't spend a lot of time going back and forth for more information.

For example, when you talk to guests about making a dinner reservation, get all the information you need to get in one conversation: their price range, food preferences, whether anyone will join them, their second and third choices if the first restaurant is booked, the time or range of times they'll consider dining, and how far they want to travel.

When you make the reservation, you'll first need to check on availability for the number in the party and their desired dining time. Place the reservation under both the guest's name and yours. For example, when Park makes a reservation for, let's say, our old friend Gayle and her party of four, he would place the reservation under "Benchmark-Gayle." This provides greater recognition for the property and may help ensure that your guests get top priority. If your guests request a restaurant that you're unfamiliar with, let them know they'll be your guinea pigs.

Inn the Know

Obey the five-minute rule! Most conversations with your guests should be conducted while standing and last no more than five minutes. That's enough time for them to feel as if you're paying enough attention to them and it fits into your schedule, too!

B&B-eware!

Make reservations for guests only at restaurants that you or reliable sources can recommend. This also goes for sightseeing tours, theater companies, comedy clubs, and other kinds of entertainment. If a guest has a bad experience while staying with you, it can result in a tarnished image of you and your house (whether deserved or not).

Follow up immediately with the guests after you make reservations. Slip a confirmation under their door, leave a message on their in-room voicemail or, if you know they'll be out all day, get their cell phone number or have them call you in an hour to confirm the plans.

Providing Local Info

Provide brochures, maps, flyers, and local publications for guests in a common area. Set up a table or shelf just for this purpose so that people know they can take copies for their personal use.

If there's a guidebook that guests can borrow for bird watching or hiking trails, you might want to get a couple of copies so that guests can take them on day trips. If your area has a tourist center, post its location or phone number in plain sight for guests who might want to do some more digging around.

At Beck and Call

When are you too accommodating? Are you watching a guest's kids while they're out for the evening because you can't say no? Most guests won't ask you to go above and beyond the call of duty but there will be that occasional guest who feels that you owe him or her some extra personal service.

Coffee Talk

"Don't try to be all things to all people," suggests Dennis Radtke, General Manager of County Clare—an Irish Guesthouse and Pub in Milwaukee, Wisconsin. "Define your concept, your amenities and services, and stay true to them. This is not to say that your guests can't have special requests and that you can't oblige them, but if you cater to every whim of every guest you run the risk of being like a restaurant with 50 items on the menu. You know that the food can't be that great because it would be impossible to have everything freshly and carefully prepared. The same concept applies to this business. Better to find your personal niche and be leery of changing it for the sake of change."

You might find it difficult to say no to people—who doesn't? But to save your sanity and strength and to concentrate on all your guests, be firm (but congenial) with pushy guests. They won't be happy with anything you do, so it's best to stop them from making a dozen unreasonable requests by not accommodating the first one. Most people will back down when you make them realize that something is unreasonable and that you have a house full of guests to attend to. Try compromising with guests so that they feel as if they got the service and attention they were after. For example, let's say you have guests who arrived late for a dinner reservation; they don't have a car and they urge you to drive them to and from a restaurant during a downpour. Offer to order them a taxi and call the restaurant to inform them that your guests will be arriving shortly. If you feel these guests will not be pleased with your solution, offer to take them outbound only, and give them your business card with the number of a reliable cab company on the back for the return trip.

Offering Business Services

Tapping into the business traveler market means providing services that they need to do their job. If you find that more and more suits are staying with you on extended business trips, you might want to convert your least-used room into an extra common room and meeting place. Most likely, you'll just need to provide things such as a fax machine and an easy way for folks to get their messages (data ports would be extra nice). Some of the equipment and services you might want to add are as follows:

➤ **Fax machine.** You obviously don't need one in every room. Have one out for guests to use in a common area or keep it in your office so you can control how much it's used. Keep in mind that you'll need a dedicated line for the fax if you keep it in the common area.

➤ **E-mail and the Internet.** Just think, in a few years, 24-hour Internet access probably will be a standard service! For now, figure out whether you want guests to have in-room access or if it should be available in a separate area. Will you have a computer set up for guests to use whenever they want to or will they need their own laptops? Again, think about your clientele. Grandpa George from Tulsa doesn't need Internet access at 3 A.M. nor might he want it—ever. Your area might already be hooked up with high-speed Internet access. Check with your cable or telephone company to find out.

Coffee Talk

"As hotels have become more costly and competitive over the years, we have tried to hold the line on price but not on service," said Jay Lesiger, Chelsea Pines Inn in New York City. "We now serve homemade bread every morning as well as fresh Krispy Kreme donuts (guests love them). We continue to add more and more amenities to the inn; our latest will be an e-mail server in the breakfast room so guests can check their mail while they're traveling. Our main aim is to keep guests happy and eager to return and since half our business is from repeats and referrals, it must be working!"

➤ **A good phone system.** If you have a lot of business travelers, get a good phone system with voicemail. That way they can leave an outgoing message and can pick up messages from wherever they are. Hotels provide this service and that's the reason business folks stay with them (well, one of the reasons). You might argue that most business travelers will have cell phones, or at least pagers; this is true, but cell phones are not always reliable, especially if the user is 2,000 miles away from home base or in a remote area.

➤ **Computer printer.** This is nice to have on hand. Business folks who know you have this in advance will be happy if they need to print out files from their laptop. Just be sure they know what kind of printer you have and that it's color (get inkjet or laser—they're just better). Remember that ink cartridges (particularly color) are expensive, so think twice before you offer this service full-time.

➤ **Mailing services.** Have FedEx, United States Postal Service, DHL, or Airborne Express envelopes and slips on hand for business travelers. You won't be charged for their standard shipping envelopes and guests can pay for mailing charges with a credit card number. USPS packages will need to be dropped off by you or your staff but some of the other courier services can schedule pick-ups (depending on location and their respective criteria).

Even folks who are not business travelers might appreciate having a fax machine available and, at the least, a voicemail phone system so they can get their messages.

Try not to get ahead of yourself when implementing services. Don't burn out early on; in time you'll be able to determine what is really beneficial to your guests and will help you keep your sanity.

The Least You Need to Know

➤ The level of service you provide should match what you charge in room rates. Increase your services gradually as you find out which ones guests make use of.

➤ A concierge-type personality includes traits such as stamina, speed, efficiency, and a pleasant nature.

➤ Making reservations and providing local information are basic services that are easy to offer and will be appreciated by your guests.

➤ Providing business services is a growing trend; yours can be as simple as having a fax machine or as involved as adding data ports to every room.

Housekeeping Basics

What keeps you on your toes, never goes away, and won't get more exciting over time? No, it's not your Uncle Carl. It's laundry and dishes and vacuuming and sweeping and dusting and ... well, the list goes on and on, and so will your enthusiasm—right? Hardly. Let's get real: You won't like it. No one does, and that's okay. You don't have to like it but you will have to do it. Day after day, hour after hour, you'll be doing something to keep your B&B looking, smelling, and feeling good.

Keeping House Every Day

You might think, "Why have these crazy authors dedicated an entire chapter to cleaning?" It seems odd; after all, most everyone knows how to take care of their own house. The difference in taking care of a building used by others is that you need to clean above and beyond average. When people enter their room, they want to feel as if they're the first ones who've ever stayed in it—not consciously, of course—but any evidence of previous guests will be a huge turnoff.

Staying on Top of It

Housekeeping is one of those very important things that can easily get away from you. The best way to stay on top of cleaning guest rooms, common areas, outdoor areas, bathrooms, hallways, and the kitchen is to attack it piecemeal, whenever you can.

You might recall the "day in the life" scenario we concocted in Chapter 3, "What It's Really Like." If you go back and look over that schedule, you'll find that laundry and cleaning were the two tasks that came up on and off throughout the day, every day, whenever possible. That's the only way to stay on top of housekeeping—and stay sane.

If you sit down and tell yourself, "Okay, I can clean everything from noon until 3:00 today," the task will seem so daunting that you'll never get to it; not to mention that you'll be interrupted 30 times during those two hours—because you're an inn-keeper. On the other hand, if you know you're going to clean only one room and then move on to something else, you won't put it off; you'll get it done so you can move on to other things.

Whipping Staff Into Shape

That's whipping staff *into shape,* silly; flogging staff is not recommended, and is highly controversial—well, in most parts, anyway. You'll need to keep an eye on staff, especially when they first start, to make sure things are polished and details aren't missed. You will have high cleaning standards for your B&B because it's your house. Your staff, on the other hand, might be less than eager to get things perfect because it's not their place.

Inn the Know

Always organize cleaning times around guests' schedules. If most of the guests plan to be away for most of the day, you'll have time to get to every room in a small or even mid-size B&B. It might seem overwhelming to get rooms cleaned when all the guests leave the house at once, but actually this can be fun in a "beat the clock" kind of way. You can leave all the doors open and crank up the tunes!

When a staff member starts working at your B&B, take the person through the cleaning procedures as you do them. Clean a few rooms together and have Sally or Sam clear off breakfast while you observe. As you go along, point out certain things such as fixing the blinds so that guests will have sunlight on entering the room and go through the order of how you clean things. Do a spot check when staff members, new or old, clean a room to make sure they're doing everything to meet your standards. This might seem like micromanaging but it's a very good way to impress upon the staff how important perfectly clean areas are to you and the guests. Stay out of your staff's way most of the time; it will show them that you have confidence in their work. For more on working with staff, see Chapter 20, "Help Wanted."

Getting Rooms Ready

When you're cleaning, there are some things that it's absolutely out of the question to leave behind: dust in any form (whether as bunnies or the filmy kind), human hair, streaky mirror, wet countertop or floor, an unsparkling toilet, or dirty floor or carpet.

The Stages of Clean

Have a system for getting rooms ready. If you think about it, you won't do a full clean every time someone checks in. You'll do it when they check out. So, what kind of clean do you do in the time you have between the departure of one guest and the arrival of another who will occupy the same room? When do you clean a room during a guest's stay? Have a system so you and your staff will know the cleaning status of each room from day to day. Consider Park's method:

➤ **Make-ready.** This is the big clean right after someone checks out. Replacing sheets and towels, dusting, disinfecting, vacuuming, and anything else to make the room totally ready to go happens during a make-ready.

➤ **Ready.** This means the room has been cleaned (has gone through the make-ready stage) but no one is checking in to it right away.

➤ **Ice.** This is a room that's ready, but now that someone is checking in, it needs ice. During an "ice," walk through the room to make sure nothing was missed during the make-ready. Also, take care to open a window, turn on the ceiling fan, check the thermostat, put music on low, or do anything else that will make the guest's first entry into the room more pleasant.

Inn the Know

Pick up a copy of *How to Clean Practically Anything,* published by *Consumer Reports.* From stain removals to high ceilings, this book has it all.

Shoestring Solution

Some hotels still change sheets daily, but given environmental and economical concerns, every other day or every third is fine. Towels usually are changed every day but you can try getting guests to reuse them by posting an environmental alert sign, available through supply companies such as American Hotel Register. Here's an example of one sign: "Dear guest: In an effort to conserve water and energy, please consider using your towel more than once. Please decide for yourself: A towel on the rack means 'I'll use it again,' whereas a towel on the floor, shower, or tub means 'please exchange.'" These signs are available as tent cards, static cling (to apply to mirrors), or in a variety of other styles.

➤ **Fluff.** This clean happens after the first night of a guest's stay. General tidying up, straightening, towel change, and light cleaning are done.

➤ **Fluff-plus.** This is a fluff clean plus a change of linens. For guests staying four nights, a fluff-plus is done after two nights; guests staying longer get linens changed after three nights.

➤ **Flip.** A combination "make-ready" and "ice" after one guest checks out and another is expected in a few hours.

You can call these stages Larry, Moe, Shirley, and so on for all we care, as long as you have a system. Be sure you post the status chart (an erasable marker board works great) where it's accessible to all the staff.

Where Do I Start?

You will come across a pigpen guest now and then, have no doubt about it; and there will be times when personal items you find in a room will make you uncomfortable. Do your best to clean around people's things unless they're all over the place. If you do move things, fold clothes neatly and be sure to put money, dresser items, bags, and shoes where people will see them right away. Tucking things away will appear invasive to a guest, who then might rummage through the room to make sure everything's there.

B&B-eware!

Some people don't seem to mind if their things are tidied up to get them out of the way but others will mind a lot. If you get a sense that some guests are nervous about leaving their stuff in their room, make an extra mention of the room safe (if there is one) or, on their first day, tell them exactly where their belongings were placed when you cleaned the room. You also can offer the house safe for their valuables.

If you move efficiently but thoroughly through an average-sized room, it should take you about 20 to 25 minutes for a typical cleaning, 30 to 35 for a fluff-plus, and 40 to 45 for a flip or a make-ready. The more you get used to cleaning the rooms, the quicker it will go. For a bigger room or one with several occupants, figure on a little more cleaning time.

You might assume that the longer folks stay with you, the more they tend to settle in and spread out, making a bigger mess. Actually, during longer stays people get a chance to see how hard you and the staff work, and guests generally are more mindful of the mess they make. This doesn't always happen, but most of the time it will.

Shoestring Solution

You're going to be cleaning a lot, so search a wholesale store for a concentrated disinfectant you can live with. Orange or lemony scents are better than pine or institutional smells. These industrial-strength cleaners often can be diluted with 20 parts water, so by using them you'll save hundreds of dollars yearly.

When you start out, you might find it helpful to make a checklist for yourself and the staff of what should be done for a make-ready and in what order. Here's an example:

- ❏ Fold up guests' belongings and set them aside on a chair.
- ❏ Put away ironing board and things that can be tucked away.
- ❏ Remove dirty bedding and ball it up.
- ❏ Dust tops of shelves and tables.
- ❏ Sitting areas: Tidy up reading materials, fix pillows (there's always a possibility that guests will come back for something and will talk to you for a bit, so it's nice to make the sitting area, if there is one, inviting).

Inn the Know

Having small storage areas in your bathroom will save you time and energy. Use an under-the-sink cabinet to store toilet paper and facial tissue. Complementary toiletries should go where guests can see them. Items you shouldn't keep under your sink are cleaning supplies. Buy tasteful toilet brushes that can be tucked behind the toilet so you're not lugging one from room to room.

Shoestring Solution

If a room won't be used for a few days, adjust the thermostat to low during cold periods. Why keep the heat on when no one's using the room? Better to keep those heating bills down. Remind staff to check on the thermostat, too.

❑ Kitchen nook areas: Do dishes, put them away; check mini-fridge for any spills; clean up coffee maker (you can always reuse rags for bathroom after they're used in kitchen area but not vice versa, which is why the kitchen area is taken care of first).

❑ Clean bathroom: Pile up dirty towels, consolidate guests' items, clean sink, wipe down counter, squeegee shower area, clean toilet, wipe down floor, empty trash, and place clean towels on shelf. Remember this order: sink, tub, toilet. It just makes sense.

❑ Remake bed.

❑ Empty trash into larger trash bag.

❑ Wipe down mirrors and windows if necessary.

❑ Vacuum carpet or sweep floor.

❑ Fix blinds, windows, and curtains depending on the weather, sunlight, and time of day.

❑ Sanitize phone and doorknobs (not on a day-to-day basis, but this is good to do once every week or two).

❑ Working fireplaces: Pulling out ash is a messy job, so make sure it's done before vacuuming!

❑ Last check of the room: This is your last chance to not let your previous guest make your first impression. Check the bathroom and bed area carefully for hair.

Choose a cleaning order that works for you, but try to be consistent. You'll be more efficient when you can move from one step to the next without having to double back because you forgot something.

Common Areas

As guests will be in and out of your sitting areas and breakfast room, you'll be fixing and straightening things in those areas throughout the day. Avoid any major cleaning around guests who are relaxing in your common areas as it will make them very uncomfortable. If you do need to clear away breakfast plates or tidy things up, talk with your guests while you do it so they feel more at home. Halls and stairways also are best cleaned when guests are away from the house. You don't want them tripping over the vacuum cleaner or waking up to the sound of it.

Eating areas should be cleaned right away. If your breakfast area also is your sitting room, make sure that the tables and floors are cleaned thoroughly. Crumbs and leftover morsels kicked under the couch and into corners are an invitation for pesky bugs and rodents. If you serve a buffet-style continental breakfast, place a tray or cart where guests can put their trash and dirty dishes. As guests mill down at different times, clear the tray periodically throughout breakfast to keep the breakfast area looking neat.

Inn the Know

Have those cleaning supplies ready and waiting. Buy some sturdy plastic buckets that contain everything you need to clean a room: sponges, all-purpose cleaner, glass cleaner, dusting spray and cloth, squeegee, and paper towels.

The Big Clean

Set aside time in your year to clean those ceilings, walls, and windows. This is best done as needed and before your peak season. Get out that Murphy's Oil Soap for wood and your concentrated disinfectant for everything else. Don't forget those dusty ceiling fans!

There are some items that need cleaning every few months. Have a back-up supply to rotate in when the following items are busy getting fresh and clean again:

Shoestring Solution

Save money on paper towels by cleaning your windows with newspaper. Not only will it save you money, it does a better job.

➤ Zippered pillow protectors, mattress protectors, and blankets should be cleaned every three months.

➤ Synthetic comforters can be sent out for cleaning twice a year. Down or feather comforters should be protected with covers that are cleaned every three months or as needed.

Mattresses should be flipped every three months. You can write on the mattress the date you bought it and the dates it should be flipped. Choose time frames that fit into your seasons (flipping more in busier times), at least three to four times a year. Replace pillows at least every two years (three for down). Most towels can become rags but your local animal shelter might be able to take old bedding off your hands.

Laundry Again?

The difficulty in doing laundry is not that it takes too much time, as the machines do most of the job (except for folding—wouldn't a folding machine for home use be a great invention?), but that it uses so much hot water. Doing laundry is out of the question in the morning and again in the evening, peak times for guests to be showering. Consider doing the laundry yourself during slow times and using the laundry service when you really need it.

Laundry services typically charge by the pound. Turnaround service should be next day, but you might try getting a lower rate for off-peak. To save time and trips to the chiropractor, find a service that picks up and delivers. Ask if your commercial laundry service will do a same-day-service wash and fold for guests. If they won't, find out which laundry service is the fastest in town so you can recommend it to your guests.

Kitchen Duty

Keeping your kitchen spotless should never be compromised, especially if guests have access to it. Having a sparkling kitchen all the time also will be a coup if the health department shows up to see how you're doing.

As we mentioned in Chapter 6, "Legalities and Liabilities," your local and state health departments will have food and cooking guidelines. Make sure you find out what they are and get used to following them to the letter.

Some food preparation rules might include keeping your fridge at 38 to 40 degrees (necessitating a thermometer) and dishes washed at a certain temperature. Most household water heaters are set at 120 or 125 degrees; if they are set above that, you run the risk of scalding your guests. If you have a commercial operation, you might have to boost your temperature to between 140 and 160 (check your local codes) for washing dishes. Some residential dishwashers have a built-in temperature boost. Sweep your floors regularly and wash them once a week. Pests are most likely to come in through the kitchen.

Outdoor Upkeep

Overgrown grass is a menace, and who wants to sit on patio chairs that are dirty from a recent rain? Outdoor areas sometimes are neglected because most of your focus will be on the inside. Make sitting areas and gardens inviting for guests to hang out in.

> ➤ **Garden and sitting areas.** No one wants to sit on gritty chairs. Keep the chairs tipped during rainstorms and towel them off in the mornings. In warmer weather, put out umbrellas and lounge chairs. Instead of ashtrays, try using small buckets of sand. They look nicer, they're safer, and they're easier to clean up.

> ➤ **Guest parking.** Driveways deteriorate into dips and potholes. Stones get shuffled into grassy areas. Tar cracks. For your driveway and parking areas, try to find material that can stand up to cars and is easy to maintain. Crushed stone is a good option and so are crushed seashells (if you live by the seashore).

> ➤ **Walkways.** Keep these areas swept and the overgrowth cut back. Check for cracks and raised stones that can cause tripping.

Your guests will appreciate fresh-air common areas, so it's worth the extra time and energy it takes to keep them clean, attractive, and safe.

By now you've gotten the hint that cleaning is important and will account for most of your daily chores. The trick in everyday upkeep is to make sure it's done behind the scenes as much as possible. Guests will want to see your place in its polished state, and not witness how it got there!

Inn the Know

A dishwasher is a must. If you run a larger operation, consider getting two. You might not need to run them at the same time, but you can load them and have them ready to go. Some health departments will be wary about your sanitary conditions if you don't have a dishwasher, as dishes must be cleaned at a certain temperature.

B&B-eware

Don't forget those front walks and steps. Find a few times—early morning and early evening work well—to sweep these areas and keep them neat and unobstructed.

The Least You Need to Know

➤ Cleaning is something that should be attacked in regular, brief periods of time, so that it doesn't get away from you.

➤ Make sure your staff maintains your high standards and pays attention to details so that cleaning is consistent for every guest.

➤ Cleanliness and organization are equally important in your kitchen, laundry, and office areas.

➤ Give the same attention to your outdoor areas that you give to your house so that everything's in top shape.

Help Wanted

Help! You just sat down for the first time in what's now a 14-hour work day—and it's not over. You still have to pay some bills, check your e-mail, clean the now empty suite 3 (which you tried to get to all day) and prepare for next morning's breakfast. You've thought of hiring someone to help you out but you don't think it's worth it for only six rooms. If you're doing all the work yourself—or even if you have a partner who helps out—and you have the income to support hiring one or more employees, seriously consider this option.

Having good, reliable staff to take on the housekeeping, cooking, bookkeeping, publicity, office work, landscaping or anything else you need will let you concentrate on the guests. Spending more time with guests means you can kick up your services a notch; and you know what that means—higher room rates.

Knowing When You Need Help

Let's say you're the only person operating a six-room B&B. As a new owner, you're just coming out of your low season and you're on the brink of high visibility through recent links to your Web site. Most of the time you can handle the work but it's wearing you thin. And how will you cope during the forthcoming higher occupancy times? Can you make it—physically and mentally—at this pace for another year? Is the business already starting to suffer?

If you find that things are gradually slipping (breakfast is served late or you're too exhausted to even attempt to look chipper), your business is heading in the wrong direction. Don't think that you'll be able to handle it after you get some rest and a day off. If you have the income to support staff, consider making it the next step in growing your business.

Even with high room rates, if you have fewer than six rooms and you're just starting out you probably won't have the income to support full-time employees year-round. Try hiring seasonal staff or part-timers with minimal hours; or hire people for one or more limited tasks such as cleaning your own quarters or doing your gardening. Think of jobs that can be done by outside people and don't require much supervision. It's a good way to ease into the job of being an employer so you'll be extra prepared to handle full-time staff when the time is right.

Coffee Talk

"The first thing we did when we bought the inn was hire a publicist," said Ken Burnet and Greg Nemrow, owners of Gaige House Inn in Glen Ellen, California, who bought the house turnkey. "We knew we would be doing things differently and we wanted to get that out to the press. We did, and still do, almost no print advertising. Our marketing budget is spent on the publicist and on the Web. After four years we have created enough demand for the property that we can afford to run it the way we like!"

Hiring Reliable Employees

If you have a high occupancy rate and income to support even one employee, he or she might turn out to be your salvation. Finding that someone who's just right for the job, however, is another story. Hiring competent staff will depend mostly on you. Weeding out those who are not suited for the job requires some strategic interviewing and a whole lot of patience.

Placing an Ad

If you need to hire full-time help, placing an ad is your best bet. Stating your requirements in a newspaper ad will eliminate the need to weed out the unqualified candidates you'd get if you just put the word out around town that you're looking for some help. Use language in your ad that will get the right people interested. Here's an example of an ad for inn-keeper's assistant:

> WANTED: Inn-Keeper's Assistant. F/T position May-Nov. Possible part-time/year-round. Competitive salary for service-oriented individual who is enthusiastic, energetic, and possesses good organizational skills. Involvement includes all aspects of inn-keeping with a heavy emphasis on housecleaning. Housing might be available.

B&B-eware!

Think twice about hiring a couple or two or more people who are friendly with each other as a package deal. Cohorts can form a united front and challenge your authority. If they get into a comfort zone, their efficiency will decline, and if one slacks off, do you fire both of them? It can get tricky; you can find yourself worrying about being the bad guy and hoping that your guests don't notice the power struggle.

By telling candidates that they'll have a hand in "all aspects of inn-keeping" you can hope to pique the interest of someone who wants to learn about the business and eventually move up in rank. At the same time, using the phrase "a heavy emphasis on housecleaning" will head off any surprises about what the job entails. If you have housing space for one individual, it's good to say that it "might" be available. You don't want to promise housing if it's for ma, pa, and the whole crew squeezed into one room!

You also can spread the word among colleagues who might know of people who are looking for work and are experienced in the business. Someone might have turned away a qualified candidate who wasn't a good fit for any number of reasons, but would fit in just fine at your place.

The Interview

Before you set up interview sessions, get as much information as you can from the applicant over the phone. Ask potential employees about their current job, why they responded to the ad, where they live, and how long they've lived in town (or if seasonal, how long they plan to stay). Describe the job and some of the duties involved. Try to get a back-and-forth conversation going about what you'd expect of them and how their past experience fits in with your needs. Also take note of how prospects sound on the phone. Are they easy to understand? Can they respond well to questions? Are they relaxed, friendly, and sharp? These are all qualities you'll want staff to demonstrate with your guests, so make sure they come through to you.

B&B-eware!

There are some things you cannot ask about: race, religion, marital status, sexual orientation, and pregnancy. If you ask an applicant about these personal things and then decide not to hire the person, you can get called on the carpet for discrimination.

Conduct in-person interviews when there won't be any guests around. Refer back to your phone conversation, only this time dig deeper. Try to ask questions that make candidates think instead of those that evoke yes or no answers. Giving people situations to react to is a great way to find out if they can think on their feet. For example, let's say you're interviewing Doris for the position of cook: Ask her what she would do with an overabundance of eggs left over in the fridge. If she responds with some great quiche or custard recipes or other ideas for using up the stock, you know she's good at pitching in and economizing.

Whatever interview approach you use, be sure to get the following information from each candidate:

➤ Experience in the service industry.

➤ Familiarity with the duties of the job.

➤ The craziest inn-keeping experience the person has ever had (loosens people up and can lead to other discussions).

➤ Willingness to pitch in at any time for any task.

➤ Reason for applying and reason for leaving his or her previous job.

➤ His or her favorite position at a past job and why.

➤ How active the person is in his or her off time and what he or she does to stay healthy.

➤ Where the person sees him- or herself in a few years.

➤ How flexible the person is in working hours.

➤ If the person has a driver's license.

➤ If you have a pool, ask if the person can swim and whether he or she has CPR or lifeguard certification.

➤ What his or her special skills are.

If you're interviewing for a management position, add these to the list:

➤ Description of previous management positions

➤ What he or she thinks it takes to manage other staff

➤ Specific things he or she would do in your absence

➤ How the person has gone out of his or her way for guests in previous positions

Have potential staff fill out an application so you have a written record of them for your files. You'll need information such as Social Security number and mailing address to do a criminal background check. It's also a chance for you to see a handwriting sample; if a staff member needs to leave a note for guests, you'll want to know that his or her writing is neat and readable! You can find job application forms at office supply stores or make your own.

If you go through a few candidates and have a hard time pulling information out of them, it could be the way you ask the questions. Avoid using "do you," "are you," or "have you" to start off questions. If you ask someone, "Do you think you're the right person for this job?" the response will be "yes." Why would someone say no? If you ask, "*Why* do you think you're the right person for this job?" the applicant will have to dig deeper for a meatier response.

Inn the Know

When an interview goes exceptionally well, put your prospect to the test. Have the person clean and make ready a room or take him or her to a room and ask what the room needs or what he or she would do differently with it. Whether or not you like what the person did, give him or her $20 for the effort. Do this only for prospects that you're seriously considering!

B&B-eware!

For your own peace of mind, do a criminal background check on anyone you might hire. States have different procedures for employers to follow. Call your local police department to find out how to go about it.

Be sure to get at least three references from each qualified person—two of them from past employers—and call them all. Try to get particulars from the past employers using details that the candidate gave you such as "Christy Hoosawhatsy says she had the chance to take some reservations for you; how well did she do?" If she was lying about taking reservations, you'll know in a minute; if she wasn't, you'll get more details on her abilities.

Try to be consistent from interview to interview. Ask the same questions so you can compare answers and make notes on things that stick out as both favorable and not great.

Send a letter—promptly—to anyone you interviewed that you will not hire. It's only fair and it will make your inn look professional to the locals.

You're Hired!

An employer in the outside-of-the-home "real" working world locates, interviews, sets policies, reprimands, and fires employees. The B&B world is no different, except that doing these tasks is a bit more difficult. Because your place of employment is a house (a place where people normally go to relax), it can be tough to find employees who'll behave in a professional manner. Some inexperienced candidates might take a job in the lodging industry because it seems like easy work, so you have to make more of an effort to weed out the slackers. Also, because B&Bs have a more family-cozy atmosphere, it's difficult for owners to lay down the law with employees. Maintaining a manner with your staff that's somewhere between congenial and authoritative can be tricky.

After they're trained and you have some confidence in them you'll obviously be able to let staff work more independently, although you'll still need to provide guidance and support and keep a keen eye on their abilities. Guests see you and your staff as a package deal. If the quality of your service slips because of one employee, it'll make you and your entire operation look bad.

Inn the Know

Now that you've hired staff, you'll need to make some adjustments. Having people assist you can be both a blessing and a curse. With staff you'll be free to do other things but you'll also need to take time to make sure they do their jobs.

Staff Policies

Just as you have to have guest policies, you have to have rules for the staff; particularly in the service industry where everyone who comes in contact with guests must be personable and professional. As the owner, it's up to you to help staff cultivate the type of image you want. Plus, people generally work better with guidelines in place. Knowing what they can and cannot do gives staff a structure to work around.

The following are some policies to consider implementing:

➤ **Trial and error.** Set up a trial period for new staff to see how they'll work out. Two to three months for full-time staff and two weeks for seasonal usually are good cut-off points. Tell them what the probationary period is and that it will end with a review. Hiring new staff on a trial basis gives you an easy out if someone's just not right for the job. It also keeps new staff on their toes; they'll pay more attention to the way you operate knowing that their new job is not set in stone.

➤ **No off-time socializing with guests.** If you're extra strict about any rule, this is the one. Staff needs to know that "on-time" friendliness cannot extend any further. How will employees be able to concentrate on their jobs if they're busy fraternizing with the guests? It's easy to build relationships with guests, particularly those who return often. Make it clear to staff that their relationships to the guests are as service providers; it cannot go beyond that.

➤ **Clock on, clock off.** Punctual staff will make your business run smoothly. Make sure staff arrives 10 minutes earlier than their shift starts. This will give them time to check in with you and other staff about any new developments or about what needs to be done that day. A few minutes of settling-in time will ensure that staff is ready to roll when the clock strikes one (or two or three ...). These extra minutes can add up to almost an hour per week of unpaid time so reward their enthusiasm by offering breaks or letting them leave early when possible.

➤ **Let them eat cake—somewhere else.** As an employer you're required by law to give staff breaks, but the number of breaks will depend on how many hours they work (check with your state regarding guidelines). Make sure your staff (except those who live on site) have a place to go during breaks: the kitchen, an outside area, or any area where they're not likely to run into guests. This is as good for them as it is for your business. Employees who have uninterrupted break times will feel refreshed and be revved up for the next few hours of their workday.

Inn the Know

Be firm and consistent with your rules but stay open to change, too. If a staff member suggests that something isn't working, look into it. If the person is right, change it; if you don't think a change is necessary, explain your decision. Being flexible won't make you look spineless; it will encourage a direct and open relationship with your employees and they'll respect you for considering their opinions.

➤ **Take good care of yourself.** A staff member, Rachel, who works the morning housekeeping shift, comes in bright, shiny, and ready to roll. By late morning, it's all she can do to keep her eyes open and drag herself around. Tell staff that they need to keep fit and should come to work with a full belly. Everyone needs energy in the morning, especially those who work at a B&B.

➤ **No flip-flops, no tube tops.** Have a dress code that will suit your B&B. You don't need to require a uniform but you could suggest to staff that you prefer clothing without advertising, simple-style polo shirts in solid colors, khaki shorts or pants, sneakers or comfortable shoes, and definitely socks. Tell them that clothes smelling of smoke or hooch are not allowed.

Defining Roles and Duties

Everyone plays a part at their place of employment. That's the reason you hire people—so you can farm out duties that you don't have time for or aren't able too handle as well as someone else. When you hire people, define their duties and responsibilities and tell them how you expect them to approach their work. Stick to your side of the bargain, too. Don't ask your cook to clean rooms and vice versa. There will be times when you'll need someone to pitch in on something that's normally "not his or her job," but don't stray too far into this territory. If you expect too much more from an employee than the work he or she was hired to do, the person's original duties and responsibilities might be getting short shrift. It's sometimes easy for an owner to forget just how long it takes to go to the store or clean the common areas when it's not something you do anymore. Finding the balance is key. Keep in close contact with your staff so you can pick up on how efficient and thorough they are in their work.

If you find that one staff member is great at one task and so-so at another, change his or her duties. If an employee is perfect at readying rooms but not as thorough when taking reservations, why make the person handle the desk? Your staff's strengths and weaknesses will surface over time. Stay alert to people's abilities and you'll be able to get the most out of their work efforts.

B&B-eware!

Don't assume that hardworking staff can work without sufficient breaks when they need them. This business is volatile, and neither you nor your staff will always be able to take breaks or time off when you want to. To compensate, give your employees unexpected breaks during slower times, when you can handle the house yourself.

What to Pay

The old adage, "you get what you pay for," applies to employers, too. Good staff won't work for low pay. If they do accept a job with pay that's not equal to their worth, they'll eventually lose their eagerness to work for you.

In touristy areas where there are several B&Bs and owners are scrambling for help, you'll have to increase your pay to compete. Usually, housekeeping staff (if strictly housekeeping) is paid hourly and managers and cooks are put on salary. Wages will vary a little bit in each area and trade. Check out a few Sunday papers and online job sites to find out what other employers are paying.

Doing payroll yourself is a tricky business. As we explained in Chapter 9, "Setting Up Your Business and Financial Structure," the employer is responsible for more than just writing out checks. You'll need to take care of withholding the right taxes, matching federal taxes, and sending taxes off to the right places. Based on the options you take, a payroll company will do these things for you at a cost of anywhere from around $15 to $50 per week, varying with the number of employees.

Coffee Talk

Jeffrey Houston from Advanced Payroll, Inc., in Provincetown, Massachusetts, says that looking for a payroll company with a good track record is important. "Find out how long they've been in business and if they have experience in your particular industry. Most payroll companies will write out the paychecks, handle wage reporting and tax deposits, and can advise you in most of your employment-related issues. One of the most popular options is direct deposit, which saves you and your employee a trip to the bank. The best thing about a payroll service is that it makes sure the different tax deposits are calculated correctly and deposited on time. Avoiding costly mistakes can easily justify the expense of using a professional payroll service."

Learn Your Staff Right

You'll need to pull out some extra time and patience during training hours. How much training each staff member needs will depend on the job, the person's experience, and whether you have other staff. The first time you train someone is always the toughest, particularly if you're still getting your feet wet, too.

Make sure your staff doesn't count on tip money as part of their pay. Gratuities should be considered extra pocket money and not an even source of income from week to week. Tips will vary depending on people, season—and, oh yes—your service. Come up with a system for splitting up tips. The easiest way to divvy up the loot is to split it evenly or according to staff hours (full-timers get more than part-timers). Make sure that employees know that the tips are shared by all and that pocketing a tip will result in their being fired. You should not be in on the tip jar. It's inappropriate for B&B owners to accept extras, just as the owner of a hair salon would not take tips from clients.

Work at a B&B is 90 percent hands-on, so one-on-one training is the only way to do it. As an employee gradually takes on more responsibility and you gain more confidence in the person's ability, you can loosen the reins.

Have patience with anyone you train, and be thorough when it comes to relating even the smallest details. Try not to patronize staff by belaboring the obvious, but do explain things they might not consider such as closing doors softly to keep noise down in the morning or shutting the hall window during a storm because rain usually floods the floor.

If you're hiring housekeeping staff, take them on several different types of room cleans (see Chapter 19, "Housekeeping Basics"). For a cook, work in the kitchen, make shopping lists together, and organize the kitchen space so that it makes you both happy. Have office staff attack smaller projects while you're there to answer questions. A manager will already be practiced in the service industry but will need time to adjust to your way of doing things.

Team Spirit

Functioning as a team is important in any workplace. At a B&B, all employees must make teamwork a top priority. You and the staff should be a united front to guests; if one of you knows something about the operation you all should know it. As meetings are impossible on an everyday basis, everyone will have to keep everyone else informed of the details. For example, a guest will catch one staff member in the hall about setting up a wake-up call and then maybe talk to you later about checking out early the next day.

How do you keep track of everything and make sure that information is passed around? One great way to transmit information among staff is to write it down where everyone can see it. A large board with erasable markers works great. Have a spot for each room and an open space at the bottom to write things such as "running out of cleaning rags." This board is a great tool for keeping track of the status of each room including when guests are checking in and out, which determines what kind of cleaning needs to be done in each room (see Chapter 19 for more on different categories of readying a room). Make sure staff dates each note so that old stuff can be erased a few days later. To keep your operation running smoothly you need everyone who works for you to be motivated to continually update the board so that everyone stays informed.

Also have your staff carry around pocketsize notepads for making notes as they work that they'll transfer to the board when they have the chance. Keep the board in an area just for staff; the kitchen is a great place. If guests have access to the kitchen find a spot that's just for staff such as an office area or even a basement stairwell.

Coffee Talk

Try some tactics to pump up the staff's motivation. Michael MacIntyre and Bob Anderson, owners of the Brass Key in Provincetown, Massachusetts, have an incentive program for the desk personnel: They've set a revenue goal for a particular period; if the desk staff meets the goal they get a trip, compliments of the Brass Key. In 1999, all the desk personnel went to Sydney, Australia, for 10 days (in the off season, of course). "It works out great for us. The employees get to see how other hotels operate (they come home with new ideas for the Brass Key) and they have a good time, which generates high morale!"

Hiring Seasonal Staff

If your B&B is located in an area with a very high tourist season and minimal activity in slower times, you might need to hire seasonal staff. Hiring reliable temporary help can be difficult. Short-term staff won't have a long-term stake in working for you so their motivation is not as high; it also is a challenge to get staff to stay on until the agreed-upon end date.

Create some incentives to keep seasonal staff coming back. Michael MacIntyre and Bob Anderson, owners of the Brass Key, are back with another incentive program that has worked well: a bonus based on years worked. When employees return for a second year Brass Key gives a bonus at the end of the season equal to 2 percent of their gross pay. The third year they receive 3 percent; the fourth year, 4 percent; and the fifth year, when the bonus is capped, 5 percent. If employees continue to work in future years they still get a higher year-end bonus because their salary has gone up. Becausethe Brass Key encouraged good employees to return, 15 of the 18 employees from last year returned for this year's season. The current staff has become so efficient that MacIntyre and Anderson have been able to cut back on the overall number of employees (and this means no additional training time).

Coffee Talk

Staff incentives work. "It's a win-win situation," says Michael MacIntyre of the Brass Key. "In the long run, I've actually decreased payroll expense, I have better employees, and the employees who work for me get more income."

B&B-eware!

Don't pay employees under the table, even part-timers. The IRS will catch up with you!

College kids from the area or visiting for the summer can be a good source of employees for peak times. Some might work out fine—particularly those who pay their way through school—but others might be unreliable. You'll need to screen young adults carefully.

If you're in a resort area where the workforce is tapped out, consider recruiting overseas. People from Eastern Europe and the Caribbean could be looking for work during high season. A lot of foreigners come to the United States for part of the year under a work visa. Because money earned here can go a longer way in their respective countries, most foreigners head back to their own countries and live on the wages they earned here for the rest of the year. There's some red tape on your end, including putting an ad for the position in the local paper; this will satisfy the government requirement that you attempt to fill the position locally. If you use a payroll company, they'll know the system and all the steps you need to take in your state.

Inheriting Employees

If you're buying a turnkey business you'll need to decide whether to inherit the staff that comes with it. No doubt, the staff will be nervous about their jobs, and about you, too. You'll be skeptical of them but hopeful that you can keep them on for a smooth transition.

If you're looking for a clean start with new employees, think twice. The staff you retain will save you time spent in digging up past information or figuring out quirks in the house. You'll need to lay down the law a bit with employees who think they might have the upper hand because you're "new"; so before you take over from the previous owner, sit down with the staff and the previous owner to discuss how things worked in the past. Tell staff that they'll be working on a trial basis for three to four months so you have an "out" if someone doesn't work well under you.

There's bound to be some friction between you and the inherited staff. Some employees might even feel bitterness toward you because of the change in ownership. Try to interact with them as much as you can in the first few months to build relationships. Remember, you're the new stepmommy or stepdaddy, and they've got to get to know you.

Hiring an Inn-Sitter

For your first year or even longer, it will be difficult for you to leave your B&B to take a vacation. If you can't handle being away from the operation, don't do it. Your stress will wreck your vacation and your family or friends will never ask you to go along with them again.

When you do find the courage to leave your "baby" for some extended time off, getting a professional inn-sitter is the best way to go. As when hiring an employee, get references. Make sure candidates have actually held management positions and talk to the owners they've worked for.

Shoestring Solution

If you're not sure about hiring an inn-sitter, consider temporarily promoting a staff member to take over in your absence. It makes the most sense to choose someone who you took out of heavy housecleaning and gave more office duties to. The person will know all the ropes and will have the incentive to keep moving up. Start small by going away on short trips at first, or even just out for an evening. You could have the employee you're considering help organize and work a party so you can see how take-charge he or she is. A staff member would have to be working for you for at least a month before you could move the person in this direction.

Finding an inn-sitter might be more difficult than hiring staff. Some professional inn-sitters will travel, so you don't need to find someone in your area, but this also makes it difficult to find them!

Providing Perks

Health insurance for small businesses is getting easier to find, but it's still extremely difficult, and it'll cost you. If you have a partner who works outside the home and has health insurance you'll most likely (why wouldn't you?) attach yourself to that policy. If you don't, and you have four or more employees and get a group rate that won't break you, it can be a good perk for you and your staff.

Try giving other perks such as more time off, bonuses, and annual wage percentage increases that aren't Scrooge-like. Even if you can pay staff higher than the industry norm, bonuses and vacation time will be truly appreciated. If you have living quarters available to house a full-time manager or some other upper-level staff person, doing it can be a great way to keep turnover down. However, steer clear of exchanging a free place to live for some or all of an employee's pay. It's not an even exchange and the staff member soon will become unmotivated. Try to keep the two separate; offer a modest rental rate or try paying the person a bit less for free living quarters. Whatever the arrangement, motivate the employee with whatever bonuses and wage increases you usually give.

Consider matching an employee's contribution to an IRA or the return on a CD in exchange for a year's commitment. You also can offer incentive programs that will boost morale and work to the benefit of the business. Create a competition among staff for the most reservations booked per week or ask them to come up with ideas to cut back expenses. Make it well worth their while by giving them a cut of the money they brought to or saved the business.

Shoestring Solution

If you need to lay off staff in the winter, bump up their pay for two quarters before the lay-off and then drop salaries down to the minimum that will allow for the highest amount of unemployment. That way, they should be able to earn close to a regular salary. Also, schedule paid vacation time for them at the end of the unemployment period, shortly before they return to full pay. Rested and happy, your employees will be ready to renegotiate their contracts and start the busy season. You've saved money during your low season and prevented staff turnover.

Schedule a meal out with an employee from time to time. It gives people a chance to sound off to you and it allows you to connect with them more than you can when you're cleaning up breakfast or passing them in the hall. If something's bothering an employee, you have a better chance of hearing about it over lunch than during the workday.

Before you reach for a pink slip for an employee who is not working out as expected, try discussing your concerns with the person in private. If the employee responds favorably to your wishes, set up a plan of action for how things will change. If this employee continues to lose face with you and is detrimental to the business, you may not have any choice but to let him or her go.

Handing Out Pink Slips

Firing staff will be difficult. Maybe you'll never have to send someone packing but chances are you will. You might be reluctant to do it because you've had a hard time finding reliable employees or you don't have the time to train someone new. These are legitimate concerns, but remember that your reputation is at stake. If an employee slacks off, or worse, it will be you who looks bad.

So, how do you fire someone? Never do it in front of guests or other staff, and doing it over the phone might seem easier, but it's a very bad idea. The person's having to return to the B&B (to pick up personal items and turn in a key, for example) would be an awkward situation for you, the employee you fired, and the staff.

When you do decide to give someone the boot, approach the person as soon after your decision as you can and ask to speak to him or her privately. Say that he or she had not worked out as you'd hoped and explain why. Say that you'll have the person's last paycheck mailed (preferably certified) and show your former employee to the door.

Sounds easy enough, right? Some of you will have a tough time letting people go. Who wouldn't? Just remember that if an employee is inadequate, it's not your fault. Repeat after us, "It's not my fault." There, now you're ready!

It might sound funny but overseeing staff can be a lot of work. The goal is to have extra hands that will help the daily operation run smoothly so you can concentrate on the business and the guests. Like everything in small business life, though, this goal will not be reached right away. Have patience with your staff, who will need guidance, and also be tolerant with yourself, especially if you're a first-time employer!

The Least You Need to Know

➤ Before you hire staff, determine the kind of help you need and whether your business can afford it.

➤ Shorten your list of candidates by asking detailed questions and doing a thorough background check.

➤ Set staff policies and encourage staff to work as a team for smooth day-to-day operations.

➤ Provide perks that will keep staff energized and motivated and prevent high turnover.

Part 6
The Next Level

With your startup complete and your first year wrapped up (or almost), your work is done—right? You might have guessed by now that your B&B work will never *be done. The challenge of the never-ending work at a B&B also can be the fun part (well, except for the cleaning the toilets bit, and folding the laundry). Help your business grow in the direction you want it to go—and then give it a kick in the pants to get there!*

The Business in Review

How do you measure success after one year in a business that is all (or mostly) new to you? It's not easy. Most likely you'll be in the hole after a year. If you break even, you can call your B&B a success. That sounds bleak but it's a reality that all new business owners must face. While there may be little operating profit or no positive cash flow, you will probably see your property value go up 5 percent and, by making your mortgage payments, you will reduce your principal balance slightly. The best thing you can do to stay in business for another year is to review where you've been and chart a plan for future successes. In the long run, a B&B provides you with enough income to hold a very substantial appreciating asset. In 20 years it may triple in value and your debt may mostly be paid off. That's the return!

Charting Your Success

Success doesn't always come in different denominations of green-colored paper; well, not the first year, anyway. In the years to come, yes, you'll look to profit and loss as a measure of your success. For now, you'll need to review smaller triumphs, such as happy guests, and get ready to go through your paperwork to chart your future successes.

Success Comes in Small Packages

Maybe you didn't make a penny of profit in the first year—or even come close to it—but that doesn't mean you should close up shop. Consider small successes such as the following when you review your first year in business:

➤ You had endless compliments and a great turnout at your opening-day event.

➤ A local publication reviewed you and your property and people still comment on it when they meet you for the first time.

➤ You had several guests tell you that they would book again for next year and three actually have done so.

➤ You had two calls from people asking if you have any space to rent out for events.

➤ Your occupancy level was slightly above your projection for the high season.

➤ You didn't have to lay off any staff.

➤ At least half of your guests found you by searching the Web.

B&B-eware!

Don't rely on your accountant to build your books at the end of the year! Even if you hire someone to take care of your finances, you need to be responsible for everyday operations. That means keeping a logbook and holding on to every receipt, no matter how small. Check out Chapter 9 for more on developing a daily tracking system.

You might have had one of these experiences, more than one, or none at all. There are tons of other ways to chart small successes. When you review your year, make a list of all your victories, big and small. If you end up with a blank sheet of paper or there are only a few scribbles on it, you have some tough years ahead or a tough decision to make.

Getting Information Before You Need It

Just as we suggested in Chapter 9, "Setting Up Your Business and Financial Structure," keeping solid records is the only way to project the coming year's financial outlook and make whatever changes will help the business grow. You always need to see where you've been before you can determine where you're going.

If you've kept expert files on every guest, your income and expenses, and your debt management, you'll have no trouble planning for the next year. If you've purchased a turnkey B&B that had incomplete files or no files at all, you'll have to start almost from scratch. The trick in having end-of-the-year information ready to review is to collect it as you go. Were you one of those kids who stayed up late to finish a project due the next morning when you'd had three weeks to work on it? If so, change those evil ways! You won't stay in business if you're a last-minute Sally or Sam.

When It Looks Good on Paper

Check it once and check it twice: Do those figures for last year just look good on paper or do they mean you're actually in the black? Looking good on paper doesn't mean your profit was beyond what you imagined in your wildest dreams. To look good means having a healthy balance of income and profit and expenses that match the income you received. For instance, if you had a high occupancy rate during the winter ski season, you also should have a higher fuel bill.

Make sure you're accounting for everything and that your paper trails match what you have in your bank accounts. Did you forget to save receipts for gas and sometimes for groceries? If you use automatic debit (using an ATM card to pay so the money comes directly out of your account) it can be easy to lose track. If you're prone to this problem, write checks instead (and make sure you get duplicate checks) so you're sure to have a record; or reconcile your bank statements to the letter (well, number).

When determining whether you "look good on paper" for the first year, don't count start-up costs. They won't be included in your annual financial report in coming years, so they'll throw off your projections. Start-up costs should match up with your investment and loan money. As long as you account for every deposit, withdrawal, fee charged, and amount of interest posted in your bankbooks, you'll have an accurate report of how your business is operating.

What to Expect After One Year

Expect the worst and hope for the best. You can expect to be dead tired and hope to have bits of down time to recoup. You can expect to be flat broke and hope to have a few extra pennies to eat dinner out once in a while. You can expect to be discouraged about certain aspects of the B&B business—or even the business as a whole—and hope to appreciate the fact that you're your own boss.

Coffee Talk

Nancy-Linn Nellis, owner and inn-keeper of 1794 Watchtide by the Sea in Searsport, Maine, suggests that you anticipate unexpected predicaments. "No matter how long you're in this business, how much you've learned, and how well you've anticipated every problem, some new one *will* come along. You're at your most creative when coming up against new situations that you'll have to circumvent."

Some of your expectations will be the same ones that everyone who's started a B&B has had. Your first expectation probably was that you'd have a good time doing it, which we certainly hope for! If you didn't, don't give up, at least not right away.

But if you hate getting out of bed in the morning to make breakfast for strangers maybe nothing about this business will make you happy. If you're completely unsatisfied in every way with this kind of work, it might not get any better, so you should seriously consider your next move. Don't let that old failure bug creep in and make you sick to your stomach. It's not your fault that you don't like it. Do you feel like a failure because you don't like broccoli? Nonsense! As we said in the beginning chapters, you won't know what it's like to run a B&B until you actually do it. Feel good about taking the chance you took to find out.

What Guests *Really* Think

It's a little tough to determine what someone's really thinking; you have to judge that by their actions. If by the end of your first year you received even a handful of guests referred by people who'd stayed with you in the beginning, you're in good shape. If you didn't, consider whether you or the business could be the problem. Did guests leave extra happy and make it a point to say goodbye? Or did they rush out with a quick "thanks"? Think back to your typical interactions with guests during their stay and when they were departing. Was there a general feeling of "eh," or were guests happy to see you, talk to you, and tell you what you were doing right? When you're all wrapped up in daily chores it can be easy to discount a few encounters with guests that didn't go very well. Make an effort to stay tuned in to guests' reactions to you and to the B&B so you can head off any serious dissatisfaction in the future.

Inn the Know

Try to get as much feedback as you can in little bits during a guest's stay. Finding out at departure time that a guest wasn't satisfied or had real problems is the worst; you have no way to make it up to the person when he or she is rushing out the door and out of your life for good.

Getting Good Feedback

Staying in tune with your guests is key to uncovering what pleases them; reading faces and observing body language can be very useful devices. Try to get sincere feedback from guests. If you ask how the meal was or how the evening went and you get a lukewarm response, try the somewhat probing "Was everything else okay?" If in response you get a litany of complaints that don't seem reasonable, the guest could be unhappy because of a personal predicament or problem, not because of you or your house.

When guests leave, always ask if they enjoyed their stay and say that you hope they'll return. Try not to expect too much of a response from everyone; some people might have had a very pleasant time but they're just quiet or shy, and won't feel comfortable talking about it. Others will spill their guts about every little "problem" they had. Over time, you'll be able to weed out the true complaints from the nit-picking ones. As long as you stay sharp and tuned in, you'll know which complaints to ignore and which ones can hurt the business if they're not addressed.

How do you avoid complaints? Don't give guests a reason to complain! Something will always go wrong on one day or another. But if you work hard to provide services and amenities that match guests' expectations of your place and you maintain an obliging and cheerful manner, you can't go wrong. Well, 99 percent of the time, anyway!

Providing Guest Response Cards

Guest response cards are not necessary but they can be useful, particularly in larger houses where you might not have interaction with departing guests. In a smaller house you might feel silly providing a card when you've had plenty of conversations with your guests. Response cards can be great for that guest who feels the need to thank you in writing and for those … you know … quiet types.

If you provide cards, keep the questions short and let the guests do all the talking. Some questions to ask could be…

> ➤ Did you enjoy your stay with us?
> ➤ Is there anything that could have improved your stay at (your B&Bs name)?
> ➤ What did you like best about your room? Our services?
> ➤ Will you consider staying with us again?

You can ask if guests will recommend your place to friends but it's a little pushy. If they respond that they'll consider staying with you again, that's as good as a referral because these guests will spread the word among their friends. Don't forget to leave a blank space for people to add comments. Have a spot for the guest's name and the date, too. Try to have questions on one side only so that you can write notes about which room the guest stayed in and what additional comments they might have made on the way out. You can keep these cards separate (as long as you have the name of the guest so you can refer back to the reservation confirmation) and review them from to time. You also can match them with a mailing list when you send out promotional materials. Would you send out a flyer to someone who wasn't happy with your place? Don't bother.

Inn the Know

When guests tell you they particularly enjoyed a service or a meal, write it down on their reservation form. Also note particulars about their stay such as the name of a restaurant they went back to several times. When the guests return, they'll be amazed when you ask them if they'd like dinner reservations there.

If you decide to have guest portfolios (see Chapter 18, "Guest Services with a Smile"), consider including the response card in the guest's packet. The downside to this is that guests might leave it behind when they check out. If you have staff but don't provide a guest portfolio, have whoever cleaned the room most recently place the guest response card with a business envelope in a visible spot. The envelope will be a subtle suggestion to leave a gratuity and the response card will be more eye-catching because it won't stand alone. Staff also can write a personal note on the envelope to draw even more attention to both items. If you do turndown, place a guest comment card on the bed the night before checkout. Don't forget to provide a pen!

Growth in the Years to Come

Start-up costs are a killer, and getting through the first year expenses can seem brutal. Contractors underestimate costs, your kid needs braces, fuel prices skyrocket, or your prodigal younger brother moves in with you. You can't predict the unpredictable in that first year—or in the years that follow, for that matter.

When you're estimating growth for future years, be sure to take it slow. Maybe you were like our old friend Dominick from Chapter 8, "The Business Plan," and you estimated occupancy levels at 75 percent for the high season, 50 percent for mid-season, and 20 percent for low season. If your real percentages turned out to be 65, 40, and 10 percent, would you raise projected levels to 90, 60, and 30 percent for the second year? Hardly. Stick with your original estimations for the first year and those numbers will begin to fall into place.

If you bought an operation already in business, charting future growth should be less of a headache. Particularly if you're renovating and updating the place, you'll be able to estimate projections slightly higher than the past owner's occupancy levels. Just to be safe, though, you might want to use the past owner's occupancy levels from last year for your first-year projections. If you come in ahead you'll know where to go from there.

Obviously, predicting business growth is a lot easier when you have a past record to follow. If you're starting from scratch, predicting the first year's growth will be tough, but not impossible. Estimating as much as you can about the first year's profit and loss at the beginning of that year will give you a good indicator for years to come. In your second year, you might look back and decide that you underestimated your profit (a very good thing) or that you expected too much. Re-examine what your inn offers, your location, the area economy, and your competition. You might have overestimated your rates or the tourist flow. Maybe your area had a bad year or your competition added some amenities that moved them up to your level. Whatever factors apply to your situation, be sure to make the appropriate adjustments for the coming year. As always, stay humble. Wait until you're at 100 percent occupancy levels to get smug!

The Least You Need to Know

➤ In the first year, appreciate small successes (such as happy guests) and look forward to big ones (operating profit and increased equity) in the years to come.

➤ Expect the worst and hope for the best. Chart gradual growth for the years ahead and *always* underestimate your profit until the business stabilizes.

➤ The only way to know how successful you were in your first year is to keep solid and complete records of your income and expenses from the very beginning and review them in detail.

➤ Find out what guests really think by observing them closely, interacting with them, and leaving guest response cards in their rooms.

Chapter 22

Expanding the Business

In This Chapter

➤ Planning for future expansion

➤ Organizing how you spend your funds

➤ Finding ways to expand the business in stages

➤ Choosing a secondary business that makes sense

You're probably thinking, "How can they talk about expansion when I just poured my life savings into starting the business I have?" It sounds like crazy talk, but don't give up on us just yet. You might not be able to expand in the next year or even in the next five years, but planning for growth now will help send you in the right direction.

As your B&B inches along, you'll always need to be making decisions about where to put your energy and spend your funds. If you think about future development now—maybe you want to add another business or more rooms—you'll have set goals to work toward. You can always change them later if things that make sense now no longer do or the numbers just don't add up. If you construct a plan for possible future improvements now, though, you'll be more likely to make them happen when the time comes.

Where to Spend Your Cash

There are a lot of ways, big and small, for B&Bs to expand. Where you spend your cash will depend on your location, your guests, and your own interests. You might even find that, instead of you directing the business, it will direct itself and tell you where to go! This actually is a good thing. If your business starts to take off in a direction you didn't expect, run with it. Go with the opportunities that come up and when the time is right you can get back to the kind of business growth you had planned on.

Raise Your Standards

One of the best ways to expand the business is to work with what you've got. Take your services, amenities, and overall appeal to the next level when you have the funds. Returning guests won't mind spending more if you've really added to the house. They'll love coming back to see all the changes you've made and will even feel as if they've been a part of your business growth. Most expansion with B&Bs occurs gradually.

Offering More Services

Providing more hotel-like services that match your clientele can help the bottom line if you can spare the time and effort. In featuring services, you'll need to find ones that guests really pay for and/or use. If you offer business services but most of your clientele are singles or couples traveling on vacation, those paid-per-use services are less likely to generate additional income. On the other hand, services such as wash-n-fold and baby-sitting can be provided with little investment from you. Hosting functions (weddings, bar mitzvahs, and so on) for small groups may require little upfront money and generate good future interest. Larger events may be wildly profitable but will necessitate catering-type hardware and nerves of steel.

To find out if offering a service is worth your time and labor, start off small and then work your way up. If you think your clientele will pay more for having their personal items laundered, try it out during a slow time or when you have business travelers for long stays. This way you can get a small dose of the effort you'll need to expend in offering an extra service before you put it in full swing. When you do add a service that you will charge extra for, make sure you advertise it well on your Web site and highlight it when guests call to make reservations. If you're trying to hook a potential but indecisive guest, you can throw in a mention of your new service; if the person says "Oh, that sounds great," you know you have a keeper.

Adding Appealing Amenities

The same concept of adding services applies to amenities. However, because amenities will (in most cases) cost you more than any service, you'll need to take extra care in your choices.

For instance, do you think guests would really go for access to health and fitness equipment? Before you run out and spend money on a total gym to put in your spare room, try it out this way: Call up a local fitness center and find out how much it would cost for day passes. They might give you a discount if you buy a book of 20 to test the idea; or they might offer some kind of group membership card that guests could use. If it works for enough guests, consider adding a gym. Before you make any moves, though, check with your insurance agent about all the possible liability issues and costs. Most clubs will require people to sign a disclaimer waiving the club's responsibility for injuries, but that might not work for your B&B's gym.

Here's another idea for starting out small: Add a small kitchen area to your middle-of-the-road suite to bump it up. Consider doing the renovation at the end of your high season so you can watch how it sells during a less demanding time. During your high season, people might take that room because they have fewer choices. Being able to sell a room with new amenities during a low season is a good indicator of its value. If it works, plan on gradually adding kitchen areas to other rooms.

Remember to first determine whether adding things such as a small kitchen conforms to your zoning. Putting in a wet bar–type unit with a microwave is less costly, but some municipalities consider this combo a kitchen, and therefore it may not be an authorized use of your lodging license. Even though it's not legal, however, it's done anyway.

Giving the House a Make-Over

If you have big plans for a house before you open but soon discover that they're just not financially possible, don't give up. Do what you can to the house now and leave some things for later when you have more income. Try to concentrate on the major work such as rewiring, updating plumbing, and things that will be installed in the walls.

Shoestring Solution

TVs and TV/VCR combos are dirt cheap at the big discount warehouses, but expect VCRs to go the way of the 8-track tapes in the not-so-distant future, replaced by DVDs. If wiring all your rooms for cable is cost prohibitive, you might choose to set aside your smallest room as an extra lounge. If the room shares a bath with another guest room, that guest room instead could have a private bath (even if it's off the hall), and you'd have an additional entertainment area. Do some calculations. This arrangement might allow you to bump up your amenities—and revenue—at little or no cost!

Maybe you have a large bathroom in one room that could accommodate a whirlpool tub, but the tub that's there is clean and in good shape. Determine how much guests use the tub itself before you add an expensive amenity such as a whirlpool. If you have a sturdy queen size bed that you can use in one room but the head- and footboards are less than attractive, remove them and dress up the room in other ways. Wait until you have more dough to replace the bed if you do so at all. Do you have some attractive (not valuable or antique) head- and footboards but feel the room would be better served by having more usable space? Store or ditch the footboard and frame. Affix the headboard to the wall with four or more heavy-duty screws in spots where they won't be seen when the bed is made. If you've decided to ditch the rest of the bed, you can saw off a good portion of the legs so that the metal frame on wheels or glides (for carpet) can butt to the wall just below the headboard. You've managed to give the room a larger, more streamlined (though not necessarily contemporary) appeal and made it even easier to clean under the bed.

Another way to save money when making over your guest rooms is to make do with less in your own quarters. If it's a choice of income over comfort, living with your space in near-to habitable condition can save you thousands!

Entertaining the Idea of Dinner

Serving dinner to guests and nonguests has been mulled over by more than a few B&B owners. We're not going to lie to you; here's some hardcore advice: Don't do it. Okay, so that's not advice for all of you. Serving dinner will work well for some large inns, inns in areas with few restaurants, and owners who choose to serve dinner on a limited basis (or only to guests) as a means of controlling costs. For the rest of you, particularly if you have a smaller operation, consider this option—and then reconsider. The costs and the headaches most likely will far outweigh the extra income you'd gain. In addition to determining whether you have the finances to start serving dinner, you'll need to ask yourself some other questions to see if this option makes sense for you:

➤ **Does your property make it possible?** Do you have enough space in the kitchen and in the dining areas to accommodate all your registered guests and some nonguests, too? Take into consideration room to move around for wait staff and the comfy factor of seated guests. You might need to renovate to do this; for example, by adding a common bathroom or expanding the kitchen to accommodate the commercial appliances you'll require.

➤ **Can you serve dinner in a way that will ensure it's consumed?** If you're just serving to your guests, make dinner a package deal. You'll need to promote this heavily so that guests know why your rates appear high. If you don't make dinner a package deal you could run into trouble with guests who say they want dinner when they make their reservation with you over the phone and then decide that they don't after they arrive.

➤ **How will dinner late at night affect guests in their rooms?** Noise and dinner smells will go beyond their designated area and it will be annoying to guests who are in their rooms trying to keep the world out.

➤ **What is the competition like?** Are you surrounded by restaurants, hotels, and inns? Even if there are only a handful of restaurants in your area, there might be a reason for it. The restaurant business is extremely volatile. If you decide to serve dinner to guests and your competition is high, provide one meal as part of a package deal or on special occasions in guests' rooms. This way you'll know who's coming to dinner and you can budget accordingly.

➤ **Will you need to hire a chef and other staff?** Maybe you can cook; but can you cook at restaurant quality? Can you cover when employees inevitably quit or call in sick?

➤ **Do you have the space for dinner?** You can get away with serving breakfast without a dining room, especially if you serve continental, but not dinner. Guests will expect dinner at your B&B to be a sit-down, elegant affair. That's what they'll be looking for from a restaurant, which is what you are considered to be if you serve dinner.

➤ **Do you have the energy?** Even if you hire staff to help you out, it will be difficult for you to relax in the evenings with guests and staff buzzing around. Guests will want to take their time at dinner, which might mean you'll be doing late-night clean-up after staff has gone home.

➤ **Can you handle the extra management?** Is there a food distributor near your area? There'll be a lot more paperwork, supplies to order, staff to supervise, and dealings with the feds. If you're spending time in the office working on these extra business affairs, the interaction between you and guests will be compromised.

B&B-eware

B&Bs that just serve breakfast are not held to the strict rules and regulations of restaurants. Adding another meal, however, will classify your B&B as a restaurant operation to authorities. You'll need to get a separate restaurant license, adhere to very strict health regulations, and have enough space inside and outside (for parking) to accommodate the new traffic flow.

Coffee Talk

Nana Phinney, Park's oft-visiting aunt, suggests giving dinner a whirl before committing. "Consider the once- or twice-a-year special occasion meal such as a New Year's Day brunch or summertime barbecue. You'll get a feel for the amount of preparation and clean-up required to carry off this type of affair again and again."

279

Shoestring Solution

Decide how elaborate a dinner you'll serve before you plan your kitchen. A *prix fixe* (set menu) with only a couple of options each for appetizer, salad, entrée, and dessert might allow you to get by with fewer appliances, utensils, cookware, and storage space. Providing a variety will require more work, more skill in preparation, more groceries—and more potential waste of food.

For many B&Bs, the serving of dinner in a home setting is a dream come true. Dinner is a great idea and can make sense in the right place. Before you invest in everything that serving dinner requires, though, figure out if dinner at your place will be the sure thing.

Other Second Businesses

Obviously, it's best to attempt a second business only when the B&B is running smoothly and when you have staff to help you with the house or with the additional business. Getting zoning to approve a second business on the property might take some persuasion. If your property is zoned for mixed use, you'll probably have an easy time. You will need to get a separate license (in most areas) for the second business.

Check with your insurance agent to see if you'll need more liability coverage when adding a second business. If your intention is to have a second biz from the get-go, ask your realtor about the prospect. If one day the idea just hit you that you'd like to sell some hand-painted hollow eggs, you'd better check with those town government boys and girls in the building department. If you don't like, trust, or understand their response, keep trying. Get as much support as you can from town officials you do know, and go at them again. If it's a total no-go, exercise business expansion options that are possible in your area.

Some second business ideas that can work great with B&Bs are...

➤ **Selling antiques.** Even if the antiques are in a barn or other separate building, you could handle the stragglers yourself during the weekdays and might need an extra hand only on the weekends or the busiest times. You'll have to know something about antiques and spend ample time scouting out dealers. Or, if you have a big enough building, consider renting it out to vendors instead. That way you have income without expending your time, energy, or staff resources, and you've increased the appeal of your property.

➤ **Selling artwork or other wares.** If you (or someone you know) is lucky enough to have a talent for baking home-baked goodies or building funky birdhouses why not sell the stuff? Happy guests love to take home reminders of their stay and are more apt to impulse buy when they're on vacation.

Coffee Talk

Part of the reason former owners Peter Garza and Christopher Covelli moved to Provincetown, Massachusetts, to open Christopher's by the Bay was to give Peter a beautiful backdrop for painting. Selling his art (and his sister's) at the B&B then became part of the business. "We started by putting a list of the art for sale in the dining area, but it didn't work too well. Then we displayed art for sale in the common areas so that every guest could see it. We then put little signs on the paintings with their titles and prices, and that worked very well. Because our primary business was hospitality, and not selling art, we always kept the art sales low key and never pushed."

➤ **The gift shop.** Have a little room at the front of the house that you don't know what to do with? A gift shop is a great idea if you have the capital to get it going and staff to help you out. You can order extra items such as terry cloth robes with the name of your B&B on them and sell them in the shop along with area wares and necessities such as toothpaste. Gift shops, big or small, work really well in larger inns where there's a better chance of high inventory turnover. Shoe polish does go bad after sitting on a shelf for a while.

➤ **Renting out the living room.** You might be in an area with a lot of socially or politically active people with nowhere to meet. Or maybe you have a room that's perfect for out-of-office conference meetings. As long as these groups don't interfere with your guests' stay, this can be a great way to earn extra income. You can even provide light catering for their meetings and charge more. Most gatherings require light fare such as muffins, croissants, fruit, and beverages for breakfast meetings and nibbly snacks for afternoon or evening.

➤ **Renting out the backyard.** Small weddings or other events can be a good way to pull in income but organizing these affairs can be taxing and can take up quite a bit of space. Even if someone else does the catering and you rent out the space, your life will stop when these events take over. Plus, if you don't rent out rooms to the event-goers, your other guests might either be neglected or feel secondary. Before you head in this direction, make sure the income is worth the hassle, your space can handle the traffic, and your B&B business won't be compromised.

Coffee Talk

Michelle and Allen Kruger of Arbor House Bed and Breakfast at Kruger's Farm Winery in North Stonington, Connecticut, built their unique B&B one business at a time: "The Victorian farmhouse was already approved by the town as a B&B. The winery took longer to start because we needed to obtain licenses at the town, state, and federal levels, which took approximately one year. Because cider is classified as a wine, manufacturing was permitted in our facility; so we began to make Chester's Hard Apple Cider. Renting out the facilities for special functions was a natural follow-up to those businesses. To date we have not actively solicited clientele our operations; all of our customers have found us by word of mouth or the Internet."

In any second business that you consider, make sure the numbers add up. Don't forget to consider yourself in that equation, too! If you're dog-tired from the B&B, how will you manage more work? Even if you hire staff, you're still the primary employee in every way. Consider adding a business only if the income you'll derive from it makes it worth your while. Even seemingly low-maintenance sidelines such as selling antiques will take your time away from the primary business. Be certain that you can afford the staff resources, that you have a facility that will work well for it, and that you can accommodate the second business without sacrificing the happiness of your B&B guests.

The Least You Need to Know

➤ Where you decide to spend your cash depends on what guests will really use, what your interests are, and what your property can handle.

➤ Renovating or adding services or amenities are some of the ways to expand the business, allowing you to bump up rates.

➤ Serving dinner is a plausible idea only for businesses that have the perfect conditions to make it worthwhile.

➤ Other sideline businesses can be profitable as long as you have the funds, time, and energy to spare.

Stay in Business!

The minute you decide to enter the world of owning a bed and breakfast, the startup of that business will consume your life. For months or maybe even longer, you'll be focused on gathering funds, making the business legal, and getting your house pretty. During those start-up days there's a huge build-up to opening day. When you have most everything in place and you open your doors you might not quite know what to do with yourself. This won't last long (the laundry can't wait and neither can your guests!) but it will take you a while to get into the swing of everyday B&B life.

Be prepared for this transition to be weird and concentrate on shifting your thoughts. Instead of thinking of your projects as wrap-ups as you did during renovation, you'll need to think of the business as an ongoing, living thing. Instead of working toward a finished project, you'll be building the business step by step. During startup, the more you concentrate on things such as setting up marketing strategies and practicing your hosting skills the easier it will be to stay in business down the road.

Staying Focused

As we noted in Chapter 1, "Open, Sez Me!" one of the biggest misconceptions new-comers have is that the hard work is over when renovations have been completed. You might already have found out just how great a misconception this is. If you plan on staying in this business for a long time you'll need to find ways to keep up the same energy levels you had at the beginning. Even if you don't plan to keep your B&B and will be flipping it for profit in a few years, you'll need to work just as hard (maybe even harder) to get a good sale price. Often your target sale date may be de-layed by high interest rates, recession, and the like. Your four years could easily be-come seven so be prepared to work and wait.

Inn the Know

Who'll take care of your guests if you're sick? There are times when you just can't head it off. If you don't have staff, make sure you have someone available—a partner, a relative, a close friend—who's willing to learn something about the business and fill in when necessary. If your substitute won't accept pay, show your appreciation with nice din-ners out or other nonreturnable gifts.

Saving Your Strength

Taking good care of the business means taking good care of yourself. Running a B&B is physically demand-ing work. It's stair-climbing, floor-scrubbing, errand-running, hot-stove-slaving, forced-smiling kind of work. Your mind and body both need to be up to the challenge. That means eating right, exercising, and getting enough sleep.

A bleary-eyed host with low energy has no ability to take care of guests. Listening to guests is tough when you're yawning! Most people need a good six to eight hours of sleep to function the next day. If you can live on less than that, you'll do great in this business be-cause some days you'll have to! However, as has been proven, you can't completely "catch up" on sleep. Do yourself and your guests a favor and get as much shut-eye as you can.

Keep Guests Coming Back

If you have a good circle of friends, do you ignore these pals completely so you can go out and make new ones? Nah. You hang out with your good buddies and invite more friendly folk in as they cross your path. Think of your business as an old friend that people will want to visit—they just need a reminder to do it once in a while.

Keep your business going by giving your guests reasons to come back. During the off-season send e-mails with a promotion for returning guests. Alert past guests of events happening in your town. When guests are staying with you, describe how different occasions throughout the year are celebrated in town and give details about the town's "big event" (if there is a big event, of course).

What is the best, the absolute number one way to get guests to come back? You already know what we're going to say but this one can stand some more book time. Here goes: Treat them right in the first place. Treat all your guests as if they're your number one priority and they'll be yours for life. Apart from the handful who will take advantage of you, the rest will appreciate your efforts in the house, your breakfast, your services; and they'll appreciate you—your hospitality, your conversation, and how you help them to relax away from home. What are friends for?

Shoestring Solution

Send out holiday cards to your top returning guests and guests who were extremely satisfied with their stay. Be sure to make notes in their file or, if you're really organized, photocopy their reservation form and slip it into a separate file. Sending a card keeps you fresh in guests' minds and is a tax write-off!

The Juggling Act

As you might have discovered already, you need to use different skills at different times of the day. Depending on your particular arrangement you might need to be a cook in the morning, a house-cleaner in the mid-morning, front desk staff for check-in and check-out, reservation-taker all day, and manager every minute.

Aside from juggling your day, you'll need to learn how to juggle the change in seasons. Because most of you will have a shift in occupancy during the year, you'll need to learn how to change your habits during each season to make it through. And then there's the juggling act of your personal life—if you can preserve one!

Making It Through a Low Season

Do you have a slow off-season but don't want to shut down? Take a part-time job. Start a hobby that could turn into an off-shoot of the business later on. If you do decide to shut down for a few weeks or months, consider doing some inn-sitting (see Chapter 20, "Help Wanted"). When you're up and running and you want to tell people what this business is all about, become a consultant.

If you don't shut down during your low season and you have the funds to focus on the business, do just that. Take some time off to clear your head, whether you go away or not, and then do some things that you don't have a chance to do in the high or mid season such as:

➤ **Clean the heck out of the place, top to bottom.** Get those drapes steam-cleaned, the carpet professionally cleaned, the rugs cleaned, and get a duster into those hard-to-reach places.

➤ **Concentrate on marketing.** Now is the time to review, revise, and put your marketing plan into action.

➤ **Spend some quality time in your rooms.** Look over every nook and cranny. Find things that are out of whack that might have been missed by you or staff during the busy times such as chipped baseboards or wall cracks.

➤ **Get to know your guests all over again.** Review your guest records and the notes you made during their stays. Were there any comments made on a particular breakfast? A particular room? Did guests make any negative comments or provide good suggestions for improvement? Were they right? You'll be amazed when you review your records—if you keep good ones—at how much you've forgotten.

➤ **Improve yourself.** Change some decor around, move furniture, buy new pieces to add to rooms while they're empty and you can clearly see what they need. Also, take a seminar and attend a conference.

➤ **Hit the road.** Visit other B&Bs, hotels, resorts, or any and all destinations to borrow their ideas. Nothing can be as important as exposure to other places and cultures. You'll come back with new ideas of what works—and what *doesn't*—to improve on your own little piece of heaven.

Coffee Talk

"I've seen a lot of people enter this business only because they think it will be fun and they like to entertain," said Tari Hampe of Tari's, a Premiere Café and Inn in Berkeley Springs, West Virginia. "Only a true idiot would do it for those reasons. It's business. It's work. We've all seen television shows with those happy little B&B fairies. How do they look so good after cleaning toilets? Why are they smiling when they just got a plumbing bill for $2,450 to unclog a drain because someone flushed their socks?"

Stay in Business Because You Want To

Most of you will find that there's some aspect of this business that you could easily live without. As your business moves along, pay attention to the little things that irk you. Maybe fulfilling simple guest requests really gets on your nerves or you find it almost impossible to make another bed. These little things might go away as you get used to running the business and start making more money—or they might not.

Irksome things just might seem to be multiplying all over the place. Soon you'll be snapping "duh!" at your partner who wants to know if you want more coffee (well, maybe you're not a morning person). If you reach a point where you have nothing good to say about the business you're in, why stay in it? If you decide to get out, don't feel guilty—or worse, have thoughts of failure. Be grateful that you learned a lot of things about yourself and that you learned you'd rather be doing something else.

If you decide to tough it out, do it with all your might. Sometimes giving in to a way of life can release a lot of pressure and lift that invisible weight from your shoulders. Pretty soon you might be able to gloss over those irksome things and get to the things you really enjoy. By the way, that's, "Yes, I'd love some more coffee, sweet love of my life." This line actually will get that cup refilled—try it!

The Least You Need to Know

➤ Taking good care of yourself and keeping guests coming back are key to staying in business.

➤ Spend your time wisely during the low season by doing things such as reviewing the business, fixing up the house, or taking a class.

➤ Learn to love owning a B&B or call it quits. Either way, make a decision that will make you happy!

Glossary

amenities   Extras that increase the appeal of your B&B.

Americans with Disabilities Act (ADA)   Dictates regulations that businesses must follow to accommodate those with disabilities.

B&B   If you had to look this one up, you're *really* starting from scratch!

business plan   Written proposal explaining your plans for operating the business and your goals for the future.

cash disbursement journal   Another term for expense log.

common areas   Rooms and other areas in your house (or outdoors) where guests are allowed to roam free.

concierge   Member of the hotel staff in charge of various services for guests.

construction loan   Lending institution agreement to loan a set amount of money but release it in portions as each level of renovation is completed.

convection oven   Oven that uses a fan component to evenly distribute heat.

corporate structure   Business that operates as a separate entity from a group of investors.

domain name   You know, your www.

duvet   French term for comforter.

fictitious name statement   Registering your business name to make sure it hasn't been taken and won't be taken by anyone else.

flip   Building or property bought for the purpose of renovation and subsequent sale for profit.

guarantee hold   Keeping a room in a guest's name until a specified day or hour.

guesthouse   Another name for B&B. Sometimes used because breakfast is not served.

guidebook   Lists accommodations in particular areas and what each offers.

homestay   Very small (three rooms and under) lodging. Homestays do not always operate year round, and the guest rooms are secondary to the private quarters of their residents.

income operating statement   Form that helps determine how much you can afford for a mortgage on a property based on estimated income and expenses.

inn   Different from a B&B because dinner or meals other than breakfast are served to guests and nonguests, although this is not always the case. Some owners use the term *inn* because their establishment is larger than a B&B.

inn-keeper   You, silly!

inn-sitter   Professional who sleeps around ... er, fills in for weary inn-keepers when they need a day, two weeks, or a season off.

lawn gnomes   Far more PC than lawn jockeys.

liability insurance   Covers anything that could happen to someone while in your house or on your land.

market value   What you can get for a product (your house, for example).

micromanager   Manager who does not delegate appropriate minor responsibilities to staff.

mise en place   French for "everything has a place." Used in the kitchen, it denotes preparedness.

niche marketing   Not to be confused with quiche marketing. Marketing to a particular segment of the population.

occupancy rate   Actual or estimated percentage of nights your rooms can be rented out.

ordinance or law replacement insurance   Covers costs of rebuilding or renovating under newly applied town ordinances.

owner-occupied   B&B in which the owner or inn-keeper lives in or on the property.

planning and zoning committees   Town board (sometimes split up and sometimes one board) that makes decisions on town's development.

Portuguese sweet bread (*Bolos Levedos*)   Overgrown English muffin that is sweetened with lemon and sometimes raisins. Readily found in the Northeast. Yum, yum!

proof   Verifiable copy of a printing order on which alterations or corrections can be made before multiple copies are produced.

property insurance   Covers the house, everything in the house, and everything used to maintain it.

real-time booking   Reservations done online as though you are making them with a reservationist over the phone.

rentable nights   Nights in the year when owner will accept guests.

reservation service agency (RSA)   Charges commission per referral and sometimes other flat fees for booking guests with you.

room rates   The prices of the rooms you rent.

schtick   *See* spiel.

seasons   Terms used to describe high (on-season or peak), mid (shoulder), and low (off-season or off-peak), periods in which the most and the least number of tourists traipse through your area, and the periods in between.

sole proprietorship   Business that is privately owned.

spiel   *See* schtick.

startup   As the term suggests, a business started from scratch.

treasury tax   Any tax an owner charges clients and then passes on to the government.

turnkey   Business that is already in operation upon purchase. Just turn the key and go!

turnover   In business terms, the rate at which workers are replaced. (Or, a flaky fruit-filled pastry.) Or, you just dreamt that you owned an inn in Vermont!

umbrella policy   Insurance coverage that is an extra blanket of coverage and also kicks in when your other policies are maxed out.

worker's compensation   Insurance coverage for injuries suffered by an employee during work hours.

zoning   Town or city areas sectioned off to designate what takes place in those areas (residential, commercial, or mixed-use).

zymurgy   The branch of applied chemistry dealing with fermentation, as in brewing. Have one on us—if you've gotten through the book and you still want to be an inn-keeper, you deserve it!

National and Local Associations

Contact information changes frequently, so be sure to phone or check out Web sites before you write to the associations in this appendix.

National Associations

Listed with the following major organizations are Web sites that are online guidebooks; they also have information helpful to inn-keepers and travelers.

American Bed and Breakfast Association
www.abba.com

National Bed and Breakfast Association
PO Box 332
Norwalk, CT 06852
Fax: 203-847-0469
Web site: www.nbba.com
E-mail: info@nbba.com

Professional Association of Innkeepers International
PO Box 90710
Santa Barbara, CA 93190
Phone: 805-569-1853
Web site: www.paii.org
E-mail: info@paii.org

State and Local Associations

Many of the state association Web sites were created through larger sites such as Bed and Breakfast Inns Online (www.bbonline.com). This means that sometimes they can be contacted only by e-mail or voicemail because there is no "office," only a Web site. Some are mainly online guidebooks that might charge a fee and might require credentials before including listings (some are PAII associated so they can use PAII standards). Check out www.bbonline.com and www.paii.org for updated lists of state associations.

There are a gazillion more regional associations within many states, so many that we don't have room to include them all! Do some snooping around with the state associations and on the Net to find the smaller organizations that are even closer to home.

Bed & Breakfast Association of Alabama
PO Box 707
Montgomery, AL 36101
Web site: www.bbonline.com/al

Arizona Association of Bed & Breakfast Inns
PO Box 22086
Flagstaff, AZ 86002
Phone: 1-800-284-2589
Web site: www.bbonline.com/az

Bed & Breakfast Association of Arkansas
PO Box 250261
Little Rock, AK 72225-0261
Phone: 501-253-2246
Web site: www.bbonline.com/ar

California Association of Bed & Breakfast Inns
2715 Porter St.
Soquel, CA 95073
Web site: www.innaccess.com
E-mail: info@cabbi.com

Bed & Breakfast California
Phone: 408-867-9662
Fax: 408-867-0907
Web site: www.bbintl.com

Bed & Breakfast Innkeepers of Colorado
PO Box 38416-Dept W
Colorado Springs, CO 80937-8416
Phone: 1-800-265-7696
Web site: wwww.innsofcolorado.org
E-mail: info@innsofcolorado.org

Florida Bed & Breakfast Inns
PO Box 6187
Palm Harbor, FL 34684
Phone: 281-499-1374 or
1-800-524-1880
Web site: www.florida-inns.com
E-mail: innroute@florida-inns.com

The Great Inns of Georgia
541 Londonberry Road, NW
Atlanta, GA 30327
Phone: 404-843-0471 or
1-800-501-7328
Fax: 404-252-8886
Web site:
www.bbonline.com/ga/greatinns
E-mail: gainns@bbonline.com

Hawaii Island Bed & Breakfast Association
PO Box 1890
Honokaa, HI 96727
Web site: www.stayhawaii.com
E-mail: hibba@stayhawaii.com

Illinois Bed & Breakfast Association
PO Box 82
Port Byron, IL 61275
Phone: 1-888-523-2406
Fax: 309-523-2349
Web site: www.go-illinois.com/
E-mail: info@go-illinois.com

Iowa Bed & Breakfast Innkeepers Association
707 Harrison Street
Emmetsburg, IA 50536
Phone: 1-800-888-4667
Web site: www.bbonline.com/ia

Kansas Bed & Breakfast Association
PO Box 71
Enterprise, KS 67441
Phone: 1-888-8KS-INNS
(1-888-857-4667)
Web site: www.kbba.com
E-mail: info@kbba.com

Bed & Breakfast Association of Kentucky
Web site: www.bbonline.com/ky

Louisiana Bed & Breakfast Association
PO Box 3988
Baton Rouge, LA 70821
Phone: 504-346-1857
Fax: 504-336-4154
Web site:
www.louisianatravel.com/lbba
E-mail: lbba@ltpa.org

The Maryland Bed & Breakfast Association
PO Box 23324
Baltimore, MD 21203
Phone: 410-235-MBBA
(410-235-6222)
Web site: www.bbonline.com/ky

Michigan Lake to Lake Bed & Breakfast Association
444 Oak Street
Holland, MI 49424
Phone: 616-738-0135
Web site: www.laketolake.com
E-mail: innfo@laketolake.com

Minnesota Bed & Breakfast Guild
305 E. Roselawn Avenue
St. Paul, MN 55117
Phone: 651-778-2400
Fax: 651-778-2424
E-mail: info@hospitalitymn.com
Web site: www.hospitalitymn.com

Note that this Web site is an umbrella organization for the entire lodging and service industry in Minnesota, the only one of its kind in the United States.

Bed & Breakfast Association of Mississippi
Web site: www.bbonline.com/ms

Bed and Breakfast Inns of Missouri
204 East High Street
Jefferson City, MO 65101
Phone: 1-800-213-5642
Web site: www.bbim.org
E-mail: info@bbim.org

Montana Bed & Breakfast Association
2986 Highway 93 South
Stevensville, MT 59870
Phone: 1-800-453-8870 (for voicemail)
Web site: www.mtbba.com
E-mail: beds@mtbba.com

Nebraska Association of Bed & Breakfasts
7 Valley View Heights
Kearney, NE 68847
Phone: 308-234-1670
Web site: www.bbonline.com/ne
E-mail: nabb@bbonline.com

Bed & Breakfast Innkeepers Association of New Jersey
PO Box 108
Spring Lake, NJ 07762
Phone: 732-449-3535
Web site: www.bbianj.com

New Mexico Bed & Breakfast Association
PO Box 2925
Santa Fe, NM 87504
Phone: 505-766-5380 or
1-800-661-6649
Web site: www.nmbba.org
E-mail: info@nmbba.org

Empire State Bed & Breakfast Association of New York
PO Box 616
Buffalo, NY 14209
Phone: 716-882-6116
Web site: www.esbba.com
E-mail: mail@esbba.com

North Carolina Bed & Breakfasts and Inns Association
PO Box 1077
Asheville, NC 28802
Phone: 1-800-849-5392
Fax: 281-403-9335
Web site: www.bbonline.com/nc
E-mail: ncbbi@bbonline.com

North Dakota Bed & Breakfast Association
RR 2, Box 15A
Scranton, ND 58653
Web site: www.bbonline.com/nd

Ohio Bed & Breakfast Association
5310 East Main Street, Suite 104
Columbus, OH 43213
Voicemail: 614-868-5567
Web site: www.ohiobba.com
E-mail: obba@travelohio.com

Oklahoma Bed & Breakfast Association
766 DeBarr Avenue
Norman, OK 73069
Phone: 1-800-676-5522
Web site: www.bbonline.com/ok

Oregon Bed & Breakfast Guild
PO Box 3187
Ashland, OR 97520
Phone: 1-800-944-6196
Web site: www.obbg.org

South Carolina Bed & Breakfast Association
PO Box 1275
Sumter, SC 29150
Phone: 1-888-599-1234
Web site: www.bbonline.com/sc
E-mail: scbba@bbonline.com

Bed & Breakfast Innkeepers of South Dakota
PO Box 7682
Rapid City, SD 57709
Phone: 1-888-500-INNS
(1-888-500-4667)
Web site: www.bbonline.com/sd

Tennessee Bed and Breakfast Innkeepers Association
5431 Mountain View Road, Suite 150
Antioch, TN 37013
Phone: 1-800-820-8144
Web site: www.bbonline.com/tn
E-mail: tbbia@bbonline.com

Historic and Hospitality Accommodations of Texas
PO Box 1399
Fredericksburg, TX 78666
Phone: 1-800-HAT-0368
(1-800-428-0368)
Fax: 512-353-4900
Web site: www.hat.org
E-mail: info@hat.org

Bed and Breakfast Inns of Utah, Inc.
Utah Travel Council
Council Hall/Capitol Hill
Salt Lake City, UT 84114
Phone: 1-800-200-1160 (Utah
Travel Council)
Web site: www.bbiu.org
E-mail: info@bbiu.org

**Bed & Breakfast Association
of Virginia**
PO Box 791
Orange, VA 22960
Phone: 540-672-6700 or
1-888-660-BBAV (1-888-660-2228)
Web site: www.bbonline.com/va
E-mail: bbav@bbonline.com

Washington Bed & Breakfast Guild
2442 NW Market Street, PMB #355
Seattle, WA 98107
Phone: 1-800-647-2918
Web site: www.wbba.com
E-mail: info@wbbg.com

**Mountain State Association of Bed &
Breakfasts (West Virginia)**
17 Center Avenue
Weston, WV 26452
Phone: 304-269-7902
Web site: www.wvonline.com/bandb
E-mail: mabb@bbonline.com

**Wisconsin Bed & Breakfast
Association**
108 South Cleveland Street
Merrill, WI 54452
Phone: 715-539-9222 or
1-800-432-TRIP (1-800-432-8747)
(to obtain a free copy of brochure)
Web site: www.bbonline.com/wi

**Wyoming Homestay & Outdoor
Adventures**
PO Box 40048
Casper, WY 82604
Phone: 307-237-3526
Fax: 307-237-1290
Web site:
www.wyomingbnb-ranchrec.com
E-mail: whoa@coffey.com

More Resources

Consider this a hodgepodge of resources for your business.

Online Guidebooks and Booking Sites

Some sites will charge advertising rates and will set up a link to your site; others are RSAs (reservation service agencies) with real time booking, which will mean an upgrade in software. We've noted which sites list inn-keepers outside the United States with a "USA+" because some sites do not have a completely international reach (will list only Canadian B&Bs, and so on). Check out www.paii.org/travelers for other listings of PAII-associated online guidebooks (most are listed here) and continual updates.

American Automobile Association
www.aaa.com

Mobil Travel Guide
7373 N. Cicero Avenue
Lincolnwood, IL 60712
Phone: 1-800-653-0220
www.mobil.com/mobil_consumer/travel/guides

Aaron's Travel Resource (USA+)
www.travelhero.com

American Historic Inns, Inc. (USA+)
www.bnbinns.com

B&B Getaways
www.bbgetaways.com

BedandBreakfast.com (USA+)
www.bedandbreakfast.com

Beds, Breakfasts, and Inns (USA+)
www.bedsbreakfastsandinns.com

Bed and Breakfast Network (USA+)
www.bedandbreakfastnetwork.com

Bed and Breakfast Inns of North America
www.bestinns.net

Bed and Breakfast Inns Online (USA+)
www.bbonline.com

BnBFinder.com
www.bnbfinder.com

Border to Border Bed and Breakfast Directory (Inns of Oregon, Washington, and California)
www.bbexplorer.com

Cruising America
www.cruising-america.com

1st Traveler's Choice (USA+)
www.virtualcities.com

HotelCity.com (USA+)
www.hotelcity.com

innformation.com (USA+)
www.innformation.com

The Innkeeper B&B Network, Inc. (USA+)
www.theinnkeeper.com

Innroads (USA+)
www.inns.com

Innseekers
Phone: 1-888-INN-SEEK
(1-888-466-7335)
www.innseekers.com

InnSite (USA+)
www.innsite.com

Inntopia.com (USA+)
www.inntopia.com

InnWeb.com
www.innweb.com

Lanier Travel Guides (USA+)
www.travelguides.com

The National Network (USA+)
www.go-lodging.com

New England Innkeepers Association
www.newenglandinns.com

Professional Association of Innkeepers International (USA+)
www.innplace.com

Select Registry: Distinguished Inns of North America
www.innbook.com

Travel Pick (USA+)
www.travelpick.com

111 Travel Directory (USA+)
www.triple1.com

TravelData (USA+)
www.traveldata.com

Rave Reviews (USA+)
www.rave-reviews.com

USInns.com
www.usinns.com

Selected Hotels
www.uswelcome.com

Wakeman and Costine's North American Bed and Breakfast Directory
www.bbdirectory.com

Accommodations Search Engine Network (USA+)
www.ase.net

International Bed and Breakfast Pages (USA+)
www.ibbp.com

The Register (USA+)
www.travelassist.com

Bed and Breakfast Online Canada
www.bbcanada.com

B&B Info Canada
www.bandbinfo.com

Canada's Coast to Coast B&B Registry
www.bbregistry.com

Western Canada Bed and Breakfast Innkeepers Association (WCBBIA)
www.wcbbia.com

Seminars and Conferences

These just scrape the surface of educational seminars and conferences that aspiring inn-keepers and those already in the business can check into. As always, sniff around other inn-keepers, national and local associations, and nearby universities.

➤ PAII (www.paii.org) puts on an international conference where you can attend all sorts of seminars and visit with vendors and B&B Web site and RSA staff.

➤ The University of South Carolina Beaufort has developed B&B education seminars exclusively for aspiring inn-sitters or inn-keepers of small B&Bs. USCB also offers a follow-up intern program. Check out their Web site at www.learninnkeeping.com.

➤ Bill Oates and Heide Bredfeldt conduct weekend seminars several times a year at their Three Mountain Inn in Jamaica, Vermont. They also offer apprenticeship programs and consultations. Check out their Web site: www.inns-for-sale.com or give them a call at: 802-254-5931.

➤ Nancy-Linn Nellis conducts four-day seminars at different times of the year at her B&B, 1794 Watchtide by the Sea, in Searsport, Maine. Check out her main Web site (www.watchtide.com) and the direct link for seminar information at www.inn-formation.com.

➤ Carol and Tom Edmondson, owners and inn-keepers of The Captain Freeman Inn in Brewster, Massachusetts, offer an "Innkeeping from the Innside" seminar and cooking school on weekends. Check it out at www.captainfreemaninn.com.

➤ David Caples and Helen Cook conduct workshops at Amelia Island, Florida, through their company LodgingResources.com. Call at 1-888-201-7607 or check out their Web site: www.lodgingresources.com.

➤ Nadine and Carl Glassman run both apprenticeship programs and inn-keeping seminars at their Inn School at the Wedgwood Inn in New Hope, Pennsylvania. Give them a call at 215-862-2570 or send an e-mail to stay@new-hope-inn.com for more information.

➤ Tom King offers hands-on seminars at his Queen Anne Bed & Breakfast Inn in Denver, Colorado. Call for upcoming dates: 1-800-432-4667 (except Colorado); 303-296-6666.

➤ Helen Bartlett, previous B&B owner, conducts seminars in Hot Springs Arkansas. Call her office at 501-623-9829 or check out the Web site at www.bednbreakfastconsult.com.

➤ New England B&B Consultants and Sales offer one-day and weekend seminars throughout New England and also are a listing agency. Their home base is in Whitefield, New Hampshire. Call 603-837-9320 or check out the site at www.nebbc.com.

➤ Lynn and Del Mottaz, owners of The Meadows in Brooklyn Park, Minnesota, conduct seminars for inn-sitters. Call Meadows Seminars at 612-315-2865 or check out their Web page at www.bbonline.com/innkeeper/meadows.

Online Magazines and Helpful Sites

In addition to the large associations and some of the online guidebooks that provide information on inn-keeping, check out these sites:

Innsights
www.bandbmagazine.com

Bed and Breakfast Inns Online INNkeeper INNformation
www.bbonline.com/innkeeper

Bed and Breakfast for Sale
www.bedandbreakfastforsale.com

LodgingResources.com
www.lodgingresources.com

Books

Some helpful books for small business owners and B&Bs:

Barlow, Janelle, and Claus Moller. *A Complaint Is a Gift: Using Customer Feedback as a Strategic Tool.* San Francisco: Berrett-Koehler, 1996.

Blanchard, Kenneth H., Harvey MacKay, and Sheldon Bowles. *Raving Fans: A Revolutionary Approach to Customer Service.* New York: William Morrow and Co., 1993.

Caselton, Margaret. *The Gracious Table: The Art of Creating a Beautiful Table.* New York: Rizzoli International Publications Inc., 1996.

Cobb, Linda. *Talking Dirty with the Queen of Clean.* New York: Pocket Books, 2000.

Gerber, Michael E. *The E Myth Revisited: Why Most Businesses Don't Work and What to Do About It.* New York: HarperBusiness, 1995.

Gray, William S. *Uniform System of Accounts for the Lodging Industry by the Educational Institute of the American Hotel/Motel Association Hospitality Accounting.* Upper Saddle River, NJ: Prentice Hall, 1995.

Greco, Gail, and Lynne M. Kopick. *Secrets of Entertaining: Tips from America's Best Innkeepers.* Guilford, CT: Globe Pequot Press, 1996.

Gross, T. Scott. *Positively Outrageous Service.* Boston: Warner Books, 1994.

————. *Outrageous!: Unforgettable Service ... Guilt-Free Selling.* New York: AMACOM, 1998.

Kippel, Edward. *How to Clean Practically Anything.* Yonkers, NY: Consumer Reports Books, 1996.

Koehler, Dan M. *The Insider's Guide to Small Business Loans.* Central Point, OR: Psi Research-Oasis Press, 2000.

Levinson, Jay Conrad. *Guerrilla Marketing Excellence: The 50 Golden Rules for Small-Business Success.* Boston: Houghton Mifflin, 1993.

McKeever, Mike. *How to Write a Business Plan.* Berkeley, CA: Nolo Press, 2000.

Ohrbach, Barbara Milo. *Tabletops: Easy, Practical, Beautiful Ways to Decorate the Table.* New York: Clarkson Potter, 1997.

Professional Association of Innkeepers International. *PAII's Guide to the Inn Guidebooks* (check out their Web site at www.paii.org).

Wolfman, Peri, and Charles Gold. *Great Settings.* New York: Clarkson Potter, 1996.

Wolosz, Joe. *Hotel and Motel Sales, Marketing and Promotion: Strategies to Impact Revenue and Increase Occupancy for Smaller Lodging Properties.* Infinite Corridor, 1997.

Zemke, Ron, and Dick Schaaf. *Taking Care of Business: One Hundred One Ways to Keep Your Customers Coming Back (Without Whining, Groveling or Giving Away the Store).* Minneapolis, MN: Lakewoods Publications, 1998.

Cookbooks

Once again, these are only a few of the many cookbooks helpful for B&B owners:

Cool, Jesse. *Breakfast in Bed: 90 Recipes for Creative Indulgences.* New York: HarperCollins, 1997.

Frieberg, Carol. *Breakfast in Bed Cookbook: The Best B&B Recipes from Northern California to British Columbia.* Seattle: Sasquatch Books, 1990.

Leahy, Donna, and Jerry Orabona. *Morning Glories: Recipes for Breakfast, Brunch, and Beyond from an American Country Inn.* New York: Rizzoli International Publications Incorporated, 1996.

Maynard, Lucian, and Julia M. Pitkin. *The American Country Inn and Bed and Breakfast Cookbook: More Than 1,700 Crowd-Pleasing Recipes from 500 American Inns.* Nashville: Rutledge Hill Press, 1993.

McNair, James K. *James McNair's Breakfasts.* San Francisco: Chronicle Books, 1998.

Murphy, Martha Watson. *The Bed and Breakfast Cookbook: Great American B&Bs and Their Recipes from All Fifty States.* Owings Mills, MD: Stemmer House Publishers, 1997.

Smith, M. J. *The Low-Fat Bed and Breakfast Cookbook: 300 Tried-and-True Recipes from North American B&Bs.* New York: John Wiley and Sons, 1998.

Stein, Catherine. *Breakfast in Bed: Health Smart Recipes for Muffins, Cakes and Breads.* Charlottesville, VA: Howell Press, 1996.

Reservation Software

Guest Tracker by Munsenware
19050 Industrial Boulevard, Suite 4
Elk River, MN 55330
Phone: 763-441-7512
Fax: 763-441-6797
Web site: www.munsenware.com
Sales e-mail: gtsales@munsenware.com
Support e-mail: gtsupport@munsenware.com

Avail by Digital Rez International, Inc.
Rathomill Rockley New Road
Rockley, Barbados, West Indies
Phone: 1-800-811-5988
Fax: 250-836-3560
Web site: www.digitalrez.com
E-mail: software@digitalrez.com
Support e-mail: support@digitalrez.com

Easy Innkeeping by Grace Software
GraceSoft
PO Box 42237
Houston, TX 77242
Sales: 1-888-781-1086
Support: 281-495-1911
Support fax: 281-495-3196
Web site: www.easyinnkeeping.com
E-mail: info@gracesoft.com

GuestAll by Applied Technologies
Applied Technologies
PO Box 771132
Orlando, FL 32877
Phone: 407-888-4482
Web site: www.guestall.com
E-mail: whr@guestall.com

Online Booking Agencies

WorldRes.com (USA Headquarters)
1510 Fashion Island Boulevard, Suite 100
San Mateo, CA 94404
Phone: 650-372-1700
Web site: www.worldres.com

Note: This is the biggest online reservation booking agency but it is primarily for hotels and big establishments.

Availability Online
PO Box 307
Pawlet, VT 05761
Phone: 1-888-487-1456
Web site: www.availabilityonline.com
E-mail: info@availabilityonline.com

Webervations
Phone: 740-385-4444
E-mail: info@webervations.com
Web site: www.webervations.com

InnRes
Web site: www.innres.net
E-mail: info@InnRes.net

Index